WORLD WAR II

BATTLE ON LAND

All six contributors to the text are, or have been until recently, members of the prestigious Department of War Studies at the Royal Military Academy, Sandhurst.

Dr Duncan Anderson, chapers 6, 9, 14 and 19. Senior Lecturer with Special Responsibility. An Australian by birth, he took his higher degrees at Queen's University, Ontario and at Oxford University and held a number of university posts before joining the Sandhurst faculty in 1987. HIs special interests lie in nineteenth- and twentieth-century civil-military relations and military history.

Dr Stephen Badsey, chapters 3, 15, 17 and 18. Senior Lecturer. Educated at Cambridge University, where he received his doctorate for a thesis on British Cavalry, he was formerly a research assistant at the Imperial War Museum and had considerable experience as a freelance researcher and writer for television before joining the Sandhurst faculty in 1988. He recently published *Normandy, 1944* (1990).

Mr David Chandler, General Editor, chapters 2, 7, 8 and 13. Head of Department. Educated at Oxford University, he spent four years in the army before coming to Sandhurst.He is President of Honour of the British Commission for Military History, was recently appointed a Trustee of the Royal Tower Armouries and serves on the Councils of both the Society for Army Historical Research and the Army Records Society.

Dr Paddy Griffith, chapters 10 and 11. Senior Lecturer for many years at Sandhurst before becoming a freelance author and publisher in 1989. He took his Doctorate at Oxford University and is the author of a number of books, including (with Colonel Elmar Dinter) *Not Over by Christmas* (1983). He has a special interest in the American Civil War and War Gaming.

Mr Sean McKnight, chapters 1, 4, 5 and 20. Joined Sandhurst as a Temporary Senior Lecturer in 1989. Educated at Oxford and London universities, he has taught History in Bedfordshire, Singapore and Dubai. He is presently engaged in research for a higher degree on the British Army Staff in World War I.

Mr Gary Sheffield, chapters 12 and 16. Senior Lecturer with Special Responsibility. A graduate of Leeds University, he is currently researching a higher degree on officer-man relationships in World War I at King's College, London. He has published three books, including (as co-editor) *Warfare in the Twentieth Century: Theory and Practice* (1988) and *From Vimy Ridge to the Rhine: the War Letters of Christopher Stone, 1914-1919* (1989).

Photography
UPI/Bettmann
Keystone Collection
Peter Newark's Military Pictures

Design
Sally Strugnell

Commissioning Editor
Andrew Preston

Publishing Assistant
Edward Doling

Photo Research
Leora Kahn
Kenneth Johnston

Editorial
David Chandler
Fleur Robertson

Production
Ruth Arthur
David Proffit
Sally Connolly

Director of Production
Gerald Hughes

Director of Publishing
David Gibbon

MALLARD PRESS

An imprint of BDD Promotional Books Company, Inc,
666 Fifth Avenue, New York, N.Y. 10103.

Mallard Press and its accompanying design and logo
are trademarks of BDD Promotional Book Company, Inc.

CLB 2430

Firstpublished in the United States of America
in 1990 by The Mallard Press.
Printed and bound in Italy by New Interlitho.

ISBN 0 792 45374 3

WORLD WAR II

BATTLE ON LAND

Edited by
DAVID G. CHANDLER

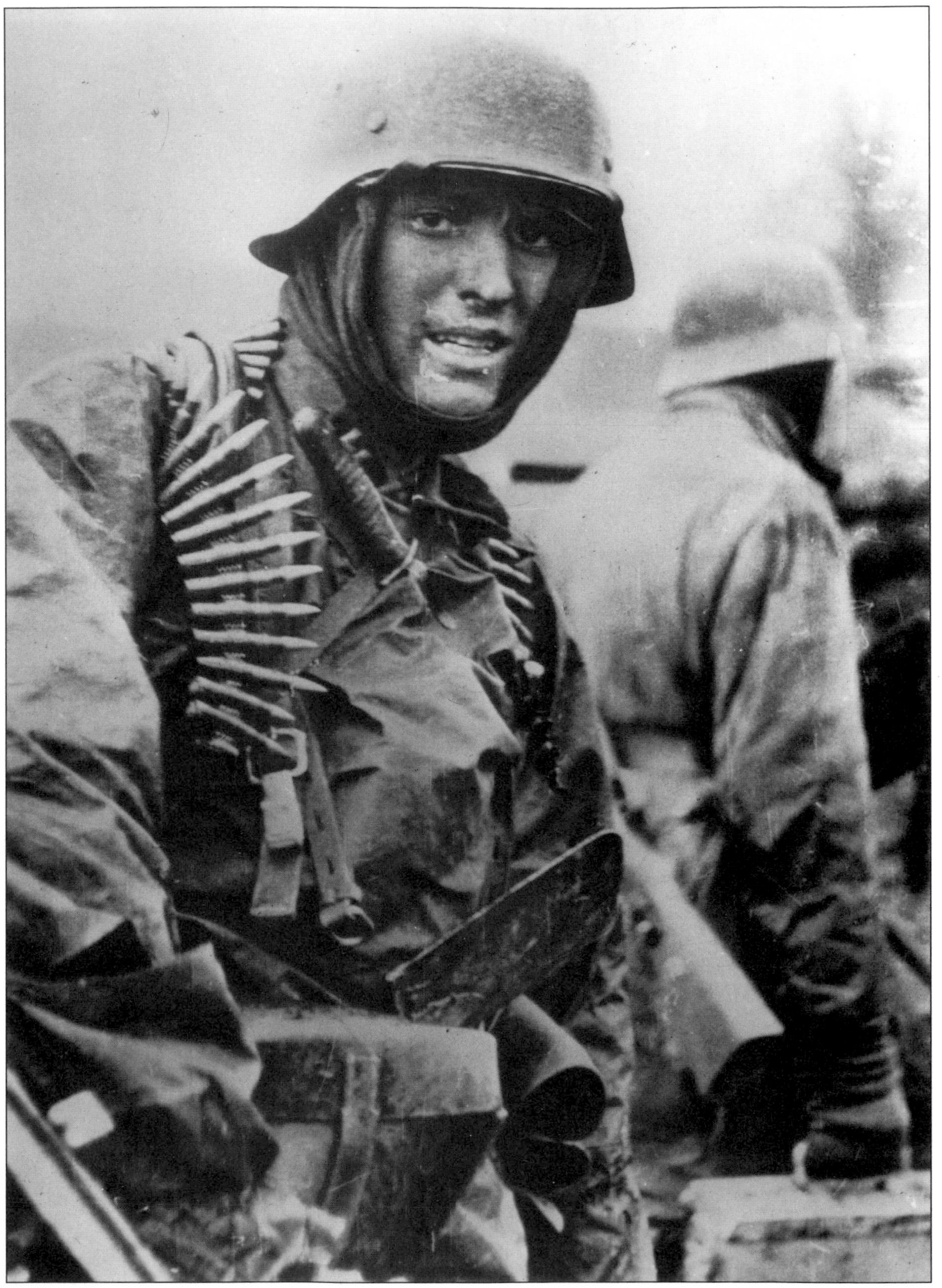

A German soldier during the Battle of the Bulge, his nation's last great offensive of the war.

CONTENTS

INTRODUCTION

'War is Hell,' stated William Tecumseh Sherman after the close of the American Civil War, and so it has always been from the dawn of history. On the other hand, there are, unfortunately, worse human-motivated circumstances of misery – genocide, enslavement and deliberate aggression amongst them– that have from time immemorial caused individuals, tribes, peoples, nations and great alliances to accept the challenge of warfare as the lesser evil. Although it is doubtful whether there has ever been a totally 'just' war – causation is invariably complex – the Second World War became inevitable when Hitler invaded Poland on 1st September, 1939. By its close, over five million British citizens had donned uniform, and one twentieth of those had become casualties – not including the 63,000 civilians, men, women and children who were victims of bombs. Yet, compared to the Soviet Union, Germany, China and Japan, Great Britain and its Commonwealth and Empire came off lightly.

Winston Churchill once stated that he remembered two vital dates during the Second World War, both in 1941. On 22nd June that year (the day the Germans invaded Russia), he said he knew that we would not lose the war. On 7th December, 1941 (the day the Japanese attacked the American fleet at Pearl Harbour, thus bringing the United States into the conflict), he knew that we would win it. But before 'V-E Day' in May, 1945, and 'V-J Day' three months later, mighty battles had to be fought on land, sea and in the air before Mussolini's Italy, Hitler's Germany and Tojo's Japan would concede defeat.

This volume sets out to describe twenty crucial land battles during that long and terrible struggle. The first six relate to Allied defeats – French, British, Russian and American – as the Axis enjoyed the advantages conferred by possession of the initiative in the war. There were occasional victories on land to be sure – General O'Connor's eliminiation of the Italian X Army in Libya, and the conquest of Italian East Africa by generals Cunningham and Platt for example – but they were few and far between, and for most of those early years the news made dismal reading.

Then – with the battles of El Alamein and Stalingrad – came the turning of the tide. Allied armies began to regain lost ground, slowly at first, but then more rapidly. Vast amphibious landings in North Africa, Sicily and Italy prepared the way for the opening of the 'Second Front' – the Allied invasion of northwest Europe on 'D-Day', 6th June, 1944. In Russia, the relief of Leningrad after one of the longest sieges in history and the winning of the largest tank battle in all history at Kursk heralded the collapse of German power on the Eastern Front, where almost half the war's casualties were inflicted. Away in the Far East, General Chiang-Kai-Shek absorbed the attention of two-thirds of the Japanese Imperial Army, General Slim clung doggedly to the Indo-Burmese frontier before launching his huge, ultimately victorious counter-offensive, while in the Pacific the Americans clawed back island after island from Guadacanal onwards at heavy cost and against fanatical Japanese opposition.

Hitler won a little time by his defensive victory at Arnhem, but then lost his last large offensive in the Ardennes. Four months later he was was dead by his own hand, Berlin was occupied by the Red Army, and Germany was destined to be split into four zones between the victorious British, American, French and Russian powers – setting in train a series of events that would cause the Cold War and dominate the European and world scenes until forty-five years later. The dropping of two atomic bombs on Japan ended the fanatical resistance of Emperor Hirohito's imperial forces, and probably saved the Allies another million casualties and Japan twice that number. Finally, after the conclusion of a Soviet offensive in Manchuria, fighting ceased throughout the world and men and nations began to face up to the hardly less daunting problems of peace.

Below: in a hopeless but gallantly defiant gesture, a British soldier takes a pot shot at German dive-bombers as they shriek down, their banshee sirens screaming, to bomb the beaches at Dunkirk. Although the odds against hitting an aircraft with a single rifle bullet were huge, it helped morale to be striking back, however futiley.

This dramatic picture shows how close some destroyers came to the beaches. As a line of men, with water up to their shoulders, wade out to grasp the scrambling-nets and climb aboard, other soaking soldiers patiently look on. The destroyers were sitting targets until they could be floated off at the next high tide.

Much has been written – and doubtless will continue to be written – on almost every one of the twenty land battles discussed in this book. Yet tales of men in battle are ageless and require constant commemoration, if only in the hope that the rivalries and mistakes of policy and human judgement that made inevitable such terrible destruction and misery may never again occur on such a scale. Nevertheless, it may be a trifle fanciful to hope that '...battle has abolished itself' in the light of today's potentially cataclysmic weaponry, for until mankind's pugnacious nature is finally tamed it is all too likely that wars will continue to bedevil human history – indeed, there have been over 200 of them since 1945. For sure, there is no denying the interest engendered by warfare: as Thomas Hardy wrote in *The Dynasts*: 'War makes rattling good history; but peace is poor reading,' and in that fact is reflected much of the tragedy of mankind. Yet perhaps today, at last, the prospect for peace is a little brighter.

David Chandler
R.M.A. Sandhurst

BLITZKRIEG IN THE WEST

Heinz Guderian (front left) inspecting *Panzer* troops in training. Appointed Inspector General of *Panzer* troops by Hitler, Guderian developed the doctrine of mechanized war used with such devastating effect against France in 1940. His charismatic and aggressive leadership of XIX *Panzer Korps* ensured that they triumphed in their crossing of the River Meuse at Sedan.

In 1933, the Treaty of Versailles still limited German strength; a *Reichswehr* of 100,000 and no air force meant Germany feared Poland, never mind France. Just seven years later, French might was humbled by *Wehrmacht* superiority in strategy and resources. For the second time in seventy years France was prostrate before Germany and the name Sedan linked to defeat.

Hitler's rearmament programme gave Germany superiority in anti-tank guns, self-propelled artillery and anti-aircraft guns. Their six-to-one advantage in anti-aircraft guns included 2,600 versatile '88s', a weapon illustrating Germany's qualitative edge. The *Luftwaffe* had nearly double Allied numbers, while its Ju52 transport planes gave it greater operational mobility. Discounting the neutral forces of the Low Countries, the Allies were even at a disadvantage in terms of manpower.

To some peoples' surprise the figures show an Allied numerical lead in tanks. However, Germany had a slight lead in tanks capable of engaging other tanks. Even the best Allied tank was badly designed for tank-to-tank combat, lacking a radio and placing too many demands on the man in the turret. Allied tanks were primarily infantry-support weapons, while German strategy concentrated tanks into an integrated team with other mechanized forces. To the punch of these *Panzerdivisions* was added range and mechanical reliability, producing a formation capable of exploiting a breakthrough in battle.

The combination of firepower and mobility in the German mechanized forces made *Blitzkrieg* a possibility. Concentrations of *Panzerdivisons* would rupture enemy lines and, supported by mechanized infantry divisions, exploit this breakthrough. The *Luftwaffe* could provide close tactical support, driving enemy planes from the sky and co-operating with ground forces as 'aerial artillery'. Speed of attack and chaos in the rear denied the enemy the chance to form a viable defence, allowing large enemy formations to be enveloped. In essence, *Blitzkrieg* paralysed both the enemy's will and their ability to find an appropriate response.

General von Manstein's persistence and Hitler's intuition and luck lead to the adoption of the *Sichelschnitt* or 'sickle cut'. It was calculated that an invasion of the Low Countries would pull in the Allied armies and fix' them against the German's Army Group B. Having drawn the Allies, German Army Group A, with most of the *Panzerdivisions*, would crash through the Ardennes and reap four Allied armies in an enormous 'sickle cut'. Conservative generals warned against the plan, but, like

The Fall of Sedan, May 1940. The speed of the German *Blitzkrieg* amazed the French High Command.

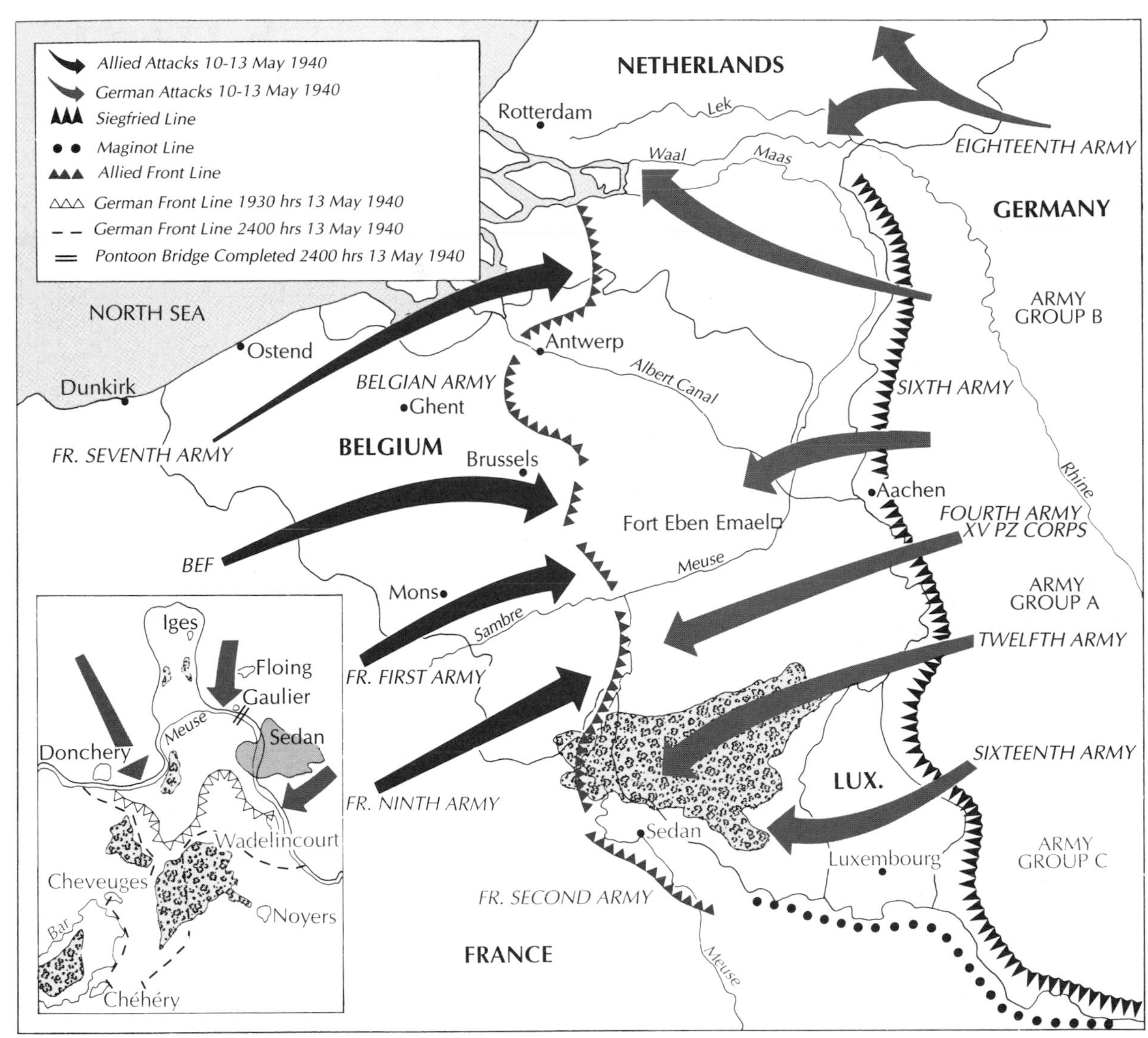

Hitler, the man leading the sickle's cutting edge was a bold gambler. The moment had arrived for the commander of XIX *Panzer Korps*, Heinz Guderian – his aim was to cross the Meuse at Sedan.

It is easy to point to Allied inferiority in resources and strategy. The French Army prepared for trench warfare and Britain contributed minimally to ground forces. Tanks were wasted in dispersed defensive packets, fulfilling only an infantry-support role. Allied air forces lacked a policy of close support and co-operated poorly with ground forces. Allied assets should not be ignored, though: France had 11,200 artillery pieces, the Maginot Line secured Alsace-Lorraine and a rapid expansion of armoured forces had started. When Chamberlain said 'Hitler has missed the bus', he should have been right, for resources and strategy by themselves do not suffice to explain the defeat.

The single biggest contribution to the defeat of France was made by the French Supreme Commander, General Gamelin. A glance at the map illustrating the campaign plans makes the French reaction to the German invasion clear: they had offered a powerful thrust following the German invasion of the Low Countries, the Maginot Line had been held in strength, while the central 'joint' was weakly held. The 'joint' did not need greater strength because it was thought that the 'impassable' Ardennes protected it, and so, naturally, little had been done to add any defences here.

Facing page top: French General Gamelin conferring with senior commanders on an inspection tour of the Western Front. Gamelin was a peacetime soldier who proved incapable of handling the speed with which events moved in the 1940 offensive. His insistence on an overly bold advance into the Low Countries and his inept response to the German breakthrough were major factors in the Allied defeat.

Facing page bottom: Allied officers examining part of the Maginot line. Locked into this impressive line of fortifications was a significant portion of the French Army that would have been better employed further north. These major fortifications ended at Longwy, so at Sedan the Germans encountered weak, incomplete defences.

At dawn on 10th May an early morning call by the *Luftwaffe* ended the smug neutrality of the Low Countries. Ignoring intelligence warnings, General Gamelin ordered forty divisions into Belgium. Behind them, unseen, seven *Panzerdivisions* moved into the Ardennes – the cutting edge of the 'sickle' was about to fall on ten French infantry divisions holding a hundred-mile front in the 'impassable' Ardennes.

Guderian's XIX *Panzer Korps* had the crucial task of breaking through at Sedan. Under his command were 1st, 2nd and 10th *Panzerdivisions*, plus the *Grossdeutschland* Regiment. Following to support the breakthrough was Wietersheim's XIV Motorized Corps. Boldly lead, these elite troops were confident and highly motivated. The same cannot be said for the three French divisions defending the Meuse around Sedan; all three were under-equipped, 'B' class divisions composed almost entirely of reluctant conscripts.

Much to Guderian's relief, the enemy presented few problems during the advance to the Meuse. His vehicles, snarled in an enormous traffic jam, were not bombed, and at *Wehrmacht* High Command (O.K.H.) Halder commented 'Enemy air force astonishingly restrained'. The Belgian *Chasseurs Ardennais* performed some limited demolitions and withdrew northwards. Stiffer resistance was offered by the French light cavalry, but lacking in anti-tank guns and equipped with the under-gunned Hotchkiss 35 tank, these units could hardly even slow a *Panzerdivision*. Even the important town of Bouillon fell in a matter of hours. At last, on 12th May, the Allies made a major effort in the air, but bombing the Bouillon 'salient' failed to prevent the Germans from moving rapidly over the Semois – the last natural barrier before the Meuse. Sufficient man-made fortifications to delay the Germans had not been built – in fact, not even the simple measure of tree-felling to block roads had been tried. By the evening of 12th May the French were blowing the bridges over the Meuse. The *Wehrmacht* had arrived in half the time the French had thought possible.

Heights like La Marfée dominated the Meuse near Sedan and to this natural strength the French had added pillboxes. However, Laffontaine's 'B' class 55th Division was spread thinly over twelve miles and many of the pillboxes were incomplete. Its artillery was well placed to inflict casualties, but on the day was

Below: a German howitzer in action in Belgium. The advancing German forces brushed aside Belgian and French units in their advance through the Ardennes. Traffic jams caused the main delays - not Allied resistance.

rationed to fifty rounds per gun because Corps Commander Grandsard believed at least four days would pass before an assault. *Blitzkrieg* attacks don't pause for breath – the Germans planned to cross on 13th May.

Guderian selected 1st *Panzer* to make the main assault, while 2nd and 10th *Panzer* attempted crossings on either side. Heavy artillery from the rest of the corps and the *Grossdeutschland* stiffened 1st *Panzer*. The all-arms nature of the *Panzerdivision* is illustrated by the crossing; artillery, anti-aircraft guns, assault engineers (*Sturmpionieren*), engineers and rifle regiments all played important roles. Throughout the day the courage and leadership qualities of these men was seen at all levels.

The *Luftwaffe* put 1,500 planes into the air above Sedan and it is difficult to envisage how a crossing could have succeeded without such aerial support. From 7am to 3pm continuous *Luftwaffe* assault supplemented the artillery effort. With no Allied aerial riposte 55th's morale fell and Stuka dive bombers spread panic, especially in the badly protected French artillery positions. The bombardment suppressed French fire and made it possible to cross a big river in rubber dinghies.

Leading 1st *Panzer's* assault, *Grossdeutschland* crossed near Gaulier just after 3pm. Flak guns at the water's edge kept the pillboxes busy and several were hit through their unprotected weapons slits. Reaching the west bank, small groups of infantry pressed into the gaps between pillboxes, discovering few French interval troops. The more stubborn pillboxes were destroyed by *Sturmpionieren* attacking them from the rear with explosives. Following *Grossdeutschland*, Balck's 1st Rifle Regiment crossed and swung west, and then south towards La Marfée. By midnight Balck's men had overrun most of the hill, depriving the French of the best artillery positions to shell the bridge newly erected at Gaulier. At midnight on 13th May the bridge was complete and the tanks started trundling over the Meuse.

The day had gone well for the other crossings attempted by XIX Corps, despite their being short of artillery. Crossing at Donchery, 2nd *Panzer* had used Pzkpfw IV tanks at the water's edge to provide covering fire and once again *Sturmpionieren* had proved their worth. The audacious courage and initiative displayed by the assault troops enabled them to penetrate to their objectives, linking with 1st *Panzers* advance at about 8pm. To the north, both General Reinhardt's and General Hoth's corps had elements on the west bank of the Meuse. The 'sickle cut' was poised to thrust into the backs of the Allied armies in Belgium.

A heavy French artillery piece in action. The artillery, the pride of the French Army, was was expected to play the same dominant role as it did in the First World War. Unfortunately, very few self-propelled guns were in service, and at Sedan the French artillery performed poorly.

The Ju 87 Stuka was used to fearsome effect when Guderian's men crossed the Meuse. Functioning as 'aerial artillery' it created panic in the French artillery, while providing the Germans with the suppressive firepower they needed to cross the river. In reality it was a limited plane that owed its early success in the war to the panic it inspired.

Below: the town of Sedan immediately after the campaign. Sedan was unfortunate enough to be bombed by both sides.

Every hour that passed strengthened the German bridgehead, but an early attack could have caught XIX Corps with its tanks still on the east bank. The fate of French counterattacks on 14th and 15th May illustrates basic deficiencies in the French Army, contrasting starkly with the bold initiatives of the German campaign. Grandsard placed two tank battalions and two infantry regiments under Laffontaine's command for a counterattack. The chaos in French lines and direct disobedience to orders only exacerbated the slowness of response of an army reacting at the speed of trench warfare. The counterattack went in five-and-a-half hours late, with only half its allocated forces; the alarm it caused among the Germans suggests an earlier, stronger attack by the French could have had a dramatic effect. The French were slow to exploit an initial advantage and at 8.30 were struck by 1st *Panzer,* which destroyed half 7th Tank Battalion's obsolete tanks retaking Chémery. This failure meant the dissolution of 55th and 71st divisions, which by noon were panic-stricken mobs.

Similarly Allied air forces made their efforts late – throughout May 14th, pilots fought with great courage to destroy the pontoon bridge at Gaulier. Their delay had allowed XIX *Panzer Korps* to erect 200 flak guns and the *Luftwaffe*

German engineers built sturdy pontoon bridges (facing page) with great rapidity over the Meuse. Their efficiency ensured that major German forces joined their surviving assault units on the western bank of the Meuse before the French were able to organise a counterattack.

Right: German infantry assaulting a French village on the west bank of the Meuse. The Germans showed great flexibility in their infantry tactics and small groups often took hair-raising initiatives. Much of the credit for crossing the Meuse goes to the NCOs who led small groups in daring assaults.

was able to bring about 800 machines into the air. The Allies launched twenty-seven piecemeal attacks and lost ninety planes, but to no avail. The bridge remained intact.

The best opportunity the French had for reversing the situation was General Flavigny's newly formed XXI Corps, made up of newly arriving 3rd Armoured and 3rd Mechanized divisions. Unlike previous units, these divisions had tanks capable of engaging German tanks in combat. The familiar French pattern of delay meant no attack was ready till 3.30pm when the Germans already had 500 tanks over the Meuse. Flavigny cancelled the attack and dispersed the tanks over a twelve-mile front. It was not until the afternoon of 15th May that the XXI Corps attacked in three separate actions. *Grossdeutschland* provoked the first attack by taking the hilltop village of Stonne and only just held off French tanks with their self-propelled anti-tank guns. The second attack, at 5.30pm, was based around a battalion of 'Char B' tanks that thrust towards Chémery, raising alarm at Guderian's HQ. The final action – an attempt of two companies of 'Char Bs' to take Stonne – got into the village, but were driven out by the arrival of riflemen from 10th *Panzer*. French attacks displayed individual courage, but lacked co-ordination, both between the tanks themselves and between the tanks and the infantry.

In combat the French lacked the initiative to exploit initial advantages and, perhaps most basically, they had yet to learn the folly of using tanks in 'penny packets'. The arrival of 29th Motorized Division on the morning of 16th May settled the matter – the southern flank of the bridgehead was secured and the movement westward of Guderian's *Panzerdivisions* could continue.

The battle of Sedan was, in effect, over. As early as May 14th Guderian had gambled that *Grossdeutschland,* reinforced by 10th *Panzer,* would hold, and had ordered 1st *Panzer* to turn west. The French in front of XIX *Panzer Korps* were in chaos; heroic defiance, such as 3rd *Spahi's* at La Horgne, was to no avail as, at the same time as they were being annihilated, 2nd *Panzer* was outflanking them with ease. On 16th May Guderian made contact with 6th *Panzer* and the three separate bridgeheads became one front. With whole divisions dissolving in panic, the *Luftwaffe* dominating the sky and the roads crammed with refugees, it would have taken better men than the French High Command possessed to retrieve the situation. Guderian's *Panzer Korps* were not to receive an attack as threatening as General Flavigny's recent failure all the way to the Channel – in fact, the German victory was more threatened by German High Command than by the French, as later even Hitler lost his nerve and tried to hold the *Panzerdivisions* back.

The qualities displayed by the men of XIX *Panzer Korps* had been extraordinary throughout the battle of Sedan. Commanders such as Guderian and Balck had inspired their troops by leading from the front. Small groups of ordinary soldiers displayed similar qualities; men like Feldwebel Rubarth who, with ten men, broke through a 300-metre stretch of bunkers at Wadelincourt, knocking out three of them and winning the *Ritterkreuz.* To this reckless taking of initiatives and quality of leadership, *Wehrmacht* training had added great skill in all arms co-operation. Yet, unfortunately for them, all the *Panzer Korps'* combat virtuosity was soon to be of no avail as their 'invincible' Fuhrer burst the bounds of restraint and summoned up enemies even their skills were unable to defeat.

Advancing German motorized forces. Despite the misgivings of his superiors, Guderian pushed his men hard to exploit their initial breakthrough. The *Panzer* forces advanced with such speed they denied the Allies the breathing space they needed to respond. In their advance to the Channel they took prisoner thousands of dazed Allied soldiers.

DUNKIRK AND THE FALL OF FRANCE

While the battle for the perimeter rages inland, British troop stolidly wait to be picked up near Dunkirk. Excellent discipline prevailed, even though some troops would have to wait three days before they could leave the beaches.

On 10th May, 1940, the storm that had already engulfed Poland, Denmark and Norway abruptly burst against western Europe. Just nine days later, German armoured units reached the Channel coast.

On the same day that the Germans attacked in the west, Winston Churchill succeeded Neville Chamberlain as British Prime Minister of a coalition government. What happened by 18th May on the central sector around Sedan and Dinant has been described in the first chapter. In the northern area, meanwhile, after four days of fighting, Holland surrendered. As the Germans of General von Bock's Army Group B attacked Belgium – serving, in Sir Basil Liddell Hart's phrase, as 'the matador's cloak' – General Lord Gort's British Expeditionary Force, almost ten divisions strong, swung forward into central Belgium, accompanied on either flank by the crack French armies – 7th and 1st – to meet what was thought to be the enemy's major offensive. They were soon made aware of their great error. 'The news from France is very bad' Churchill warned first Parliament and then the British people at 9pm on 19th May.

It was rapidly to get much worse. Changes in the Allied High Command on 18th May (General Weygand replacing the discredited Gamelin as the Allied supremo) did nothing to stop the rot. Attempts to contain the deep enemy salient failed – there was no such thing as a strategic reserve available to plug the huge gap so rapidly torn in the Allied front. German exploitation of their success was boldly and brilliantly executed; by 21st May the Allied armies were effectively sundered in two. This was *Blitzkrieg* on a scale and at a speed no-one had envisaged – including the Germans. Indeed, many *Wehrmacht* generals feared that von Rundstedt's Army Group A's armoured thrust would become exposed to a telling counterattack (as the small British action by 'Frankforce' at Arras on 21st May seemed to demonstrate), but at this stage Hitler and Commander in Chief General von Brauchitsch backed their armour specialist General Guderian's intuition to the hilt.

Meanwhile, General von Bock's Army Group B, with Holland already out of the war was thrusting deep into Belgium. By 27th May the Belgian government was considering surrender in its turn. A week earlier, Lord Gort, apprehensive that such a dire event would indeed soon occur, thus severing the BEF's links to the Channel ports, and being already dubious of

France's sustained fighting power, had secretly requested the War Office to plan an evacuation. This would mean taking his forces out of French supreme command, and, if need be, heading for the coast.

As a preliminary move, hospitals and other rear installations were already heading for Dunkirk, where the first fighting troops were embarked for England on 26th May. Next day, Gort received the British government's definitive order to regard the evacuation of as many as possible of the BEF to safety in England as his overriding priority. The scene was now set for one of the great dramas of the Second World War.

Operation 'Dynamo', as the evacuation was codenamed, was entrusted to Vice Admiral Bertram Ramsay, responsible for the logistical support of the BEF, who set up his headquarters in Dover Castle. The speed of the German advance and the intensity of enemy air activity greatly increased the problems he and Lord Gort faced. Hopes that both Boulogne and Calais would be able to supplement Dunkirk were dashed when the former fell on 24th May, to be followed by the latter two days later after a heroic defence by 1st Battalion the Rifle Brigade, which literally fought to the last round

Below: as a Lockheed Hudson of Coastal Command overflies the scene, dense clouds of oily smoke rise from the blazing oil tanks of Dunkirk's port complex, set alight by *Luftwaffe* bombing. This picture gives a clear impression of the gradually shelving beaches that made approach difficult for rescue vessels.

Left: a closer view of the blazing oil tank from adjoining Dunkirk. Although the myth of Dunkirk attributes the 'miracle' of the evacuation to the famous 'little ships', in fact the vast majority of soldiers were taken off from the moles of Dunkirk harbour by a succession of destroyers.

***Blitzkrieg* leaves the BEF trapped at Dunkirk at the mercy of a brilliant strategic manoeuvre by the Germans called the 'sickle cut'. On 25th May, Hitler called a halt to the advance, thereby allowing the Allies to evacuate to England. The decision to halt was a critical one which had far-reaching consequences. It was, arguably, the first German mistake of the war.**

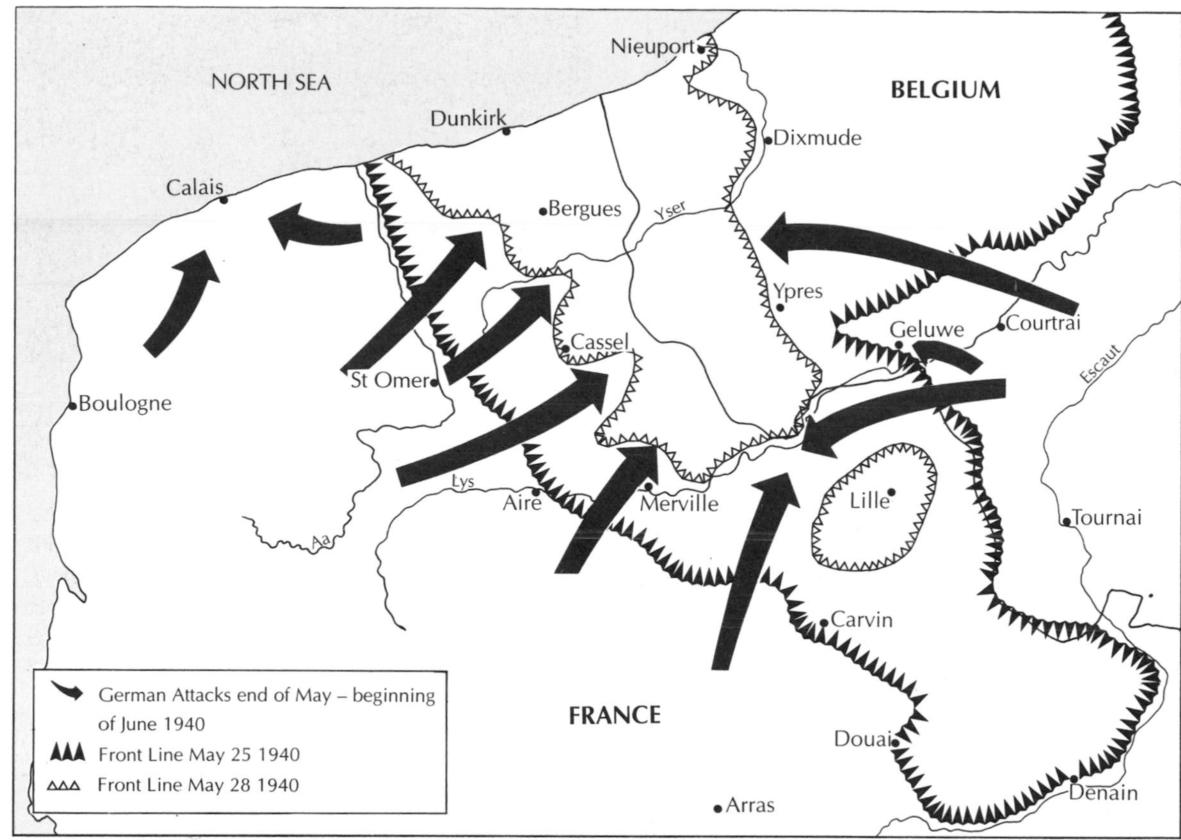

under Brigadier C.N. Nicholson before succumbing.

The main lift from Dunkirk would inevitably be the responsibility of the Royal Navy, but to supplement its capacity an appeal was issued for owners of 'little ships' – ranging from ferries and fishing boats to weekend holiday craft – to collect their craft in the Thames Estuary and south coast ports. But grim estimates claiming that at best only some 45,000 troops might be saved showed how pessimistically the situation was regarded in London.

But then Fate took a hand in the unlikely guise of Hitler himself. Remembering his own days in the muddy trenches of Flanders a quarter of a century earlier, the Fuehrer suddenly became obsessed with the need to preserve his jubilant but nigh-exhausted *Panzer* spearhead for the conquest of the greater part of France that lay south of the Somme. The savage British riposte at Arras – however small in scale – further reinforced the need for caution, while the assurances of Hermann Goering that the *Luftwaffe* alone could complete the destruction of the Allied forces in the pocket were also influential factors in decreeing a pause in land operations. Accordingly, von Rundstedt ordered his 4th Army to halt on 24th May to rest, resupply, and repair. A two-day partial lull ensued that was to prove of critical importance for the Allies.

Two further developments also helped the embattled and seemingly hopelessly trapped BEF to survive. From 24th May Lord Gort was receiving decrypted German messages from Bletchley Park, where the 'Enigma' coding machine had revealed some of its secrets. Secondly, the next day a captured document revealed von Bock's plan to exploit a wedge his troops had driven between the Belgian and British troops between Menin and Ypres. Lord Gort at once cancelled orders for two British divisions to break out south to the Somme, and diverted them in the nick of time to plug the developing gap that could have proved fatal to any evacuation. Thus, when full-scale German pressure was resumed on 27th May, the Allied defensive perimeter around Dunkirk was complete.

The third largest port in France today, in

As the lines of men on the beaches thin out, the crew of a destroyer's anti-aircraft gun maintain a ceaseless watch for the next raid by Stuka dive-bombers or Heinkel IIIs. Their beached vessel was highly exposed, and the strain upon the gunners clearly shows in their expressions. Six destroyers were sunk and nineteen damaged.

1940 Dunkirk already possessed a hundred acres of dockland and was a thriving town with a population of some 65,000. By 4th June, over eighty per cent of the town would be laid in smouldering ruins, and in 1945 it would be designated a *'Ville Héroique'*. On either side of the town lay miles of soft sand dunes running northeast towards La Panne and Nieuport and southwest towards Gravelines and Calais, with hardly any cliffs of any height dividing the hinterland from the beaches. Two important canals ran roughly parallel to the coast, linking Dunkirk with Bergues and Furnes, where both joined the Loo Canal.

On 27th May Lord Gort ordered four British divisions and neighbouring units making up about one third of French 1st Army to abandon the Lille pocket and head for Dunkirk through the Furnes gap. This move came at the last practicable moment, for the very next day Belgium surrendered, just as Lieutenant General Alan Brooke's II Corps closed the gap in the line near Nieuport. Lille was surrounded on 29th May, and a day later the Dunkirk perimeter was finally isolated. The French were made responsible for the western sector, the British for the eastern. BEF Headquarters were established at La Panne amidst the dunes. To its east, behind the Loo Canal, 4th Division held the sector nearest to Nieuport, with Major General Bernard Montgomery's 3rd Division as its neighbour around Furnes and the canal junctions. Moving westwards, the perimeter followed the line of the Bergues-Furnes Canal, 50th (Northumbrian) Division completing Brooke's II Corps. Beyond this boundary Lieutenant General 'Bubbles' Barker's I Corps' 1st Division took up defensive positions, with 46th Division taking post on its right flank as far as Bergues and its canal, running northwards parallel with Route 16A towards Dunkirk, some four miles away. The westernmost flank beyond this canal was entrusted to the French 68th Division. This completed the front line of the perimeter as on 30th May.

Closer to the sea, the remnants of six more divisions, three French and three British, stood in reserve. In a line from west to east in the rear

En route for England and safety, exhausted and sodden British, French and Belgian troops watch the dense lines of shipping of all shapes and sizes steam out of Dunkirk harbour for the short, perilous voyage across the Channel. Some ships made several such journeys.

of I Corps were the French 32nd and 60th and the British 12th divisions. Over the inter-corps boundary stood the British 5th and 23rd Divisions. Both 12th and 23rd Divisions had been badly mauled on 18th May and, apart from their 68th Division, the French were in little better state. A considerable number of Belgian troops and many refugees, both Belgian and French, were also within the defended zone. Many thousands of vehicles – tanks, trucks and artillery towers in addition to civilian transport – packed the area. In terms of men, a total of some 360,000 troops and perhaps as many more civilians were placed with their backs to the sea within a quadrangular perimeter measuring approximately twenty-four miles in length with a depth varying between five miles in the west and two in the east – an area of about a hundred square miles. Every road within this area could be commanded by German artillery fire. As III Corps began to embark the outlook for the BEF seemed bleak indeed.

The first factor that allowed the 'miracle' of Dunkirk to take place was the slowness of the Germans to test these defences. Only on the southwestern section, where General Guderian commanded 9th *Panzer* and 20th Motorized divisions of German 4th Army, and rapidly approached the River Aa, was much energy displayed at first. Remarkably, 18th and 14th Divisions of German 6th Army (part of Army Group A) did little against the centre of the Allied line, and the same was true of the formations of German 18th Army (part of Army Group B), including 265th Division facing the Furnes and Nieuport sectors on 27th and 28th May. Perhaps the meeting of the army group boundaries partly accounts for this rather than any theory that Hitler deliberately allowed the British to escape in the hope of making a quick peace.

So the evacuation got under way. The town and port of Dunkirk were heavily bombed and ablaze – particularly the oil-storage installations – from 26th May onwards, but many troops were nevertheless taken off the moles of Dunkirk and Malo-les-Bains ports for safe transport aboard naval shipping. Many vessels were hit (including eventually six destroyers sunk and nineteen more damaged, including a hospital ship), particularly from 29th May as the *Luftwaffe* attack intensified. Overhead and in the far distance the RAF fought valiantly against overwhelming numbers, displaying its skill by losing, on average, only one plane for every three of the enemy's shot down.

Fighting around the perimeter sharpened from 30th May, but most ground was held except in the east; Lord Gort was recalled to England next day, and Force Headquarters had to leave La Panne late on 1st June. Meanwhile, the armada of 'little ships' from England had made its appearance. Not only did these vessels carry much of the shore-to-ship traffic, thus permitting men to be taken off the beaches around Gravelines, despite constant dive-bombing, aerial machine-gunning and artillery fire, they also carried some 30,000 of the 53,823 soldiers taken off on 30th May (the best day) back to England. Losses to these craft were inevitably severe. Of the thousand or so ships of all sorts and sizes taking part in Operation 'Dynamo', 243 had been sunk by the end of the evacuation on 4th June.

Despite all the problems, the total of men saved rose higher and higher. Brooke handed over command of the rearguard to Major General Harold Alexander, and by late on 1st June only 46th, 1st and 50th divisions of the BEF remained ashore. By now it was only possible to use the harbour moles at night, forcing ships to sail when packed to dangerous levels above and below decks. At last, at 11pm on 2nd June,

Captain Tennant RN could signal to England 'BEF evacuated'.

By this time, the rapidly shrinking perimeter was manned by the French. On 3rd June the Royal Navy returned to take off 30,000 French troops, but many more than planned for appeared, and some confusion ensued. Despite Herculean efforts, some 40,000 Frenchmen had to be abandoned as German tanks entered the streets of Dunkirk. At 3.40am on 4th June the last British destroyer – HMS *Shikari* – set sail. The evacuation was over. At 9am the French garrison surrendered.

A brief wave of euphoria swept Great Britain, and Churchill had to warn the nation that '.. wars are not won by evacuations.' Although a total of 338,226 Allied troops (French and Belgians accounting for a third) had been brought safely to English ports, there was no concealing the fact that the BEF had lost all its tanks, transport, stores and equipment. Only a single Royal Artillery battery managed to save its guns. All the rest had to be put out of action or destroyed to prevent their use by the enemy. The wrecks of 2,472 guns, 68,879 vehicles, 20,548 motorcycles and half a million tons of ammunition and stores fell into German hands. It had indeed been a 'splendid deliverance', but it was also a potentially crippling defeat, for England now stood open to invasion.

Naturally the French government – which had moved to Bordeaux on 12th June and asked for an armistice on 21st June – did not support the British action. Vichy propagandists seized upon the fact that a total of 368,491 British troops had returned to British shores before the Franco-German armistice to insinuate that 'perfidious Albion' had saved its menfolk at the expense of its allies. In fact, British shipping had taken off 139,911 French and Belgian troops from Dunkirk, the balance of 144,171 British troops having been evacuated from other French ports – notably Le Havre and Cherbourg. These soldiers included reinforcements shipped to France after Dunkirk, lines of communication troops and representative units sent to help man the Maginot Line. Major General Bruce Fortune and the 8,000 men of 51st (Highland) Division were not so lucky, being compelled to surrender on 12th June after being trapped by Major General Erwin Rommel, commanding 7th 'Ghost' *Panzerdivision*, at St. Valry-en-Caux, west of Dieppe. Meanwhile, on 10th June, thinking it safe, Italy had joined Germany, and soon the war would spread to Egypt, Libya and East Africa.

'The harder they fall, the higher they bounce.' Distinctly cheerful 'Tommies' wait at Waterloo Station, London, for trains to disperse them throughout England. Despite the threat of imminent invasion, many were sent on 'survivor's leave'.

Churchill did what he could for France in the few remaining days of the Campaign of France. Against all advice by colleagues anxious for our ability to wage the forthcoming 'Battle of Britain', he sent RAF reinforcements over the Channel. The generous offer of joint Anglo-French citizenship was cold-shouldered by Reynaud, Petain and Laval, even in the hour of their country's extremity. The hard British decision to sink the French fleet at Mers-el-Kebir in North Africa on 3rd July to prevent Vichy from allowing it to fall under German control, killed over 1,250 French sailors. This justifiable but ruthless deed did nothing to lessen French Anglophobia, and has left its scar to the present day. Such was the 'cruel necessity' forced upon Great Britain by twentieth-century total war.

Britain now stood alone, and braced itself for an all-out *Luftwaffe* attack to be followed by the seemingly inevitable German invasion of our shores. In fact, the 'Battle of Britain' would be won in the skies over southern England by 'the Few' of the RAF, and the German Operation 'Sealion' would never be implemented as Hitler's attention turned eastwards towards the Balkans and Russia. But none of this was known in late June, 1940. Winston Churchill remained the typification of British 'bulldog' defiance, enjoining the British people to so comport themselves during the toils and perils lying ahead that future generations would declare: 'This was their finest hour'. And so it was to prove. The sacrifices of Dunkirk and Mers-el-Kebir were not in vain.

A group of 'little ships' on their way up the Thames for minor repairs after the evacuation of Dunkirk was over. Pleasure cruisers, yachts and fishing boats had all taken part, proving to be invaluable for transferring troops from the beaches to the larger vessels waiting offshore. Some small craft made the Channel crossing several times.

BATTLE FOR CRETE

The very difficult terrain of Crete. This kind of country made warfare particularly demanding for both sides, but it meant it was especially difficult for the British to mount their counter-attacks once the German paratroopers were down.

The Battle of Crete was dominated on both sides by complex issues of Mediterranean politics and grand strategy. On 28th October, 1940, Mussolini's Italy widened the war by attacking the Kingdom of Greece, and the Greek Government agreed to British troops being dispatched from General Sir Archibald Wavell's Middle East Command to defend Crete. This was known as the 'Creforce'. On 7th March, 1941, in support of Britain's new ally, Middle East Command sent to Greece 2nd New Zealand Division, 6th Australian Division and 1st Armoured Brigade, and increased 'Creforce' to five battalions, or about 8,000 men in all.

The Axis response was a simultaneous invasion of Greece and Yugoslavia on 6th April by twenty-one German divisions, comprehensively supported by the *Luftwaffe,* which over-ran both countries in two weeks. On 22nd April the Greek Government of King George II of the Hellenes transferred to Crete, accompanied by about 5,000 Greek soldiers, plus 20,000 Australians, New Zealanders and British troops who had escaped as best they could. On 30th April Wavell merged all his troops on Crete into 'Creforce' under the New Zealand Divisional commander, Major General B. C. Freyburg, who prepared his tired men for another German attack.

Adding the survivors of Greece together with the British troops already on the island, and including Cretan partisans and Greek regulars, Freyburg's force came to about 40,000 men, of which perhaps 25,000 were of any real fighting value. All these troops lacked heavy weapons, artillery, transport, radios, ammunition and, in some cases, even food and rifles. There

Junkers Ju 87 Stuka dive-bombers of 8th Air Corps pounded the defences of Crete from the air for days prior to the actual airborne assault. The extraordinary accuracy of these dive-bombers made the defenders on Crete very reluctant to show themselves when German aircraft passed overhead.

were seven medium tanks and sixteen light tanks on the island. Only thirty-four RAF fighters and light bombers, most completely worn out, made it back from Greece to Crete, and the nearest friendly airfields were 200 miles away in Egypt, too far for fighter cover. Crete in 1941 had no railways and only one good main road, running east to west along the northern coast and connecting the island's major fishing ports with the commercial harbour of Suda Bay, adjacent to the main town of Canea. The south coast was rocky, with sheer cliffs and beaches not suitable for berthing ships. All resupply had to take place from the north, through Suda, in the face of German air attacks. The Royal Navy under Admiral Sir Andrew Cunningham had three task forces, a total of two battleships, five cruisers and fourteen destroyers, to block any seaborne threat, but these were very vulnerable to air attack. By day, therefore, the *Luftwaffe* dominated the sea approaches to Crete, while the Royal Navy controlled them by night.

Despite the weakness of Freyburg's force, both signals and conventional intelligence were very good and he had a clear idea of the German battle plan. The pre-war airfield at Maleme, together with Canea and the two dirt airstrips at Retimo and Heraklion, would be seized by airborne assault, following which seaborne reinforcements would come in through Suda Bay. Freyburg in his deployment abandoned any divisional structure, slotting in troops from various nationalities and ad hoc units as required. Most of the Greek troops were allocated to the eastern end of the island, where no attack was expected. The remaining forces, including the better Greek battalions, were placed in loose brigade groups on four key locations. In the Maleme area was most of 2nd New Zealand Division (eleven battalions including Greeks) and at Canea four mixed battalions and most of the anti-aircraft artillery plus Freyburg's headquarters. At Retimo came 19th Australian Brigade and two Greek battalions, and at Heraklion a mostly British force of seven battalions. Communication between these groups was poor, being largely dependent on runners. Freyburg kept his small air contingent in Crete to contest the skies against the *Luftwaffe* for as long as possible, but on 19th May the last six remaining RAF

Facing page top: the start of Operation 'Mercury'. Junkers Ju 52 transport aircraft fly overhead as German paratroopers jump into action over their allotted drop zones. Highly trained and full of fighting spirit, the paratroops were nevertheless very vulnerable during their first few minutes on the ground.

Despite their massive air superiority, the Germans did not have things all their own way at the start of the battle (facing page bottom). British anti-aircraft fire caused serious loses to German transport aircraft as they sought to secure Malame airfield for the next stage of the island's conquest.

Right: German paratroops resting on the ground at Crete with some of their equipment containers. Difficulties in opening the parachute meant that German airborne troops usually jumped unarmed, except for a pistol, and the race to find their weapons containers on landing often decided the immediate battle.

Facing page top: the unsuccessful parachute assault at Heraklion on the first day of the battle. Some of the parachutes are carrying not men but equipment containers, and those grouped together in fours are carrying heavy equipment such as machine guns, artillery pieces or even vehicles for the airborne troops.

Facing page bottom left: German parachutists preparing for action, showing clearly their distinctive dress of parachute smock and helmet - the latter less dished than the normal German pattern - and the ammunition pouches of the officer in the foreground. The light motorcycle combination was a favourite means of moving at high speed.

Facing page bottom right: German parachutists going into action, having collected their weapons and personal equipment. Due to the uncertainty of airborne fighting, it was often necessary for paratroopers to carry heavy loads with them into combat.

fighters were allowed to fly for Egypt, and plans were made to destroy their airfields.

In the German system, airborne forces were part of the *Luftwaffe*, not the Army. Command of Operation 'Mercury', the plan to seize Crete, was given to General Kurt Student, commanding 11th Air Corps, by Adolf Hitler on 25th April. Although 7th Paratroop Division was ready, 22nd Air-Landing Division was in Roumania and the elite, glider-borne shock troops of 1st Assault Regiment were sent to replace it. In addition, the Army provided 5th Mountain Division to be flown in Ju52 transports once an airfield was secure. The total force was 22,750 men. Air support came from General Wolfgang von Richthofen's 8th Air Corps, with nearly 600 transport aircraft, 180 fighters, 280 bombers and 150 Ju87 Stuka dive bombers. German Intelligence was bad, failing to identify key defended positions and putting Freyburg's strength at no more than 5,000 troops.

The plan for Operation 'Mercury' was essentially Student's, and concerned with the strategic objective of securing the island of Crete for further airborne operations. As 'Mercury' was being planned, Rommel's *Afrika Korps* was driving Wavell's forces back towards the Egyptian frontier, and there was a revolt against British rule in Iraq. From Crete, a further attack could be mounted on Cyprus, and from there a direct airborne assault on Suez effected to link up with Rommel. Student's operational plan was – as Freyburg understood – an airborne assault on the four key locations of northern Crete in the hope of securing a landing ground and a harbour. Like Freyburg, Student abandoned the divisional structure and divided his forces into three battle groups. On the first morning, Group 'Komet' with most of 1st Assault Regiment, would seize Maleme, while in the centre Group 'Mars', with most of 7th Paratroop Division, would take Canea and Suda, with a follow-up operation at Retimo in the afternoon, while Group 'Orion' with one parachute regiment and one mountain regiment was to capture Heraklion. The heavy weapons, transport, and two mountain battalions would arrive by sea from an improvised flotilla of sixty-three assorted craft, chiefly Greek fishing vessels. The first day would be 20th May, the day on which Freyburg first gave attention to destroying his airfields.

Like all airborne operations, 'Mercury' depended on surprise and the individual fighting qualities of its troops. At 7.30am the paratroopers – most of them unarmed except for pistols – jumped from their aircraft over Maleme and Canea. Many small groups were wiped out before they could reach their weapons canisters. The glider-borne troops made crash landings on the beach or any suitable landing ground and went into action. At about 3.15pm came the second wave at Retimo and Heraklion. The complete air cover provided by 8th Air Corps made communication and manoeuvring easier for the Germans than for the Allies. But the initial plan was not a success. By the end of a day's confused fighting the landing zones were all contained, and the German force at Canea had been effectively wiped out. The one partial success was at Maleme, where the New Zealanders had been pushed off the airfield, though this continued to be disputed between the two sides.

Student then abandoned the idea of seizing Suda through Canea, and decided to push all his reinforcements through Maleme airfield, leaving Retimo and Heraklion to hold on. During the second day of the operation 5th Mountain Division resorted to the heroic expedient of flying in troops in Ju52s to land and unload on the airfield while still under fire. Although there was some loss, most of the Division was successfully transferred to Maleme. That night the seaborne invasion force tried to join the troops on Crete, but was intercepted by one of the Royal Navy task forces, and a massacre ensued. Only fifty-six men arrived to reinforce Crete. The Royal Navy itself, however, could not pursue the German force by daylight, and suffered six ships sunk and seven badly damaged by the *Luftwaffe* in three days. Finally, on 23rd May, their task forces were pulled back to Alexandria.

Major General Freyburg now saw his only chance of victory to be in wiping out the German position at Maleme, and organised a major counterattack by 5th New Zealand Brigade to start before dawn on 22nd May. Inevitably, this attack went in late and piecemeal, and although it reached most of its objectives, it failed to secure the airfield completely. By daylight the New Zealanders were forced to pull back, while the German build-up continued. Although the first forty-

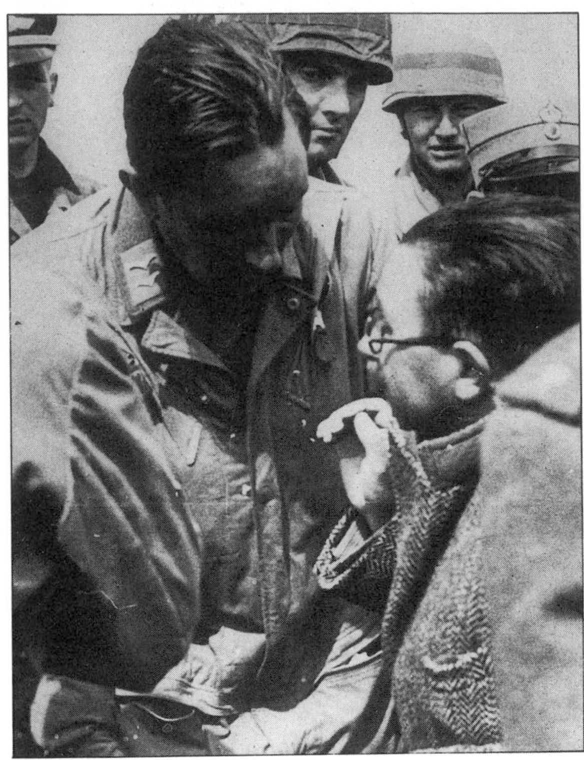

German troops on Crete demanding information from a local village headman. Cretan partisans and the few Allied troops who escaped into the hills involved the Germans in a difficult and often brutal guerrilla campaign on Crete for the rest of the war.

eight hours of the battle had been anxious, from his headquarters in Athens, Student began to sense victory. On 22nd May General Lieutenant Julius Ringel, commander of 5th Mountain Division, arrived to take over all troops in the Maleme area – chiefly his own 85th and 100th Mountain Regiments and 3rd Parachute Regiment – as a unified command. After two more days of fierce fighting, Ringel was able to mount a divisional assault on 24th May which finally drove the New Zealanders back from Maleme and made the stationing of German fighters on the airfield possible.

By this time Freyburg's men had been fighting for over seventy-two hours without respite, and brigades had shrunk to the size of battalions. As the German offensive developed it was clear that 'Creforce' would be prised away from Suda and its supply line, and there was no prospect of a successful counterattack restoring the situation. On the evening of 26th May Freyburg, fully aware of the strategic and political implications, advised Wavell that he could no longer defend Suda harbour against the Germans and that his force must be evacuated by sea.

The evacuation point was set as the little fishing village of Spakia on the south side of Crete, and a race now developed between the New Zealanders and the German's 85th Mountain Regiment as to how many of the former would escape. The troops at Heraklion were brought off directly by Royal Navy warships before dawn on 29th May. The force at Retimo, however, was completely out of touch with the rest of 'Creforce', and remained holding its position. On 30th May it was compelled to surrender, only 140 men out of 1,000 escaping. At Spakia the evacuation began on the evening of 29th May, and carried on for three nights until the early hours of 1st June. Thereafter, the Royal Navy, which had lost a further three ships sunk and eight damaged, could take no further risks. About 5,000 unwounded troops were abandoned on the island to become prisoners of war.

Operation 'Mercury' is the only example in the history of war of airborne forces winning a major strategic victory. The size and geography of Crete provided a perfect battleground for such an exploit. The result, however, was an anticlimax. About half of Freyburg's original 'Creforce' – just under 15,000 men – were taken off the island, the rest remaining as dead, prisoners or as the handful who joined the Greek forces as partisans. But 11th Air Corps had also suffered heavily. For the first time they had met an enemy every bit as good as themselves who was prepared to stand and fight. Out of 14,000 men, 7th Parachute Division and 1st Assault Regiment had lost about 4,000 dead and the same number wounded, plus a further 1,000 out of 8,750 from 5th Mountain Division. Over 200 German aircraft were also lost in the operation, nearly a third of them Ju52 transports. These losses discredited the airborne concept for the Germans, who never again launched a major airborne operation. Railways through Greece were barely adequate to supply a small garrison on Crete, and most of the German forces were needed for the forthcoming attack on the Soviet Union. The Allies, although they created their own airborne forces after Crete, made no attempt to retake the island until it surrendered at the end of the war. Strategically and doctrinally, the battle of Crete was a dead end.

BARBAROSSA–THE DRIVE TO THE EAST

A tracked vehicle pulls a wheeled trailer loaded with bicycles along one of the better Russian roads. Often termed a mechanized army, the Germans in fact suffered from a severe shortage of tracked vehicles. The much vaunted 'modern' army took 625,000 horses into Russia.

On Sunday 22nd June, 1941, during the small hours of the morning, elements from 148 divisions – totalling 3,300,000 German soldiers – were mobilized. With them were nineteen *Panzerdivisions* (excluding *Schutzstaffel* forces); 3,350 tanks; 7,184 artillery pieces; 600,000 vehicles; 625,000 horses and 2,000 aircraft – all ready to begin Operation 'Barbarossa'. They were supported by the German Navy, the Finnish Army, Rumanian armies and Italian, Hungarian, Slovak, Croatian and Spanish units. This campaign was intended to destroy the Soviet Union.

The German strategy for the invasion of Russia was indecisive: contradictory edicts from Army High Command (OKH), Armed Forces High Command (OKW) and, occasionally, direct interventions by Adolf Hitler himself combined to produce a number of unresolved aims and objectives. The campaign was launched with the hope that the bulk of Soviet strength could be trapped and destroyed by the time the Dneiper River had been reached. Further goals were to be determined in accordance with later circumstances.

Order Number 21, which established Operation 'Barbarossa' in December, 1940, gave mention to the Donets Basin and Moscow in just a single paragraph.

The forces of the Soviet Union already mobilized in the west before the implementation of Operation 'Barbarossa' were scattered through lines of first and second echelons to a depth of over 250 miles in some places. They were organized under Special Military Districts which converted to fronts (Army Groups) in time of war. To the south of the Pripet Marshes, covering a front of 540 miles, the Russian Southwestern Front and South Front defended the Ukraine. The Southwestern Front consisted of 5th, 6th, 12th and 26th armies; whilst the South Front consisted only of 9th Army and some independent units of corps' size. The best estimates break these forces down into between sixty and seventy infantry divisions, eleven cavalry divisions and twenty-eight armoured brigades. Few of the extant infantry divisions were at more than half wartime

strength and the mechanized units were, for the most part, still in the process of formation. The tank strength of the units deployed over the whole front before June, 1941, averaged fifty-three per cent of their potential force.

Moreover, Soviet forces were under dual command: on the Southwestern Front, for example, Colonel General M.P. Kirponos was the military commander and Nikita S. Khrushchev was the political commander.

Attached to the Southwestern Front was Army Group South, under Field Marshal Gerd von Rundstedt. Separated from the rest of the Front by a gap of about sixty miles because of the Pripet Marshes, its initial goal was to take the Ukraine. For this task there were two armies, consisting of thirty infantry divisions: 1st *Panzergruppe* commanded by Colonel General Ewald von Kleist and 4th Air Fleet. Italian, Hungarian, Slovak and Croation troops, equivalent to about eight or nine divisions, were also under this command. To the south, along the Soviet-Roumanian border, were one joint German-Roumanian and two Roumanian armies.

In 1941, full-strength divisional numbers were as follows: German forces incorporated an infantry of 17,734 men; a *Panzerdivision* of 15,600 men; 165 tanks, and a motorized infantry of 16,400 men. Russian military might incorporated infantry divisions across three levels of strength – their full wartime divisional complement amounted to 14,483 men. Armoured divisions incorporated about 12,000 men and 375 tanks; motorized divisions incorporated about 12,000 men and 275 tanks.

The Russian Southwestern Front put up a far more organized opposition to the German advance than was mounted against them elsewhere. Despite having 277 Russian aircraft destroyed by noon on the first day of Operation 'Barbarossa's' implementation – and having,

German infantry storming a railway station. The lack of good roads - only three percent were metalled in Russia - increased the importance of the railways for supply. As they retreated, the Russians destroyed as much line and rolling stock as they could. The Germans also had to convert the Russian gauge to suit their trains.

July, 1941: a Russian aircraft is loaded with bombs. Unfortunately, on the Southwestern Front 277 Russian aircraft had been destroyed on June 22nd; and virtually the entire air arm had been put out of action within the first two weeks of the conflict.

A Russian T-34 moves past an abandoned German anti-tank gun. The process of re-equipping the Red Army with the T-34 as its standard battle tank was in its early stages. Too few of these excellent tanks were available, while those in use were too thinly distributed to be effective in 1941.

by the end of June, virtually no air cover at all (through combat losses and simple lack of high-octane fuel and spare parts), Kirponos nonetheless managed to extricate the bulk of his forces from the line of attack by sacrificing most of his available armour in an effort to impede the advance of von Kleist.

He also managed to avoid the hammer of 6th and 17th armies in their attempt to crush his troops against the anvil of 11th Army which, with the Roumanian 3rd and 4th armies, had moved onto the offensive across the Prut River on 1st July. By 9th July, Kirponos had managed to establish a new line. The following day, Soviet Supreme Command reorganized all their southern forces and channelled them into the Southwestern Front. Marshal Budenny and Khrushchev were given command with Kirponos and General Tyulenev acting as field commanders.

Von Rundstedt's schedule had given him four weeks in which to destroy the enemy forces in the western Ukraine and take Kiev. Although this sector was regarded as the best tank country on the Russian front, summer rainstorms could quickly turn the black earth into a quagmire and the countryside would be littered with vehicles waiting for the ground to dry out – only three per cent of roads and tracks in the Soviet Union were surfaced.

Despite the German armies' slower than expected progress, by early August the Russian 6th and 12th armies had been trapped and were being destroyed in the Uman pocket, where the Germans claimed 103,000 prisoners. On 8th August, Odessa was cut off and besieged, and on 18th August General Zhukov uttered his famous warning to Joseph Stalin about the impending danger of complete destruction of the Southwestern Front as Budenny's forces were pushed back onto the Dneiper River. The danger which Zhukov foresaw was building to a crescendo, but not so much from Army Group South as from the north.

The success of German Army Group Centre

was producing worries for German High Command. Its advance to Smolensk had left flanks dangerously exposed. One third of its lorries were out of action and ammunition was not being sufficiently replenished, which brought stocks to worryingly low levels. The supply of POL (petrol, oil and lubricants) was insufficient, and subsistence supplies were

The sixty-ton KV tank was superior to anything the Germans possessed at the start of the Eastern Front War. Unfortunately for the Russians, the Red Army had abandoned the tactic of tank concentration and returned to the policy of spreading their armour out in support of infantry units.

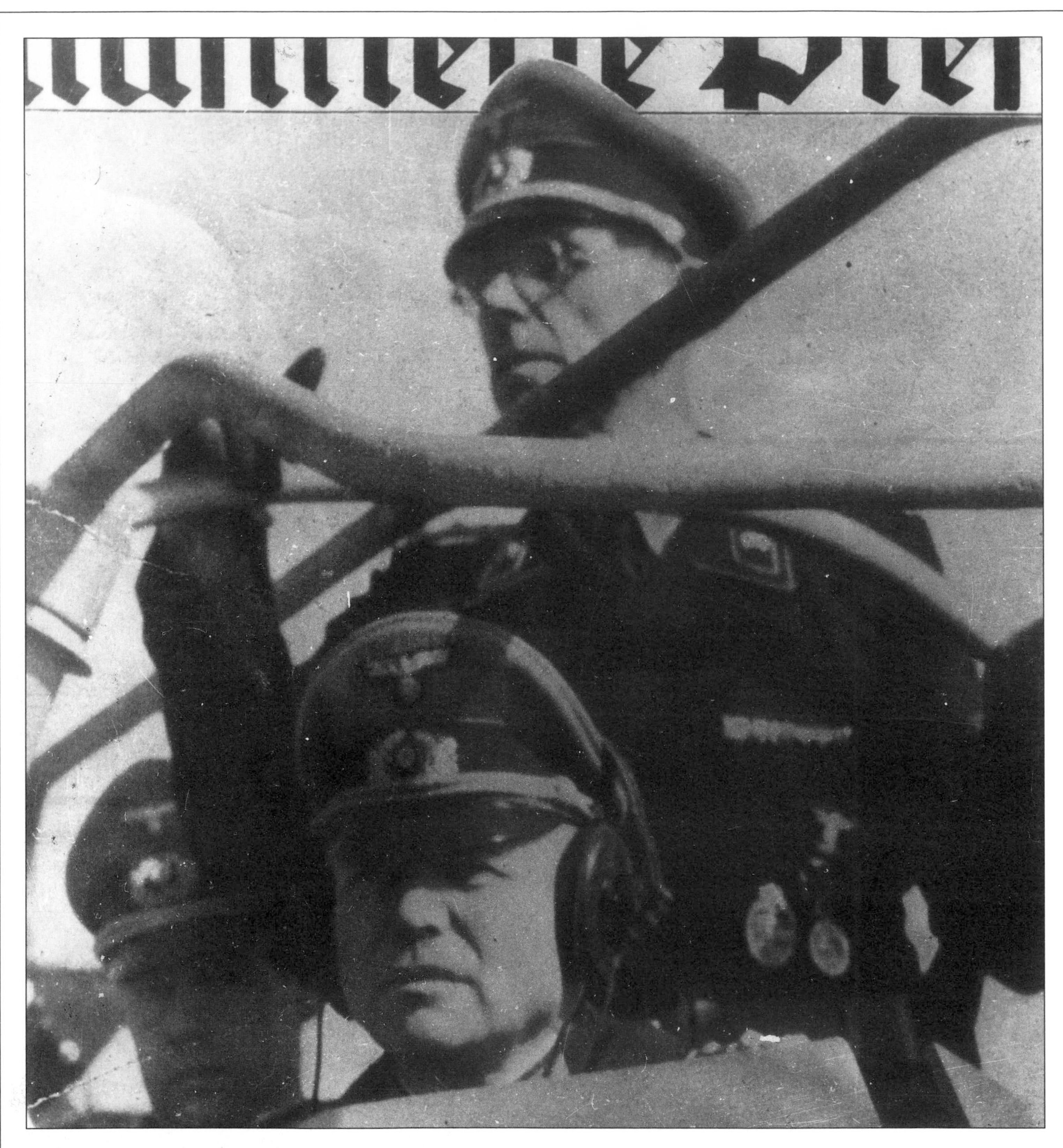

Facing page: Colonel General Franz Halder, the Chief of General Staff, OKH, stands over Colonel General Heinz Guderian, commander of the Second *Panzer* Group. As one of Hitler's favourites, Guderian was permitted to defy OKH policy and keep his entire Group together during the drive south.

The German Army's use of concentrated tank formations (below) was a major factor in their success during the first months of the war. Despite this, the 'tank lobby' continued to be in periodic conflict with traditionalists, including Hitler, who wanted as large a number of Russian prisoners as possible.

frequently nonexistent. Moreover, ferocious Russian resistance in the Smolensk pocket until 5th August and an unsuccessful battle to hold the Yel'nya salient ate into German attempts at stockpiling. By the end of July, elements of 9th Army had relieved most of 2nd *Panzergruppe* at the Front, and Colonel General Heinz Guderian could repair and replenish his units. On 1st August, XXVI *Panzer Korps* moved southwards toward Roslavl'. Its aim was to secure the Gomel-Bryansk area as the base for a 'right hook' on Moscow.

Within German High Command the lack of clear strategy with which Operation 'Barbarossa' had been launched was once more under discussion, with arguments also rising about the target priority of Leningrad, Moscow or the Ukraine. There were arguments too about the tactics of armour and infantry: should armoured divisions attack well in advance of infantry, or should the two forces stay closer to each other?

After nearly a month of disagreements a compromise was formed by Colonel General Franz Halder, the Chief of General Staff OKH, and Colonel General Alfred Jodl, Chief of Operations Department OKW. They felt that campaigns against Moscow and the Ukraine could be launched simultaneously if 2nd *Panzergruppe* was divided and the proposed formation of the Leningrad Front delayed. Their plan collapsed when Guderian visited Hitler on 23rd August and persuaded him that his own *Panzergruppe* should not be split. As a result it was determined that the Ukraine was to be taken first and Moscow would be the subsequent target.

On 18th August, Zhukov sent a telegram to Stalin warning him of the imminent threat of forty-four Russian divisions on the Southwestern Front being encircled by the enemy. He proposed that a force of army size be composed from troops taken from the Far East and the Moscow defence lines to be deployed along the Desna River. Stalin was convinced that the attack would be on Moscow and that Guderian's move south was a prelude to his turning northeastwards towards the city. On 18th August this surmise was correct. There was little possibility that Stalin could know of the

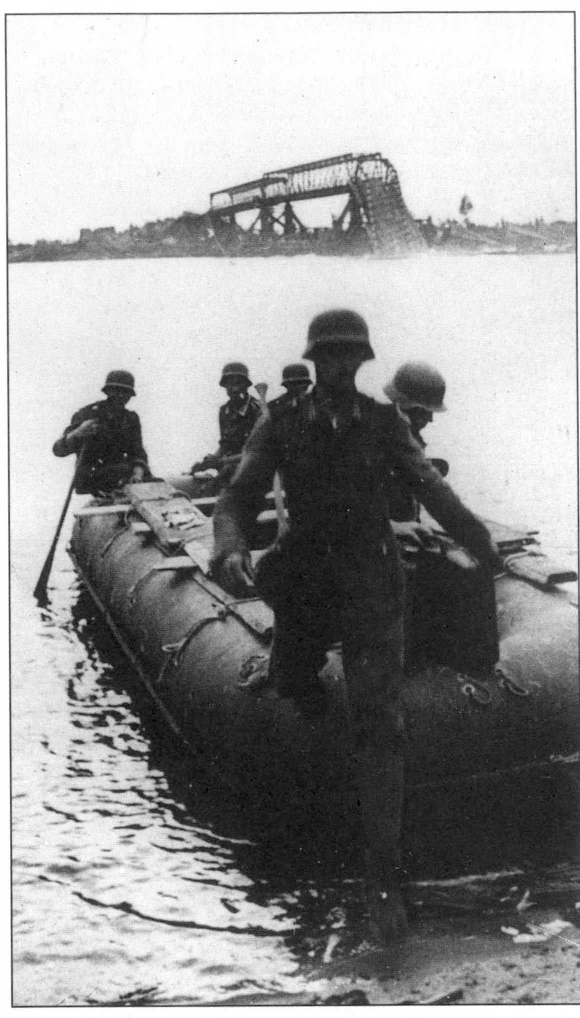

Left: German infantrymen cross the Dneiper River in a rubber boat. The advance of von Kleist's 1st *Panzer* Group from the Kremenchug bridgehead over the Dneiper met up with Guderian's drive south to close the trap that eliminated the Soviet's Southwestern Front. Rivers generally proved ineffectual as defence lines on the Eastern Front. The German infantry, slogging along days behind the glamour units in the *Panzer Korps*, had the task of mopping up the vast pockets of Red Army troops. Such cut-off units had often been left still capable of fierce resistance.

Facing page: a soldier surveys the destruction of a town in the Kiev pocket.

indecisive and changeable German target strategy. Only on 23rd August did he become suddenly terribly wrong.

The following day Marshal Shaposhnikov, who had replaced Zhukov as Chief of General Staff, informed Lieutenant General Eremenko on the Bryansk Front that he was to attack Guderian's forces as they swung to the north. That day, 24th August, 17th *Panzerdivision* was in Pochep and 3rd *Panzerdivision* had reached Starodub. The Russian 13th Army was splintering.

On 25th August, Colonel General von Weichs' 2nd Army began to push down between the Dneiper and Desna rivers, advancing on 5th Army of Major General Potapov, who had failed to turn his northern flank to defend Chernigov. On 26th August, 10th Motorized Division established a bridgehead over the Desna River, between Novgorod Seversky and Korop. Colonel General Kuznetsov, the commander of 21st Army, began to withdraw across the river but did not inform 40th Army, commanded by Major General Podlas, of his decision. As 40th Army shifted southeastwards, an gap developed. On 31st August, the last day of the month, a single 5th Army corps, 15th Rifle Corps, was the only force there to delay von Weichs. On 2nd September, an attack was launched at last from the Bryansk Front against Guderian's flank towards Roslavl'. The bulk of 2nd *Panzergruppe* was already over one hundred miles to the south, crossing the Desna River.

The northern flank of the Southwestern Front disintegrated. On 8th September, Zhukov met Stalin to warn him that Guderian would drive through it and create a pocket with von Kleist's 1st *Panzergruppe*, breaking out from the Kremenchug bridgehead. Again he urged the abandonment of Kiev. In fact it was probably already too late to get Russian forces out intact. The day before Guderian crossed the Seym River, Chernigov fell to 2nd Army, which had started across the Desna River. By 10th September, as 40th Army collapsed around Konotop, 3rd *Panzerdivision* took Romny on the Sula River. Kirponos sent a desperate request for reserves. There were none. The gap in Russian defences was now over forty-miles wide.

On 11th September, a telegram arrived at Supreme Command in Moscow, pleading for permission to attempt a withdrawal. Permission was refused. Marshal Timoshenko would replace Budenny. A suggested rescue bid with forces from the Bryansk Front was put in perspective when Eremenko revealed that he had only twenty available tanks still in battle condition. The Southwestern Front's role now was to stand its ground and fight simply in order to soak up German men, materials and time.

On 12th September, 1st *Panzergruppe* smashed through 297th Rifle Division of 38th Army. Southwestern Chief of Staff, Major General V.I. Tupikov, informed Shaposhnikov: 'The catastrophe has begun'.

The trap closed on 16th September when 1st and 2nd *Panzergruppen* met north of Lubny. Two days later, permission was given at last for Russian forces to fight their way out. Kirponos and his staff were all killed in a fire fight on 20th September, and the Russian pocket had been eliminated by 26th September.

German troops move past huge quantities of Russian equipment. As well as claiming over 600,000 prisoners, the German forces took the vehicles, guns and equipment of four complete Russian armies in the Kiev pocket.

The Germans claimed the destruction of four Russian armies: 5th, 21st, 26th and 37th, and the terrible mauling of three others: 13th, 38th and 40th. They claimed 665,212 prisoners and enormous quantities of equipment either destroyed or captured. Soviet figures give 677,085 as the number of soldiers on the Front, of whom 150,541 were outside the encirclement or escaped. German casualties in the Battle for the Ukraine numbered around 160,000.

Whichever figures are closest to the truth, the Battle of Kiev was a massive disaster for the Russians. Over half a million were dead or prisoners of war with, it transpired, a ten per cent survival rate to the war's end. The fall of the Ukraine opened up the Donets Basin and Crimea to Germany. These three areas produced over half of the Soviet grain harvest. Industrial production figures were plummetting by the end of 1941: compared to summer production figures, for example, steel production levels fell to thirty-three per cent, artillery shells to sixty per cent and aircraft to twenty-seven of their previous totals. Moreover, the black-earth region was the most important area for Russian production of coal, iron, steel, power, aluminium, chemicals and heavy engineering.

Guderian judged Kiev to be a tactical but not a strategic victory. The standard argument is that the diversion of 2nd *Panzergruppe* and 2nd Army to the south delayed the launch of Operation 'Typhoon' against Moscow by a crucial six weeks. That meant continuation of the operation into a second year, and Germany's chance of victory through *Blitzkrieg* was lost. Thereafter the contest became one of attrition.

The Battle of Kiev raises several important points. Only a maximum of fourteen to seventeen armoured and infantry divisions could have been launched on Moscow in September. This would have been insufficient. A drive by armoured divisions alone into the Moscow Zone of Defence would have been risky and unlikely to secure such a large urban area. Thus, even allowing for the consumption of resources entailed in the drive south, this campaign only contributed a couple of weeks to the delay of Operation 'Typhoon'.

Zhukov's analysis was that to leave a Southwestern Front capable of striking the flank of an advancing centre would have been courting disaster. The major industrial base of the country would also have been allowed a winter of production. Finally, would even a successful attack on Moscow have been a strategic victory? That great tactical victories may counteract a fundamental disproportion of strength between protagonists is not unknown in history, but is sufficiently rare. Even rarer would be a situation in which achieving such a victory was itself the cause of the lesser power being beaten by the greater.

THE SIEGE OF LENINGRAD

From 22nd June Army Group North advanced at a rapid pace towards Leningrad. Most of the huge losses of Soviet vehicles were a consequence of their abandonment due to lack of fuel and spare parts rather than their loss during combat. The swift overrunning of supply depots and the lack of Soviet logistical organization was disastrous for the Soviets.

Founded in 1700 to replace Moscow as Russia's capital, St. Petersburg had its name changed to Petrograd, to commemorate the birthplace of the Revolution in 1917, and Leningrad, in memory of the Bolshevik leader, in 1924. Located at the mouth of the River Neva, which links Lake Ladoga with the Gulf of Finland across the Karelian Isthmus, Leningrad was the symbolic and practical manifestation of a meeting between Western and Slavic traditions in Russia. A base for Russia's northern fleet and a major industrial centre containing almost three million inhabitants, Leningrad resented Moscow's displacement of it as Russia's premier city. Yet it was true that the advantage of its access to the Baltic Sea was undermined by its exposed position less than twenty miles from the border with Finland, albeit that the Russo-Finnish War of 1939-40 had mitigated this weakness by pushing the frontier beyond Vybord.

Leningrad featured prominently in 'Barbarossa', the German plan for the attack on the Soviet Union; its name seems to have drawn Hitler's ire in the same way that Stalingrad was to do in 1942. More practically, the aims were as follows: to secure a northern bastion for a line running south to the Ukraine from which the second phase attack could be launched; to linkup with Germany's Finnish allies; and to knock out the Russian Baltic Fleet at Kronstadt. As Directive 21 stated: 'Only after the fulfilment of this first essential task .. (including) the occupation of Leningrad and Kronstadt, will the attack be continued with the intention of occupying Moscow'. The task was given to Army Group North.

Positioned in East Prussia under Field Marshal Wilhelm Ritter von Leeb were twenty infantry divisions, three motorized divisions, three *Panzerdivisions* and 430 front-line fighters and bombers. With other forces, this amounted to half a million men divided into two armies (16th and 18th armies, commanded by colonel generals Ernst Busch and Georg von Küchler respectively), Colonel General Erich Höpner's Fourth *Panzergruppe* and Colonel General Alfred Keller's First Air Fleet. Four German divisions

On 30th June the authorities in Leningrad began to form militias for the defence of the city. The lack of officers, uniforms, weapons and ammunition meant these units were of dubious effectiveness, particularly in open battle. In street fighting in the suburbs, however, such considerations were less important.

Zhukov, the Russian hero of the Great Patriotic War - as the Second World War is known in the Soviet Union - commanded the defences of Leningrad until they were stabilized. On 6th October he was personally ordered by Stalin to return to the Moscow front to face Operation 'Typhoon'.

had been sent to Finland to support Finland's Marshal Baron Gustaf Mannerheim, who intended to reverse the result of the Russo-Finnish 1939-40 War.

Facing von Leeb on the Northwestern Front was the Russian Colonel General F.I. Kuznetsov, his 8th, 11th and 27th armies scattered across the Baltic States. Only 105 of his 1,150 tanks were new models, seventy-five per cent needed repair or servicing, while all but five of his divisions were between fifteen and thirty per cent below requirement in personnel and equipment. On the Northern Front, 14th, 7th and 23rd armies covered the frontier from Murmansk to Vyborg and here Lieutenant General Markian M. Popov was in command.

Von Leeb predicted he would be in Leningrad by 21st July. The River Dvina was reached in four days, from whence the main advance continued towards Pskov, which was entered on 8th July. A hundred miles further on, the Russians were desperately constructing the Luga Line for the shattered remnants of Northwestern Front to fall back on. Two thirds of Kuznetsov's divisions had sustained losses of over fifty per cent, few vehicles were operative and ammunition was almost exhausted. Troops were stripped from the Northern Front and thrown into the battle. Between 30th June and 7th July, 160,000 citizens of Leningrad signed up for a militia; recruitment was especially high amongst the Young Communists. With no training, inexperienced officers and little equipment, three divisions (later a fourth) were formed and sent to the River Luga. There they joined 60,000 civilians working eighteen-hour shifts to build defences. Having advanced nearly four hundred miles in three weeks, von Leeb needed to rest and replenish his forces, and his deadline passed as the Luga Line held.

Full-scale attack was relaunched by the Germans on 8th August. The arrival of 39th *Panzer Korps* from Army Group Centre secured von Leeb's southeastern flank against the Valdai Hills and allowed him to force the Line. North of Leningrad, the Finns had begun their attack on 11th July, but their major offensive wasn't launched until the last day of the month. Bled of troops, the Russians faced a two-to-one disadvantage in men, the Vyborg Line was abandoned and the front began to crumble. The enemy was closing on Leningrad from the south and north.

Leningrad was bulging at the seams. In the chaos of the first months of the war, evacuation had been ill organized. The rail network had been jammed with trucks loaded with industrial plant, while refugees had crowded in from the west. Dmitri V. Pavlov, Commissar of Trade and executive of the main administration of food supplies of the Defence Commissariat, who was sent from Moscow to take charge of food, estimated there were 2,887,000 civilians and half a million soldiers and sailors. The city had done its best to prepare for attack. Its citizens had built 18,000 miles of trenches, 450 miles of anti-tank ditches, twenty-two miles of barricades and 15,000 pillboxes.

The Germans reached Chudovo on 21st August, cutting the main rail line to Moscow; but more important was their capture of the town of Mga on 30th August. This last rail link with the outside world remained in German hands until 1944. Two days later, the shelling of Leningrad began. On the same day, the Finns reached their pre-1939 border. It was the city's good fortune that, despite great pressure from Berlin, the Finnish government adopted a policy of not advancing beyond its former frontiers. The battle in this sector became a series of skirmishes for minor strong points until the main

A camouflaged Russian machine-gun team wait for the *Luftwaffe*. The destruction of the bulk of the Soviet Union's initial air capability in the first few weeks of the war placed a great burden on its anti-aircraft ground defence until the losses could be replaced. Goering's boast that Leningrad would be destroyed by the *Luftwaffe* led to a sustained bombing campaign.

Although the main weapon used was the incendiary bomb, high explosives were also dropped (below left). The raids caused distress, but were much more strategically threatening when used against the vital supply line into the city across Lake Ladoga.

The shelling of Leningrad by German heavy artillery (facing page) was heavy and virtually continuous. Before the end of 1941 over thirty thousand shells had landed on the city, and in 1943 the Germans could still achieve a rate of over ten thousand a month.

Thor

German troops, dressed in winter white, move along a communication trench through woodland. As the battle stagnated into a siege, the fighting settled down into a static war for over two years. It was fought around buildings, thousands of bunkers and strongpoints, and hundreds of miles of trenches.

Russian advance of 1944.

When Schlüsselburg fell to the Germans in hand-to-hand fighting on 8th September, Leningrad's last land link with the rest of the Soviet Union was closed. There is strong evidence that the Soviet government considered scuttling the fleet and blowing up and abandoning the city. The airlift of specialists

Spotters for Soviet artillery keep watch in a lookout post on the outskirts of Leningrad. By 1944 the Red Army had gathered 21,600 guns, 1,500 Karyusha rocket batteries, 1,475 tanks and self-propelled guns, and 1,500 planes on the Leningrad and Volkhov fronts for the final relief of the city.

and weapons was out, not in! Only lack of pontoons stopped the Germans crossing the Neva that day. As the disaster in the Ukraine moved to its climax and Stalin's thoughts concentrated on the battle he was convinced was soon to begin for Moscow, Leningrad was left to survive on its own resources. He was prepared to loan one asset though: Marshal Georgi K. Zhukov.

Von Leeb concentrated eleven divisions, including two *Panzerdivisions*, for the assault. They fought their way through the final defence line outside the city, taking Pushkin on 16th September. The Leningrad edition of *Pravda* carried an editorial beginning: 'The enemy is at the gates ..' The following two days saw fighting in Ligovo on the edge of the city. The Russians held one last building there, Klinovsky House, and rooms changed hands several times. Zhukov seemed everywhere, ordering continuous attack and threatening execution for any retreat.

Although the Russians did not know it, the assault was about to end. Operation 'Typhoon' was a higher priority for the Germans and the withdrawal of the *Panzers* could wait no longer. On 21st September, Army Group North began to dig in. Leningrad was to be reduced by siege; the ever optimistic Goering claiming that he could level the city with his *Luftwaffe*.

A city of Leningrad's size could be expected to consume around 3,000 tons of food a day. When Pavlov arrived, his first two actions were to tighten up rationing and to take stock of all the food available. On the new ration limits, it was estimated that there were sufficient stocks of grain, flour, cereals and meat to last a month and enough sugar to suffice for two months. The only way to bring in supplies was from the Volkhov railhead downriver to Novaya Ladoga, across Lake Ladoga to Osinovets, and by truck or narrow-gauge railway to Leningrad. The trip took sixteen hours (without allowing for loading or unloading) and so could not be completed under cover of darkness. It was subject to shelling at both ends, and air attack on the lake. By 15th November, when ice stopped the boats, twenty days worth of food had been brought in since Leningrad's isolation. This wasn't replenishing consumption, and stocks had diminished to a fortnight's supply of basic food commodities. Private use of coal and kerosene had already been halted and, tragically, the winter ahead was due to be the coldest in living memory.

Worse still, though the German advance into Leningrad had been halted, their drive east had not. On 9th November, Tikhvin fell,

which meant that the closest railhead was then Zoborie, which lay over one hundred miles from Lake Ladoga as the crow flies, and much further through the forest and swamps. The food ration for troops and manual workers was cut to 1,000 calories a day. Other groups got less. Five men, a horse and a sled were sent out from the city on still-thin ice to see if there was a route across Lake Lagoda. They made it after sixty hours in a continual blizzard. On 24th November, ten light trucks set out on the trail they had blazed. Two fell through the ice and the other eight brought a meagre thirty-three tons of food. The people of Leningrad were starving to death.

On 9th December, the Soviet 4th Army recaptured Tikhvin. As a result, the six-day journey on the track cut from Zaborie was redundant, but the twenty-seven-hour ice road across the lake was still horrific. Throughout the month, little food came into the city, despite heroic efforts on the ice that cost thousands of lives. When the cats, dogs and rats had been eaten, evergreen leaves, glue from bookbindings, leather, industrial cellulose and, it was whispered, human flesh came onto the menu. In January, the last power station closed, and as a result so did the last water pumping station supplying the crucial bakeries. Volunteers were called for to meet the bakeries' needs by bucket. The destruction of all wooden houses in the city to provide fuel was ordered. The death rate reached 4,000 a day from starvation, hypothermia and diseases brought on by malnutrition. Mass graves were dynamited out of the frozen earth.

The winter grew harsher, and this was a turning point, for Lake Lagoda froze to a great depth. New, solid ice roads were constructed, and by January's end a daily average of 1,708 tons of food was being brought in. This was raised to 3,072 tons in February and 3,660 tons in March. The lorries took 539,400 people out of the city. The death toll remained high, reaching a peak in April, for starvation is a slow but, beyond a certain limit, irrevocable death. In all probability at least 800,000 died from hunger and resultant causes, and another 200,000 troops and civilians were killed in the fighting and bombardment. After a further 448,694 people were evacuated across Lake Ladoga in the summer of 1942, only 600,000 of the original population remained in Leningrad.

Although the Germans had plans to renew their attack on the city in 1942, these were forestalled by greater events elsewhere on the Eastern Front. The Soviet Union, likewise, was content simply to break the blockade, when Schlüsselberg was recaptured, with Operation 'Iskra' at the beginning of 1943. That year was spent building up 1,250,000 men to overwhelm Army Group North, commanded since June 1942 by von Küchler. When the attack came in 1944, it was part of the process of total German collapse that led the Red Army to Berlin. The official ending of the siege of Leningrad on 27th January was but a footnote, but the initial battle for Leningrad had had significance. If the city had fallen in 1941, much more of Army Group North would have been freed to sweep south towards Moscow, as the original planning of Barbarossa outlined. The loss of the Russian Baltic Fleet would have allowed the Germans to ship to a forward supply base, and use the Leningrad rail network from there. The psychological effect on both sides can only be guessed at, but it must be presumed that it would have been considerable. The Murmansk supply line to the west, quantitively limited but psychologically important, would most probably have been cut. However, the siege of Leningrad continued because of its increasing unimportance to both sides, which meant that neither committed sufficient forces to break the deadlock until the Soviet Union was advancing on all fronts in 1944. Finnish caution meant the ring was never tight enough. Other battles, at Moscow, Stalingrad and Kursk, would decide the outcome of the war: Leningrad received the Order of its namesake.

Field Marshal von Küchler's Army Group North (below), divided into 16th and 18th Armies, could muster only 385 tanks in 1944. His 741,000 men were substantially outnumbered by the 1,241,000 officers and men of the Red Army facing them. The Russian offensive that began on 14th January did not halt until the Germans unconditionally surrendered.

Facing page: a young German light-machine-gunner waits in his winter foxhole. The campaign on the Eastern Front saw the destruction of the German Army as it was bled white of experienced manpower. Its morale, likewise, seeped away into the vast expanses and cruel winters of Russia, as the sheer scale of the conflict overwhelmed Germany.

BATAAN AND CORREGIDOR

A pre-war practise of firing one of Corregidor's ten ton 12' breech-loading mortars. A good crew could fire a 1,000lb shell once every two minutes. The Japanese concentrated their massed artillery fire on the mortars' open casements and, on 5th May - the day the Japanese landed - only two were still in action.

During the summer of 1940, the Japanese Imperial General Staff started to draw up large-scale plans to destroy Western control of Southeast Asia. There were major disagreements about what to do with the Philippines. Many senior army officers were keen to by-pass the archipelago altogether and focus attacks on the British in Malaya and the Dutch in the East Indies. What could be gained, they argued, from capturing the Philippines? The islands, while still technically an American protectorate, were due to achieve complete political independence in 1945. Invading Japanese troops could scarcely pretend to be liberating an oppressed colonial people: their reception might be hostile rather than friendly. The Philippines had few of the rich natural resources which made the Dutch and British colonies such attractive targets for those who dreamed of a self-sufficient Japanese 'New Order', and an attack on the Philippines meant war with the United States - something to be avoided at all costs.

Admiral Yamamoto, commander of Japan's Combined Fleet, offered equally powerful counter-arguments for Japan's invasion of the Philippines. It was argued that it was simply too dangerous to leave the Philippines alone. Any southward move would mean war with America, a war which Japan would certainly lose unless it eliminated American naval and air power in the Pacific at the outset. At Yamamoto's insistence, the Japanese government agreed to begin their expansion with an attack on the American Fleet in Hawaii, an operation coordinated with simultaneous strikes against American bases in the Philippines. In the autumn of 1941, Masaharu Homma, one of Japan's most flamboyant generals, was appointed to command the Philippines invasion force, Formosa-based 14th Army (veteran 16th and 48th divisions) supported by an air fleet of some 500 front-line war planes.

The Americans were aware of the Philippines' vulnerability to Japanese attack ever since they had seized them from the Spanish in 1898. Exercises conducted throughout the 1920s and

Their flag of the rising sun streaming in the breeze, Japanese infantry trudge south from Lingayen Gulf on 22nd December, 1941. Japanese march discipline was poor. They straggled along, often strapping their rifles and equipment to bicycles, and that evening were ambushed by the 26th Cavalry outside Rosario.

1930s had shown that the Philippines' 7,000 islands were virtually impossible to defend. War Plan Orange (WPO-3), formulated over a number of decades, supplied a feasible strategy to ward off the Japanese. The Americans would concentrate on holding the neck of the Bataan Peninsula and the island fortresses of Corregidor and Fort Drum, denying the Japanese access to the vital Manila Bay area until the U.S. Pacific Fleet came to the rescue. It was a stop-gap measure: from 1935 onwards, Washington accelerated the plans for full Philippine independence by 1946, after which all U.S. defence obligations would cease. In the autumn of 1935, General Douglas MacArthur, recently retired army Chief of Staff, was sent to the islands to create a native army for the new, independent Philippines. MacArthur's emotional commitment to the islands – where he had served at the start of his military career in 1904 – led him to view this assignment as the fitting culmination of his life's work. He was determined to bequeath to the Philippines a large, Swiss-style citizen's army, capable of defending the entire archipelago. MacArthur was soon heavily involved in local politics. Financially dependent on the Philippine administration for the success of his cherished, embryonic Philippine army, he inevitably began to exaggerate its capability and efficiency. He tried to convince Washington to scrap WPO-3 and to authorise him to defend all the islands with his army. Initially a political ploy to gain funds and attention, by 1940 MacArthur had been convinced by his own propaganda. Some of his aides (Major Dwight D. Eisenhower among them) questioned his judgement and mental stability. Admiral Hart, commander of the United State's small Asiatic fleet, confided to his wife: 'Douglas is not completely sane, and may not have been for some considerable time'.

On 26th July, 1941, Washington abandoned WPO-3 in favour of MacArthur's strategy of defending the entire archipelago; a move which was less an affirmation of faith in MacArthur than a warning to Japan – who had recently moved into southern Indo-China – that further expansion southward would lead to conflict with the United States. The Roosevelt government made the message clear by sending reinforcements to the Philippines and promoting MacArthur from the local Filipino rank of Field Marshal to Commander American Army Forces Far East. By December 1941, MacArthur commanded 100,000 Filipino and some 30,000 U.S. regulars, including the redoubtable American-Filipino Philippine Scouts. In addition, he had 277 aircraft, including thirty-six B-17 heavy bombers and a hundred modern Warhawk fighters (the most powerful concentration of U.S. air power outside Hawaii) and Admiral Hart's Asiatic Fleet of three cruisers, thirteen destroyers, several

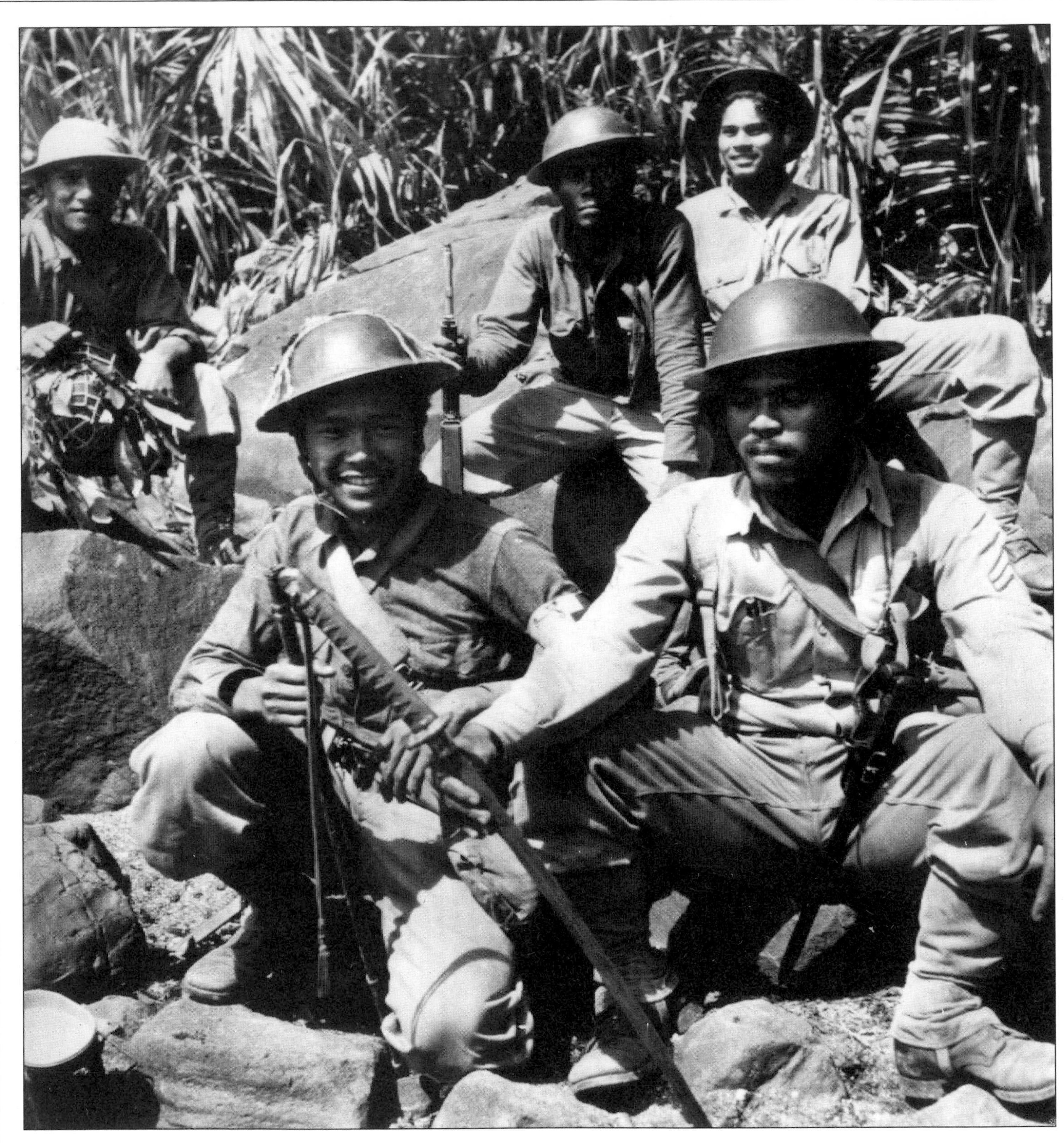

Facing page: Philippine Scouts proudly display a Japanese officer's sword, captured on 23rd January, 1942, when they repelled a landing on the western coast of the Bataan Peninsula. Unlike conscript Filipino forces, the Scouts were a regular unit of the American Army and were both feared and respected by the Japanese.

Right: closely followed by infantry, Japanese light tanks roll down a corduroy road through the wreckage of Bataan's Mount Samat line on 7th April, 1942. Although prominently featured in propaganda photographs, the tanks were of little use in the fighting on Bataan, and many were knocked out by American small-arms fire.

squadrons of torpedo boats and twenty eight submarines. MacArthur organised his forces into four commands which covered the entire archipelago; the vulnerable north Luzon region was to be commanded by Major General Jonathan Wainwright, who was allocated four divisions, about half the available manpower.

Wainwright's four divisions were responsible for the defence of about 300 miles, but both he and MacArthur knew that, apart from heavily defended Manila Bay, there was only one other place in northern Luzon where a large-scale landing could take place – Lingayen Gulf on the western coast of the Philippines, halfway between Manila and the northern city of Aparri. It was on the shores of Lingayen Gulf that both MacArthur and Wainwright believed the decisive battle for the Philippines would be fought.

MacArthur and Wainwright were correct in their suspicions: Japan's General Homma was planning a massive airstrike on Luzon's airfields. Even if the five-hour time difference between Hawaii and the Philippines meant that the attack on Luzon could not coincide with the strike against Pearl Harbour, Homma still planned to maximize surprise by hitting Luzon shortly after dawn on 8th December. In the event dense fog over Formosa prevented the Japanese takeoff and gave the Americans several hours to mobilize and prepare their defences. But the delay worked to Japan's advantage. When at midday American aircraft – including the precious B-17s – put down to refuel after a morning spent fruitlessly patrolling over Luzon, Japanese bombers suddenly arrived. Within minutes MacArthur had lost most of his air force – another Pearl Harbor, but this time with less excuse.

During the next two days Japanese aircraft launched a relentless assault on northern and central Luzon. They destroyed torpedo stocks at Cavite, Manila Bay's naval base, making reloading impossible for Admiral Hart's submarines, and drove what was left of the American air force to bases at Mindanao, the southernmost island of the Philippines. By 10th December, the Japanese had achieved control of the air. That day they landed small forces at Aparri and Vigan in the north of Luzon and two days later further forces at Lagaspi in the extreme south. Homma was trying to divert MacArthur's troops from the shores of Lingayen

Gulf – he too had realised that it was the only practical coastal landing spot – but MacArthur refused to be sidetracked. His troops were so geared up for a major Japanese landing at Lingayen that they spent the night of 12th December blazing away at a small Japanese motor boat which had entered the Gulf. By dawn MacArthur's staff were claiming a major American victory and the Battle of Lingayen Gulf received widespread U.S. news coverage.

When the real Japanese invasion of the Gulf occurred on 22nd December, American glory was not much in evidence. Hart's submarines lay in wait, but when they sighted the Japanese warships, some inexperienced captains dived deep, while others who fired watched aghast as their torpedoes hit the Japanese hulls without exploding. That night the American Navy learned that most of its torpedo stocks were defective, but, in what became one of the great scandals of the Second World War, nearly eighteen months elapsed before the defect was remedied. By dawn the Japanese convoy, barely aware of the American submarine attack, had penetrated deeply into Lingayen Gulf. The mountainous surf which met 48th Division's landing forces almost put paid to Homma's plans, capsizing scores of invasion barges, drowning hundreds of overladen soldiers and washing up others without arms or equipment. Wainright seized the opportunity and ordered a Filipino reservist division under Brigadier General Clyde A. Selleck to attack. Thanks to MacArthur's decision to keep American soldiers in the north, Filipino divisions were all that were at Wainwright's disposal at this time. It should have been a great American victory, but

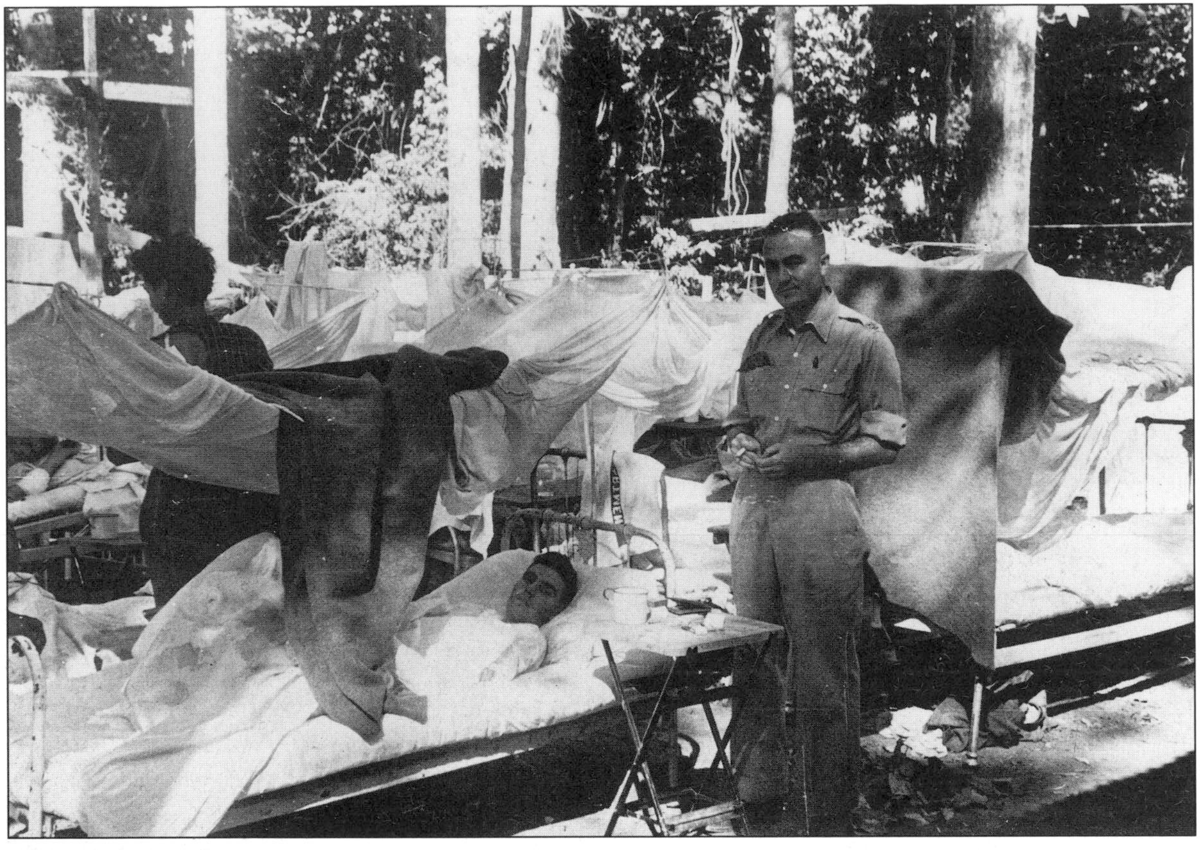

A primitive field hospital hacked out of Bataan's jungle. With few drugs, no running water and no covering for the beds - except a mosquito net -, the death rate from wounds and sickness was very high. MacArthur neglected medical arrangements in this notoriously unhealthy area - an oversight Bataan survivors found hard to forgive.

instead battalion after battalion of Filipinos refused to advance and, as the Japanese moved towards them, melted into the countryside, abandoning their equipment, including entire artillery batteries. By nightfall Homma had finally managed to land tanks and artillery and 48th Division began moving inland.

MacArthur, bitterly disappointed by the rapid disintegration of his native Filipino units, blamed Selleck and demoted him to colonel. But the fault was MacArthur's: Wainwright had never entertained any illusions about reservist Filipino fighting effectiveness and indeed had also tried to stem the Japanese advance by more reliable means - the regular Philippine Scouts whom he had ordered north from Manila Bay. For two days the Scouts, supported by a tank battalion, fought a running battle against the Japanese. By 24th December they seemed to be holding the Japanese at Rosario, a town twenty miles south of the Japanese beachhead. Wainwright intended to fall back from this position some ten miles to the Agno River, a natural defence line running across the central plain of Luzon, but that very morning came a fresh blow - Homma's 16th Division landed at Lamon Bay, a hundred miles southeast of Manila on Luzon's eastern coast, and advanced on the capital. The news of this landing, followed by Wainwright's request that he be allowed to pull his forces further south to behind the Agno River, at last galvanised MacArthur to action: within hours he had notified all American units that WPO-3, the old plan for the defence of the Bataan Peninsula, was now in effect.

Over the next eight days and nights the road around the northern end of Manila Bay to the Bataan Peninsula was packed with convoys as Americans and Filipinos belatedly moved in supplies and prepared defensive positions. All the while Japan's 48th Division continued to push south from Lingayen through the central plain, while their 16th Division advanced northwest towards Manila from Lamon Bay. In contrast to the lacklustre performance of Filipino reserve divisions on 22nd December, American and Filipino regular units now conducted determined rearguard actions which

The beginning of the Bataan 'Death March' on 10th April, 1942. Thousands of American and Filipino soldiers sit in the burning sun without food or water. As the columns staggered north such rests became infrequent. Thousands dropped from exhaustion and were bayonetted by Japanese guards.

successfully slowed the rate of the Japanese advance. It was not until 2nd January, 1942, that the jaws of the pincers slammed shut with the advance guard of the Japanese 48th Division meeting the leading elements of 16th Division in the streets of Manila. The Americans had long gone, MacArthur having declared Manila an open city on 26th December. As far as Homma and the Japanese Imperial Headquarters were concerned the campaign was now over. All that remained was the mopping up of scattered American forces on Mindanao and other southern islands, and the rounding up on the Bataan Peninsula of forces which Homma believed were little more than a disorganised mob. Indeed, so confident were the Japanese that the veteran 48th Division was ordered south to help in the conquest of the Dutch East Indies, and its place taken by 10,000 poorly trained, middle-aged reservists commanded by Lieutenant General Akiri Nara.

In fact some 80,000 American and Filipino troops were now in the Bataan Peninsula. Since 26th December MacArthur's forces had constructed a system of field fortifications which ran east and west of the forbidding, jungle-clad slopes of Mount Natib, a jagged volcanic cone which dominated the neck of the peninsula. Three divisions, backed by 200 guns, manned what the Americans called the Abaucay Line, which ran across the neck of the peninsula, except for a seven-mile gap at Mount Natib, which MacArthur believed impassable. In the eight days which had elapsed between MacArthur's decision to implement WPO-3 and the Japanese

With their few possessions slung between bamboo poles, survivors of the Bataan 'Death March' stagger into Bilibid prison. During the preceding two weeks more than 10,000 (including some 2,300 Americans) had died on the sixty-five-mile long march. Ahead lay nearly three years of brutal captivity.

Lieutenant General Jonathan Wainwright broadcasting his order for American forces throughout the Philippines to lay down their arms on 6th May, 1942. Throughout the day Wainwright had tried to confine his surrender to Corregidor but, exhausted and emotionally drained, he had finally capitulated in the face of a Japanese threat to massacre the island's garrison.

occupation of Manila the Americans had been able to move vast supplies of ammunition into Bataan, but because top priority had been given to military supplies they had stored only about thirty days' supply of food. More worrying still to MacArthur's staff was the shortage of medical supplies, particularly quinine, because Bataan was a notoriously malarial region. An additional problem was the hordes of civilian refugees who had crowded into Bataan – the Americans believed there were at least 26,000 – who made demands on supplies barely adequate for the soldiers. MacArthur's situation was anomalous: Bataan offered an excellent defensive position, but the logistic situation in everything except ammunition was precarious. MacArthur and key members of his staff, accompanied by the President of the Philippines, Manuel Quezon, soon moved from Bataan to Corregidor, the fortress island which lay two miles off the tip of the peninsula, and established a headquarters in the Malinta tunnel complex. From here MacArthur sent increasingly peremptory messages to Washington demanding the immediate dispatch of relief convoys. Unwilling to believe that America's situation was truly desperate, MacArthur urged his troops to fight on because 'help is on the way from the United States – thousands of troops and hundreds of planes are being dispatched'. It wasn't true but MacArthur didn't know this – besides, the message did serve to improve American and Filipino morale.

Confident of victory, on 10th January Nara's reservists advanced down the peninsula in two columns, one to the east and one to the west side of Mount Natib. At 3.30 p.m. a devastating artillery barrage hit the eastern column as it marched through sugar cane fields only twenty miles north of Marivales, a town at the very tip of the peninsula. By evening the western column was also involved in heavy fighting. Greatly outnumbered and without adequate air and artillery support, Nara's troops battered ineffectually at the Abaucay line for the next twelve days, while a regimental-sized task force probed and eventually found a route through the supposedly impenetrable jungles of Mount Natib. On 22nd January the Japanese burst out of the jungle to the rear of the Abaucay line. American and Filipino counterattacks on 23rd and 24th January failed to dislodge them, and a day later MacArthur's forces were falling south. It might have developed into a rout but Nara's men were too exhausted to follow – they had suffered at least 1,500 dead and wounded in the battle, the first real test of their fighting prowess since the beginning of the campaign.

The retreating Americans and Filipinos managed to form a new line along an old cobbled road running across the peninsula twelve miles north of Marivales. The slopes of Mount Samat, an extinct volcano in the centre of the line, offered U.S. gunners a superb vantage point. Homma, dismayed by the unexpectedly effective American resistance, devised a much more complex plan for the rest of the campaign. On 23rd January small Japanese forces landed well behind American lines on the western side of the peninsula, and these probes were reinforced on 26th January by the landing of a battalion-sized force. Nara's men, supported by as much artillery as could be brought forward, simultaneously hurled themselves at the Samat line. American gunfire cut them down in swathes. The landings to the south fared no better – American and Filipino rear-echelon troops managed to contain the beachheads and after three weeks of bitter fighting, on 17th February, the last Japanese positions were overrun. Homma had already called a halt to the attacks against Mount

Carefully positioned by photographers around one of Corregidor's 14' coastal guns, Japanese soldiers give a rousing banzai cheer. By this time - 6th May - Japanese civilians had become used to such scenes. It was the last they were to enjoy, for in the waters of the Solomon Islands the tide of battle had already turned.

Samat on 8th February. Now reduced to 3,000 effectives (the Bataan campaign cost him 7,000 dead and wounded and 10,000 through disease), Homma feared an American counterattack. His admission to Imperial Headquarters that the campaign had foundered in disaster and his appeal for reinforcements signalled the end of his career.

Unlike the spurious 'battle' for Lingayen Gulf on 12th December, Americans and Filipinos had now won a genuine victory. Though elsewhere the tide of Japanese conquest rolled remorselessly forward, 'Old Glory' still flew over Bataan. The American press now referred to the Philippine's defenders as heroes and elevated their general to the status of demi-god. The defence of Bataan certainly improved morale within the United States, but paradoxically the morale of the defenders was now beginning to falter. MacArthur had long realised that hopes of relief were chimerical – his continued demands for reinforcements eventually produced an order from Roosevelt that the general, his family and key members of his staff should escape to Australia when MacArthur considered the time was right. The main problem his men faced was hunger. By mid-February the garrison was subsisting on less than half normal combat rations and parties sometimes foraged deep behind Japanese lines. Malnutrition became widespread, and with it came diseases such as dysentery, beriberi and malaria. In mid-March medical officers reported that 60,000 were unfit for combat. Hunger and disease were succeeding where the Japanese had failed. MacArthur left for Australia on 11th March, appointing Wainwright to command with orders to fight to the end.

By early April Wainwright commanded only some 20,000 effectives and these now faced a Japanese army swollen to 50,000 by reinforcements. On 3rd April a massive barrage hit the lower slopes of Mount Samat, setting fire to the cane fields and incinerating American positions. A gap was torn in the American line and the Japanese surged through. Within three days they had crossed the mountains and

MacArthur as the American press saw him - the resolute hero of Bataan. Although his bungling of the campaign was well known in Washington, the Roosevelt administration did nothing to dissuade journalists from transforming him into a symbol of American resistance. The truth would have been bad for morale.

were herding a now disorganised mob of Americans and Filipinos into Marivales. Wainwright, at his headquarters on Corregidor, forbad surrender but on 9th April his subordinates on Bataan disobeyed and ordered U.S. forces on the peninsula to lay down their arms. In all, 76,000 surrendered, and the Japanese were soon marching them the sixty-five miles north to the railway which would take them to Camp O'Donnel and imprisonment. Only 54,000 reached the camp alive after what became known as the Bataan Death March.

Wainwright still commanded 15,000 men on Corregidor, but most were administration troops untrained for combat. The Malinta tunnel complex sheltered some 6,000 of them plus more than 1,000 sick and wounded. Morale was generally low, except amongst the Marines and the soldiers who manned the beach defences. Corregidor had already become used to heavy bombing but now the Japanese moved some 200 guns to the heights above Marivales, including gigantic 240mm mortars, the largest they possessed. The bombardment began on 10th April and, growing heavier each day, lasted without intermission for more than three weeks. The once lush island was reduced to a smoking moonscape. Even within the Malinta tunnel the force of the concussion caused nose and ear haemorrhages – above, the defender's heavy batteries were silenced one by one, the last, a thirteen-ton mortar, being blown 150 yards through the air by the force of an explosion. Just before midnight on 5th May the Japanese stormed ashore. The battle on the beach was short and violent, the invaders suffering heavy casualties, but shortly after dawn the Japanese were at the eastern end of the Malinta tunnel. Thousands of Americans sheltered behind the tunnel's steel gates but, unlike the men on the shore, they were little more than a frightened mob. In mid-afternoon an exhausted Wainwright met with Homma and surrendered not only Corregidor but all American forces in the Philippines. Three thousand miles to the south a furious MacArthur vetoed Roosevelt's suggestion that Wainwright be awarded the Medal of Honor.

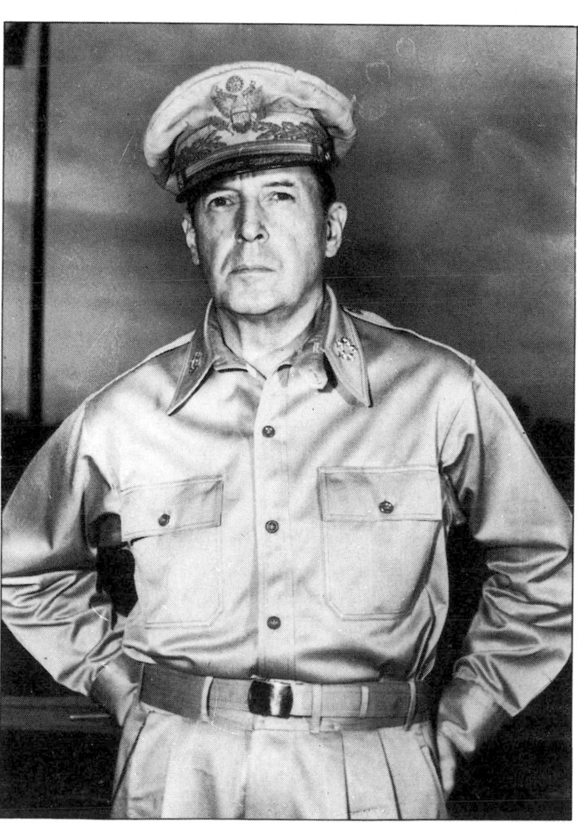

It was widely believed during the war and for many years thereafter that the Philippine campaign seriously disrupted Japan's timetable by tying up her forces in an exhausting siege and giving other Allied forces a breathing space. It is now known that except for the fillip it gave Allied moral it had virtually no effect on Japanese operations elsewhere. The Philippine campaign, however, did have a considerable effect on the way America was to conduct the Pacific War. After MacArthur's arrival in Australia on 17th March and his pledge to return to the Philippines, Roosevelt had little option other than to appoint him Supreme Commander of the newly formed Southwest Pacific Area. Over the next two years the general was to use this position and his immense popularity in the United States to force upon the joint chiefs of staff the reconquest of the Philippines, in contrast to the Navy's strategy of bypassing the islands and driving directly across the Central Pacific towards Japan. MacArthur's dispute with the Navy was long and bitter and still influences the way historians view the Pacific War. Certainly after the heroic stand made there, it would have been hard for the United States to avoid further involvement in the Philippines. Even today many Americans still feel an odd tingle in the spine when they hear the names Bataan and Corregidor.

BATTLE OF GAZALA

Colonel General Erwin Rommel (left), watches the arrival of a troop transport bringing troops for his famous *Afrika Korps*. The 'Desert Fox' proved the ablest commander of armour in the struggle for North Africa. His boldness and drive outwitted his opponents time and again, not least in the Battle of Gazala.

Facing page top: a German *PzKpfw* III for Rommel's 15th or 21st *Panzerdivision* being unloaded at Tripoli. The desert war centred around armour. This tank weighed twenty-two tons, had a hundred-mile range before it required refuelling, and needed a crew of five. Armed with a short-barrelled 5cm gun and a pair of 7.9 machine guns, it was an effective vehicle.

Facing page bottom: an Axis convoy steams into Tripoli. The battle of supply was critical to the desert war. The Axis enjoyed a short sea-route from Naples and Palermo, but had to face British naval and air forces operating from inconveniently-placed Malta. In 1942, most Allied supplies had to come from England round the Cape of Good Hope to Suez.

The long battle against General Erwin Rommel and his German *Afrika Korps* and its Italian allies for control of the Western Desert raged from April, 1941, to November, 1942. Neither side found it an easy theatre of war. Long distances over a flat and seemingly featureless desert of rock, sand, salt marsh and dust storms, hot days yet cold nights, and the lack of almost all resources, took a heavy toll on men and vehicles alike. Drinking water was as precious as petrol and disease and desert sores were prevalent – although the German troops seemed to adapt to local conditions rather better than their opponents.

It was as much a battle of supply as of shells, bullets or bombs. Owing to Axis air domination of the Mediterranean, all commodities for the British 8th Army had to be brought round the Cape of Good Hope – a distance of 11,000 miles – to its bases around Alexandria, Cairo and the Suez Canal. In contrast, only some 700 miles of sea divided Rommel's base of Tripoli from Naples, but the comparative shortness of this sea route was partly offset by the presence of Royal Navy and RAF formations operating from much-bombed, but still defiant, Malta, which took a heavy toll of Axis shipping at critical times. Within North Africa, the rival forces operated up and down the Mediterranean coastal areas, caught upon a seeming 'strategic see-saw'. The two 'goal-lines' were Tripoli and Alexandria, the important port of Tobruk, with its harbour and water-filtration plant, being halfway between the two. Any success in battle was followed by a pursuit of the defeated enemy which would end once the joyous victors could no longer ignore the length of their lines of communication, while the depression of the defeated gradually lessened the further they retired as they picked up reinforcements, supplies and munitions from their forward depots and from their ultimate bases as they drew nearer to them. The result was a period of strategic stalemate, dictated by the inexorable laws of strategic consumption (or the 'diminishing power of the offensive'), until the refurbished defender was ready to launch a counter-offensive on superior terms, whereupon the roles were reversed.

Colonel General Erwin Rommel had already been twice on the offensive and twice repulsed (by the hardy defence of Tobruk and then General Sir Claude Auchinleck's Operation 'Crusader' respectively). Now, in the late spring of 1942, he was about to launch his third and greatest effort. His forces grouped around El Agheila (where they had retreated in January) had been increased by mid-May to some 560 tanks, 704 aircraft and some 90,000 men supported by up to 23,000 more, divided between the three German *Panzerdivisions* of the *Afrika Korps, Gruppe Cruewell* (basically the Italian X and XXI Corps) and the Italian XX Corps. He was facing Lieutenant General Neil Ritchie's 8th Army of British, Indian, South African and Free French formations comprising two corps (13th and 30th) and an Army Reserve – in all perhaps 100,000 front-line troops with some 25,000 more in supporting roles. They were equipped with 849 tanks and 320 aircraft of the Desert Air Office, of which, however, only under 200 were in service in May. The stolid and well-meaning Ritchie (until recently Auchinleck's chief-of-staff) was to prove no match for the brilliant Württemberger Rommel, and was somewhat overpowered by his two corps commanders, Lieutenant General 'Strafer' Gott, and Lieutenant General Norrie, who were both far more experienced 'desert hands' than himself. Rommel's two key subordinates, lieutenant generals Cruewell and Nehring, were also first class.

The Gazala Line that was to give its name to the impending battle had been extemporized on Auchinleck's orders to serve two virtually irreconcilable functions. First, following the *Afrika Korps'* defeat in Operation 'Crusader'

late the previous year, it was intended to provide a safe shield for Tobruk against future Axis attack. Secondly, given the increasing danger of an all-out onslaught against Malta and Gozo, it was deemed essential for 8th Army, following the customary reinforcement and resupply pause, to press on westwards to regain Benghazi and the Libyan airfields within air support range of the threatened islands: the Gazala position would serve as the forward base and starting point for any such offensive. As usual, however, Rommel was destined to deliver his blow first, and, in response, the Gazala Line concept fell between two stools.

To call the position a 'line' is something of a misnomer. Sited over an area of 1,860 square miles, the Gazala defences did not entirely enclose the area they were intended to defend. The western side comprised a formidable 'mine marsh', of varying depth, which ran from the Mediterranean coast near Gazala due south into the desert for a distance of forty-three miles. To find the tens of thousands of anti-tank mines needed meant many of the perimeter defences of Tobruk had to be dismantled and re-sited. Placed within the minefield were a series of strong 'keeps' or 'boxes' – defensive positions capable of holding an all-arms garrison of brigade size. Seven of these 'boxes' were incorporated in the westward facing defences: a cluster of five defended the coast road and the area immediately to its south, the centre was protected by 150th Brigade Group Box, which overlooked two important desert tracks, and the seventh at Bir Hacheim provided the anchor at the southernmost point. South of Bir Hacheim the desert stretched away for some fifty miles to the edge of the Great Sand Sea. To guard against the obvious possibility of a 'desert hook', a secondary (but unfinished) line of 'boxes' ran east along a ridge from Sidi Muftah to El Adem. Finally, tucked away to the rear, was the thirty-mile perimeter of Tobruk's main defences, depleted of many of its mines to supply the minefield.

Dumps of water, petrol, supplies and ammunition were established within each box, but the main resources for the forthcoming June offensive were stocked around Tobruk and its much-damaged port. Ostensibly strong, in fact the design of the Gazala Line was riddled with the inconsistencies occasioned by its double set of requirements. It was not going to fool Rommel for long.

To hold this position, Ritchie placed XIII Corps in the western defences, supported by 1st and 32nd Army Tank Brigades. Major General Pienaar's 1st South African Division was placed nearest to the coast, Major General Ramsden's 50th (Northumbrian) Division was deployed in the centre, while Bir Hacheim was entrusted to General Koenig's 1st Free French Brigade. Two motorized brigades of XXX Corps were placed to the south and east of Bir Hacheim to watch the desert flank, with the rest of Major General Messervy's 7th Armoured Division positioned its brigades to the rear, with Major General Lumsden's 1st Armoured Division (again split into self-contained brigades) held a little further north. Finally, to hold Tobruk, Major General Klopper's 2nd South African Division manned the depleted defences. Thus 8th Army's resources were widely scattered and poorly integrated.

The Axis front line was around Tmimi, only twenty miles west of Gazala. There, by mid-

Left: the best Allied tank in the desert in mid-1942, the American M3 General Grant. This medium tank weighed 28.5 tons, had a range of 108 miles, and required a crew of six. Armed with a hull-mounted 75mm gun and in the turret a 37mm gun, together with four machine guns, its main drawback was the main armament's restricted arc of fire.

Below: the Duke of Gloucester, brother of King George VI, talks to General Sir Claude Auchinleck, Commander-in-Chief Middle East, while visiting XXX Corps. Auchinleck was a tough commander, but he allowed Lieutenant General Sir Neil Ritchie of 8th Army too much latitude.

A German field gun pounds General Klopper's defences, many of whose minefields had been moved west before the battle. Despite a determined defence, the Gazala Line was cracked by Rommel's superior generalship. The prize was Tobruk, with its mass of supplies of all sorts which could not be destroyed in time.

Rommel allowed for a four-day battle.

Two flaws in this plan were going to lead the Germans close to disaster, prior to their ultimate victory. Firstly, German Intelligence knew nothing about the existence of the 150th Brigade Box that blocked the Trigh Capuzzo and the Trigh el Abd trails – an early surprise for Rommel that turned into a brief, but major, logistical crisis for him. Secondly, Rommel himself erroneously believed that the battle would be over in ninety-six hours, basing his view upon his low estimate of General Ritchie's capabilities.

On the afternoon of 26th May *Gruppe Cruewell* advanced from Tmimi to make a heavy attack on the northern half of the Gazala Line. Fighting was severe, but the enemy was contained, and because it suited his estimate Ritchie informed Auchinleck that all was going well. Meantime, however, far to the south, Rommel was leading the vast sweep by the Axis armour. By the early hours of 27th May he was past Bir Hacheim, and during the next twenty-four hours the Germans defeated and scattered 3rd Indian Motorized Brigade and 7th Motorized Brigade before taking Retma and falling upon the isolated 4th Armoured Brigade in its turn. As this formation reeled back, the *Afrika Korps* smote 22nd Armoured Brigade as it attempted to intervene in the escalating battle. It, too, retreated towards Knightsbridge in disorder. In some alarm, Ritchie now realised he had misjudged his foe. So far all was going Rommel's way, but by evening he knew of two important setbacks. First, *Ariete*'s attack on Bir Hacheim had been beaten off, and second – and far worse – *Trieste* had failed to create the critical supply corridors through the minefields.

Nevertheless, Rommel decided to press northwards to exploit his initial success, gambling on Ritchie's unawareness of the growing Axis crisis. By late on 28th May he had bludgeoned his way past Knightsbridge to reach the unfinished 'Commonwealth Keep', and was almost within sight of the sea. By this time, however, both water and fuel were exhausted, and the possibility of having to surrender arose. Yet Rommel was at his best in a crisis. Leaving his parched *Panzer* crews to rest as best they could, he set off south in his staff vehicle, drove all night at reckless speed over the spring-breaking desert, passed Bir Hacheim, and then at last found an Italian supply column. Without a pause, Rommel turned it round, climbed into the cab of the leading lorry and led it back northwards through a blinding sandstorm, regaining his stranded tanks at 6am on 29th May. An hour later the *Afrika Korps* was operational once more.

Ritchie still refused to mount a counterattack, and a confused day of fighting ensued, during which the honours fell evenly. The British 2nd Armoured Brigade escaped a mauling thanks to timely help from 22nd Armoured Brigade. But the Axis position was still critical, and at this stage Rommel totally recast his operational plan. Calling off the coastwards push, he ordered his armour to regroup in a position just east of the British mine marsh, albeit that there was a newly discovered and still strongly resisting 150th Brigade Group Box in its midst. This was a very risky decision which might have led to disaster had Ritchie reacted, but Rommel gambled that its very boldness would secure success. And so it proved. He had earned a respite of four invaluable days.

General Ritchie was jubilant when he first heard that Rommel was pulling back, and prematurely announced a victory. Meanwhile, Rommel set up a ring of 88mm dual-purpose guns around his position in the 'Cauldron', completed a tenuous supply route through the minefields on 30th May, and turned on 150th Brigade Group. Brigadier Haydon fought back valiantly, but running out of ammunition after five days' incessant action (ironically, a further supply had been withdrawn from the position on the eve of Rommel's offensive), his position finally collapsed on 1st June. Rommel's supply position abruptly improved, once again just in time, for the Free French were still holding out.

Then, at last, General Ritchie assumed the counter-offensive. After lengthy preparations, and the repulse of several earlier probes against the gun ring, Operation 'Aberdeen' was launched against the 'Cauldron' on 5th June. It proved a total fiasco. The three brigades involved were ill-coordinated, and defeated by the deadly 88mm guns before coming to grips with the Axis armour. The British lost 108 tanks in piecemeal attacks, making a total of 228 since the opening of the battle). Attrition was working in Rommel's favour. At last on the night of 10th to 11th June, General Koenig was forced to evacuate his Bir Hacheim positions, which he did in style, being driven out by his girl driver.

Rommel now judged that the moment was ripe for him to break out of the 'Cauldron' and complete his victory. On 11th June he struck north with his 124 remaining tanks. His target was El Adem, and around it he proceeded to wreck 7th Armoured Division's cohesion; the 'battle of Knightsbridge' raged for seventy-two hours, Rommel accounting for a further 320 tanks. In alarm Auchinleck flew up from GHQ, but the position was hopeless. He authorised the abandonment of the Gazala position.

On 14th June the 'Gazala gallop' began. XIII Corps abandoned its positions and headed back for a new position between Tobruk and El Adem, while 50th Division took an unorthodox route westwards before wheeling away south and east around Bir Hacheim. But any chance of delaying Rommel was slim. By 17th June he had captured Sidi Rezegh and El Adem, with its important airfield. The El Adem line collapsed, and the remnants of 8th Army headed for Sollum over the Egyptian border.

General Klopper and his South Africans now stood alone within the depleted defences of the Tobruk perimeter amid a huge supply, munitions and fuel dumps. While 90th Light Division and the Italian armour pursued Ritchie, Rommel completed his plans for the *Afrika Korps* to assault this long-denied target. Early on 20th June the Germans struck at the southeast sector. Klopper fought back well, but attempts to create a diversion from within Egypt failed to materialize, and Tobruk was doomed. On the evening of 21st June, the town duly fell. Some 33,000 prisoners of war, 1,400 tons of fuel, 5,000 tons of supplies and almost 2,000 serviceable vehicles were lost to the Axis. Without a doubt, 8th Army had suffered its most humiliating defeat, having lost since 26th May about 88,000 casualties and prisoners. 'Defeat is one thing; disgrace is another' commented a distraught Churchill, visiting Roosevelt in Washington at the time the news broke. Rommel's achievement had cost the Axis some 6,360 casualties, but significantly over half that number were Germans, including seventy per cent of the *Afrika Korps'* officer strength. Adolf Hitler hastened to confer the baton of field marshal upon his most successful desert general, but Rommel was already far away to the east, in hot pursuit of the shattered 8th Army. Ahead lay Cairo, Alexandria and the Suez Canal – and beyond those were the Persian oilfields. All seemed tantalizingly within his grasp. But just short of these gleaming possibilities stood a small coastal railway station. Its name was El Alamein.

A German column moves eastwards through Benghazi following the capture of Tobruk. They are heading for the Egyptian border, behind which the 'brave but baffled' 8th Army was trying to reform. News of Rommel's success reduced Churchill to tears. Hitler rewarded Rommel with a field marshal's baton.

THE BATTLES OF EL ALAMEIN

Rommel briefs senior commanders from a half-track vehicle. Note the *Panzerarmee Afrika* symbol on the door. The Field Marshal was famous for leading from the front - he would often abandon his headquarters for the front line and, on occasion, take over personal command of encounters with 8th Army.

The triumph of Gazala and Tobruk behind him, Field Marshal Erwin Rommel lost no time in driving deep into Egypt – his goal of the Suez Canal at last in sight. An attempt by rallying elements of the British 8th Army to hold him at Mersa Matruh was shattered on 27th and 28th June when another forty tanks were destroyed and a further 6,000 disconsolate POWs began the long, thirsty trudge back towards Tripolitania.

However, four factors began to affect his brilliantly extemporized exploitation of the British defeat. First, the inexorable laws of 'the diminishing power of the offensive' began to exert their hampering influence. Second, the Desert Air Force, now operating from its nearby bases, slowed his speed of advance. Third, his pleas to the Fuehrer for just a pair of fresh German divisions to enable him to clinch his success in the Middle East, fell on uncomprehending ears, for the impending summer drive towards the Caucasus in the U.S.S.R. was taking all Hitler's attention. And fourth, in July, three out of the four Axis tankers conveying vehicle fuel to North Africa would fall victim to Allied operations mounted from unsubdued Malta.

As a result, General Claude Auchinleck was afforded just sufficient time to prepare another line – and a real one this time – seventy miles west of Alexandria. It was to go down in history as 'the El Alamein position' and, before 1942 was out, would be not only the decisive turning point in the Desert War, but also in Britain's fortunes overall in the Second World War. But none could guess this in late June 1942, when 8th Army was, although brave, both baffled and defeated.

Reconnoitered by General Sir James Marshall-Cornwall earlier in the summer, the Alamein line ran for about thirty miles from the Mediterranean coast near the small railway station of El Alamein to the cliffs edging the Qattara Depression, which was a vast area of impassable, low-lying salt marshes that effectively closed the desert flank. Flat and sandy on the coastal sector, the centre comprised a number of rocky ridges and escarpments. Both areas presented bad going for armour. Auchinleck estimated that two reinforced armoured divisions and two well-sited infantry divisions could hold this position

Winston Churchill lost confidence in General Auchinleck and sent him to India. In his place he appointed two new commanders: General Sir Harold Alexander (left) as Commander-in-Chief Middle East Land Forces, and Lieutenant General Sir Bernard Montgomery as Commander 8th Army. 'Monty' was soon to have Rommel's measure.

against superior numbers. The coast road and the railway provided good lines of communication to the rear, so long as the RAF could maintain air supremacy. Naval vessels could overhang the coast in front of the position. Lieutenant General Norrie at once put his weary and disheartened men to work, aided by troops of the new X Corps of Lieutenant General Holmes, whilst Gott's XIII Corps held the ring. Four defended localities were prepared: the largest around El Alamein; the next along Ruweisat Ridge; the third about Abu Dweiss and the fourth at Deir el Shein. The headquarters of 8th Army were close behind the Ruweisat position, where the supply dumps and airfields of Alexandria and the Delta were within easy range to the east.

To hold the area, Auchinleck could call upon 35,000 men and just 160 tanks. Reinforcements were promised – including a convoy of new American Sherman tanks provided by Roosevelt – but these would not arrive before September. Rommel could not be expected to be so helpful as to delay his next offensive until then, so could the line be held? The available troops were split into battle groups, and Auchinleck massed his artillery under Army HQ, and did what he could to create 4th Light Armoured Brigade. But to guard against disaster, he also began to prepare defences in the Delta.

Fortunately for the British, Rommel also had his problems. At the extremity of his advance he had only sixty German and thirty Italian tanks, some 1,500 German soldiers and 5,000 Italians, so small had *Panzerarmee Afrika*

The Battle of Gazala. Rommel's main swoop to the south with his *Afrika Korps* - an attempt to avoid the heavy defences of Ritchie's Gazala Line - was spotted by the British the evening that the 'Fox' set out. Ritchie, convinced the move was a feint, steadfastly believed that Rommel would strike the British defences in the centre of the Line and so initially failed to divert his armour to the south to counter Rommel.

become.

Small wonder he pleaded, albeit unsuccessfully, for reinforcements. Typically, however, he paid scant heed to the 'quartermaster's nightmare' of his position, and at once set about planning a repeat of Mersa Matruh and Gazala, which meant diversions in the north by the Italians, strengthened by 90th Light Division, combined with a drive by what remained of the *Afrika Korps* in the distant south to penetrate the desert flank. He believed this bluff would break what little he believed was left of Ritchie's nerve. Here he made a major miscalculation, for Auchinleck had replaced his army commander, and had himself devised an effective plan of defence. This was first to block Rommel's attack and then to launch counter-thrusts against the weaker Italian formations, compelling the German armour to divert from its own purposes to the task of bolstering their allies.

Rommel struck on 1st July. By last light all his attacks had petered out. The long defence by Indian troops of the Deir el Shein box and the damage inflicted by heavy artillery fire on 90th Light Division halted the diversionary attack, whilst the *Afrika Korps*, severely hampered by bad going and incessant air attacks, had to abandon its envelopment plan. But when Auchinleck launched XIII Corps in a counter-strike towards the coast on 2nd July, it made little ground, apart from reducing Rommel's tanks to twenty-six 'runners'. Risking all to gain – or lose – all, the next day Rommel threw everything against the coastal sector and broke in as far as Alam Baoshala, before again being halted. 'Our strength has faded away' remarked the German commander. Time was now on Auchinleck's side. The efforts of the New Zealand infantry and 1st Armoured Brigade had reduced the Italian *Ariete* Division to a mere five tanks. Rommel unwillingly accepted the inevitable: he ordered his formations to dig in.

There followed three weeks of attritional warfare. Applying his operational plan, Auchinleck struck time and again at Italian positions, forcing the *Afrika Korps* to dance to his tune. Rommel bided his time, waiting for the arrival of 260 reinforcement tanks from Tripoli, together with 164th Infantry Division that had very belatedly been made available to him from Crete. But 8th Army lacked real drive: the 'battle groups' were disliked, and the South African troops were critical of the fate of their compatriots at Tobruk. On 9th July, Rommel occupied 'Bel Q', jubilant to find it undefended, but the next day the new 9th Australian Division routed the Italian *Sabratha* Division at Tell el Eisa, forcing Rommel to divert 15th *Panzer* north. Two days later, Auchinleck routed the Italian *Trieste* Division and again Rommel was forced to respond. On 14th July the New Zealanders and 5th Indian Brigade routed the Italian *Brescia* Division in its turn, and all Ruweisat Ridge was cleared of the enemy. The Italian *Pavia* Division was captive or in full flight behind *Brescia* Division and Rommel, desperate, had to use his dwindling number of tanks to patch the line. On 17th July, he was about to launch an all-out armoured blow against 8th Army's centre in a new breakthrough attempt when he learned that *Trieste* and *Trento* had been routed in their turn by the Australians on the coastal sector, and

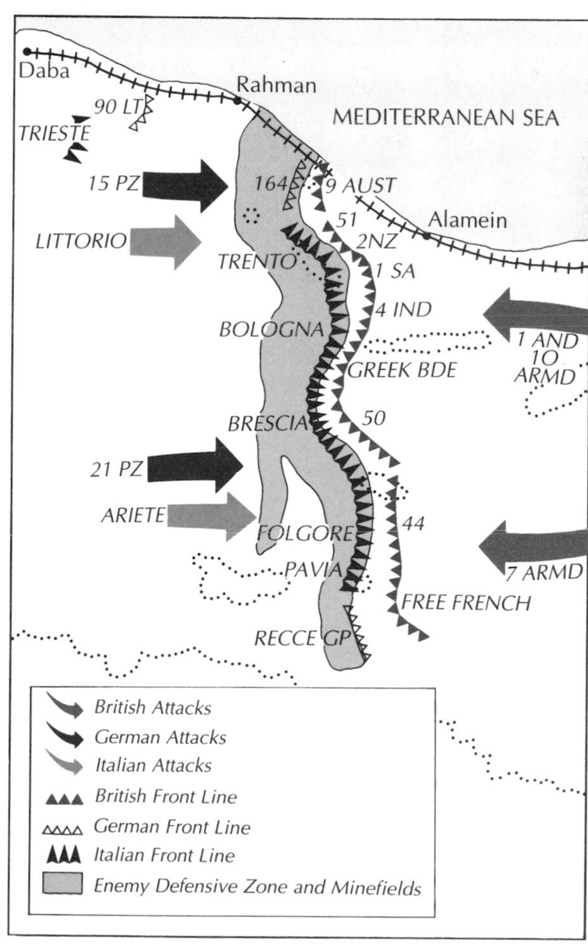

Facing page top: a feared German 88mm artillery piece in action in the Western Desert. This gun, originally designed as an anti-aircraft weapon, proved equally effective in an anti-tank role and achieved many 'kills' against British armour. The '88' was probably the most successful dual-purpose gun of the entire war.

The arrival of the first American Sherman tanks (facing page bottom) swung the advantage in armour to the British. Weighing thirty tons and boasting a top speed of thirty miles per hour, the Sherman was equipped with a 75mm main armament in a turret capable of 360° traverse. At the battles of Alam Halfa and Second Alamein it proved to be 'Queen of the Battlefield'.

Right: the battle begins as a twenty-minute bombardment by 600 British guns heralded the beginning of Montgomery's Second Battle of Alamein. Under its cover, sappers went forward to detect and lift enemy mines to create corridors for the armour of X Corps. Unfortunately, they failed to detect a second minefield area, and serious problems resulted.

90th Light Division had come off the worse in a contest with 4th Light Armoured Brigade west of Alem el Onsol, after making a limited penetration southeast of the El Alamein defended zone.

Rommel had failed. His health was breaking down – he was suffering from a liver complaint, a duodenal ulcer and severe nasal catarrh. Even worse, he found himself militarily 'off-balance'. But to convert defeat into disaster for the Axis proved beyond Auchinleck's skill. Between 21st and 26th July he used XIII Corps in a northward drive, seeking Rommel's communications; but, as General Bayerlein recorded: 'our counter-measures succeeded in preventing a catastrophe', and Auchinleck emerged with only complete possession of Meteirya Ridge to show for his efforts. Although 8th Army still possessed 119 tanks, whereas Rommel was reduced to a mere twenty-six, both armies were now totally exhausted, and five days later the First Battle of Alamein simply petered out.

Auchinleck had lost 13,000 casualties since 1st July. But he was expecting two new armoured divisions from the canal base – namely 8th and 10th – two new infantry divisions (44th and 51st Highlanders reconstituted after the disaster following Dunkirk) and a hundred self-propelled guns. Furthermore, he had inflicted 22,800 losses on the enemy, including 7,000 prisoners, and yet had managed to leave Rommel with just a sufficient illusion of success to persuade him to hold his position face-to-face with 8th Army, rather than to retire westwards to his bases.

Auchinleck was not destined, however, to reap the benefits of his achievement. On 3rd August, Winston Churchill arrived in Cairo, and five days later informed Auchinleck that he was to hand over to General Alexander, Commander in Chief of the Middle East. The Prime Minister's intention that Gott should command 8th Army was shattered when that officer died in an air crash. Instead, Churchill summoned Lieutenant General Bernard Montgomery to assume the role. On 15th August, the handovers were complete, and a disappointed Auchinleck departed to command in India.

Montgomery immediately set about creating better morale and a new army based around a *corps de chasse* of powerful armour. He courted the rank and file of Britain's citizen army like no commander before him. He brought in new generals – Brian Horrocks for XIII Corps, Sir Oliver Leese for XXX Corps, and Frederick de Guingand as Chief of Staff. He even insisted upon a new Chaplain General, hopeful of more effective prayer. The X Corps received two armoured divisions and the New Zealanders. He declared, erroneously, that he had destroyed '.. all plans for further retreat', and that he was going '.. to hit Rommel for six out of Africa'. These strident, even bombastic, claims had an amazing effect. General Sir Harold Alexander was happy to allow his subordinate his head – and large convoys of munitions were due to arrive any day. Better still, Ultra intercepts revealed that Axis shipments into Africa had dropped from 30,000 tons a month to only 6,000 tons in July.

Rommel was aware of the 1,200 miles separating him from his base at Tripoli, and knew that 8th Army was expecting important reinforcements. Already it had 767 tanks, good air support and plenty of fuel. Typically, he decided to try the mettle of the new British command without delay, in a last great fling to forestall the arrival of yet more Allied reinforcements. By late August he had amassed 226 German and 243 Italian tanks. Accordingly, on 30th August, he suddenly attacked, in what the Germans dubbed 'the Six-Day Bicycle Race', and drove for the Alam Halfa Ridge southeast of El Alamein. As Italian XX Corps attacked on the left, the *Afrika Korps* drove for the centre. From the outset, air attacks and minefields imposed delays. And Montgomery was ready for him. With XXX Corps on his right, XIII Corps on his left and with 7th Armoured Division (the 'Desert Rats') to the fore as a lure, he held Ruweisat Ridge and allowed his left wing to be pressed back towards a series of strong, new positions facing south, of which the key was Alam Halfa Ridge. Against the dug-in tanks and new 6-pounder, anti-tank guns, Rommel struck in vain. With his fuel low, on 2nd September he called off the battle and fell back to his starting positions. Montgomery made no serious attempt to follow, merely re-occupying his original line in the south. He was determined to bide his time. Rommel had lost forty-nine tanks, 2,900 men, fifty-five guns and 395 vehicles to 8th Army's sixty-eight tanks, eighteen anti-tank guns and 1,640 casualties. Montgomery also knew that a major Allied landing in northwest Africa – Operation 'Torch' – would occur west of Tripoli in November. So he played Rommel along, keeping his attention fully eastwards, whilst 8th Army grew steadily stronger.

Rommel fell for the bait, and stayed facing El Alamein, putting down new minefields and absorbing 164th Infantry Division, before departing on Hitler's order for hospital in south Germany, leaving General von Stumme in command. By mid-October the Germans had built a forty-five-mile line, faced with a double row of minefields, five-miles deep in all. On the coast stood 90th Light and 164th Infantry divisions. To its south was placed the Italian XXI Corps, strengthened by German paratroop battalions. On the right was the Italian X Corps. Close in the rear stood the armoured reserve, the veteran 15th and 21st *Panzers* and the two armoured and one motorized divisions of the Italian XX Corps in two groups – fielding in all 200 German and 300 Italian tanks, 53,000 German troops and 55,000 Italians.

Montgomery was now almost ready. On his right was XXX Corps, five infantry divisions strong. On his left was XIII Corps, two infantry divisions plus the 'Desert Rats' of 7th Armoured Division. In the rear waited X Corps – two armoured divisions (1st and 10th) with parts of a third (8th) divided between them, and the New Zealand Division. In all 220,000 Allied troops and 1,351 tanks, including new Shermans and trusty Grants, and a reinforced Desert Air Force (500 aircraft) stood waiting the order to advance and attack in Operation 'Lightfoot'. This was deliberately timed for 'Torch minus 13'. Montgomery refused all Churchill's orders for an earlier offensive. He had a master plan.

The nine infantry divisions and three armoured divisions, equipped with 285 Sherman tanks with their 75mm guns, 246 Grants and 421 Crusaders, 850 6-pounder and 550 2-pounder anti-tank guns and fifty-two medium and 832 field guns – amounted to a formidable 8th Army; in its ranks were Australians, New Zealanders, Indians, Greeks and Frenchmen, as well as British soldiers. Facing it stood four reinforced Axis armoured divisions (two German and two Italian), a pair of motorized divisions (one of each nationality) and eight infantry divisions, seven of them Italian. In overall terms Montgomery enjoyed a 2:1 advantage in manpower and a 3:1 advantage in tanks. Overhead, the Desert Air Force of Air Vice Marshal Tedder (which had been reinforced by two fighter and two light bomber groups) held undisputed sway over the *Luftwaffe* and *Regia Aeronautica*. The numerical advantage that Montgomery had demanded had been achieved. He entered the battle in an enviable position: Rommel was away sick, and come what might Montgomery could hardly lose, for once Operation 'Torch' opened in Tunisia and Algeria on 8th November, the Axis would be compelled to retreat to save Tripoli. However, there was some anxiety over the size and extent of the Axis minefields which had been partly probed in two brigade attacks on 30th September;

Facing page top left: pilots of a Desert Air Force Hurricane squadron 'scramble' to carry out a mission. By October, 1942, the British had regained the advantage over the Axis air forces, and consequently were able to harass Rommel's front-line positions and supply columns mercilessly, thus making a major contribution to the Allied victory.

Facing page top right: a Junkers Ju 87 Stuka dive-bomber crashes in flames somewhere in the Western Desert. However terrifying these aircraft were to troops on the ground, due to their relatively slow speed and limited manoeuvrability they were no match for British fighter planes. After suffering initial checks, 8th Army mounted Operation 'Supercharge' and surged through the Axis lines at El Alamein. Whilst air and armoured attacks neutralised the *Panzers*, infantry swarmed forward to occupy captured ground.

Facing page bottom: the wreck of a disabled *PzKpfw* III provides welcome cover.

A powerful self-propelled German gun captured intact during the desert battles of autumn 1942. The chassis proved to be of French manufacture and was probably made in the Renault works in Paris which the Germans had taken over.

accordingly, in tune with the latest intelligence reports, Montgomery adjusted his plan.

Originally, this had conceived of a simultaneous attack by XXX Corps in the north and XIII Corps in the south, which were to break into the Axis positions and clear corridors for the armour of X Corps to exploit; the tanks would then sever the enemy's hostile lines of communication. Now, on 5th October, he decided to attack in the north with both XXX and X corps and employ both simultaneously. Two busy weeks of final preparations and exercises ensued.

On the night of 23rd to 24th October, 1942, some 900 guns suddenly delivered a hurricane bombardment, and the mine-clearing parties moved forward. The Second Battle of El Alamein had begun. The Axis were taken by surprise, but soon rallied to their pre-arranged defensive tasks. The southern of the two thrust lines made good progress, and the New Zealanders rapidly captured Miteirya Ridge. Behind them, however, 10th Armoured Division hesitated to pass through, having run into more mines. Further north, the Australians made less progress against heavy resistance, and 1st Armoured Division became bogged down between the two minefields. The static tanks made excellent targets for the pre-registered Axis artillery. On the other hand, German General Georg Stumme died of a heart attack caused by an exploding mine. On 25th October, Rommel hurried from Germany to find the Allied operation still stalled in the north and making scant progress in the south, where 44th Division and 7th Armoured had also come to a halt.

On 26th October, Montgomery ordered a pause to adjust the plan. He now enjoined XIII Corps, led by the Australian 9th Division, to strike northwestwards towards the coast. On 27th October, some progress was made, but then Rommel's armoured counter-attacks against Miteirya and Kidney ridges, although ultimately forestalled, restricted forward progress. Churchill cabled anxiously for news, aware that 'Torch' was now imminent. So Montgomery for the second time changed his

Crusader tanks armed with 6-pounder main armaments are seen in full 'hue and cry'. The breakthrough achieved, the German *Panzers* beaten and Rommel in full retreat, it was time for the British medium tanks to sweep forward in pursuit.

plan. By Operation 'Supercharge', the Australian attack on the coast was to continue, but the main thrust would be further south. While XIII Corps pressed forward, X Corps was to strike northwestwards to distract and defeat Rommel's *Panzers*. The new assault began early in the morning on 2nd November. Rommel, his petrol almost gone, was told to 'stand and die' by Hitler. More realistically, he decided to break off and retreat, taking all Italian transport for his German troops. Victorious 8th Army had lost 13,500 more casualties and 500 tanks (150 of them destroyed), but in turn had inflicted 59,000 on the Axis and accounted for 454 tanks and 1,000 guns. It had been a battle of direst attrition, but numerical advantages had told in the end

By 4th November, X Corps was in full pursuit, but then heavy rain bogged the armour down and Rommel was free and away. Fighting bitter rearguard actions, he was pressed back through Tobruk by 13th November and Msus by 17th November, and the British re-entered Benghazi on 20th November. Montgomery paused before El Agheila where Rommel turned to face him once more, but on 13th December the Axis moved to the west again. Boxing Day found Rommel in a new position at Buerat, but on 13th January, 1943, he again pulled out just before Montgomery launched an assault. So, on 23rd January, the British at last entered Tripoli as Rommel entered Tunisia. The battle for the Western Desert was over, although much bitter fighting remained against field marshals von Arnim and Rommel who now, far too late, received strong reinforcements from Germany. But there was no denying the importance of Montgomery's victory at El Alamein. It was the only great land battle won by British and Commonwealth forces without direct American participation and, together with the German surrender at Stalingrad in February, 1943, it marked the turning point of the war. 'It is not the end', Churchill warned the jubilant British public at a review of the victorious 8th Army in Tripoli; 'it may not even be the beginning of the end. But it is undoubtedly the end of the beginning'.

GUADALCANAL

Assault groups of U.S. 1st Marine Division practise landing operations on Koro Island in the Fiji group on 28th July, 1942. Shortly after this picture was taken, the landing-craft ground onto Koro's reefs, and the exercise degenerated into a shambles. Ten days later the Marines' commander, Major General A.A. Vandegrift, approached Guadalcanal with deep misgivings.

By the summer of 1942 Japan controlled an area which extended from the eastern borders of India to the islands of the Central Pacific, and from the Aleutians to the Solomon Islands. In early June, at Yamamoto's urging, the Combined Fleet had sought to annihilate the remnants of the American Navy off the island of Midway, 1,000 miles west of Hawaii, and had suffered its first serious reverse. But even after the loss of four carriers, the Imperial Navy still dominated the Pacific. Nevertheless, this failure caused Japanese attention to turn to the South Pacific. Japan's new plan was to consolidate her hold on the Solomons, a group composed of seven large, mountainous, jungle-clad islands and many smaller ones that extended 800 miles southeast from her main South Pacific base at Rabaul. A 1,500-man garrison had already occupied Tulagi, a small island which had served the British as an administrative headquarters. Fifteen miles south of Tulagi lay Guadalcanal, one of the southernmost islands of the group. Ninety miles long by fifteen wide, the northern shore of this rugged, heavily forested island was fringed by a narrow coastal plain. On 1st July 2,000 Japanese construction troops landed on this shore at Lunga Point and began clearing an airfield. It was intended that aircraft flying from Guadalcanal would provide air cover for the next stage of Japan's expansion – the occupation of New Caledonia and Fiji that would cut the flow of American supplies to Australia.

Unknown to the Japanese, their activities were being closely observed by a team of 'Coastwatchers' – Australian and British planters and officials who had volunteered to stay behind in Japanese occupied territory. Those on Guadalcanal were commanded by Captain Martin Clemens, a Cambridge graduate and former athlete. Within hours of the landing, he had given America's South Pacific Headquarters in Noumea a clear picture of Japanese intentions. The American Commander in Chief Pacific (CINCPAC), Admiral Nimitz, responded with characteristic energy. On 7th July he ordered the only American unit in the South Pacific considered combat worthy, New Zealand-based 1st Marine Division, north to seize the airfield. The Division's commander, Major General James A. Vandegrift, protested vigorously. Apart from a handful of long-serving NCOs and officers, his division was composed of raw recruits, inexperience which showed when a rehearsal for the landing collapsed into chaos. But Nimitz remained adamant. If the Japanese were allowed to complete their air base, the strategic outlook in the South Pacific would be bleak.

On 26th July, 1942, the largest task force the United States had yet assembled in the South Pacific rendezvoused off the island of Kora, some 350 miles south of Fiji – an amphibious strike force – TF 62 – commanded by Rear Admiral Richmond Kelly Turner and composed of twenty-three transports carrying 18,000 Marines escorted by eight cruisers and fifteen destroyers, and a covering force – TF 61 – commanded by Rear Admiral Fletcher and composed of three aircraft carriers, a battleship, six cruisers and sixteen destroyers. Eleven days later, when the fleet was sixty miles south of Guadalcanal, TF 61 detached itself and remained in open waters. Meanwhile, TF 62 sped north, rounded Cape Esperance, the northwestern point of Guadalcanal, on the evening of 6th August and entered Sealark Channel, which separated the northern shore of Guadalcanal from Tulagi. About five miles west of Savo Island – a volcanic cone which rose precipitously from the channel – TF 62 divided into two groups; one heading for Tulagi, the other for Lunga Point.

At dawn the Marines of Colonel Mike Edson's 1st Raider Battalion stormed ashore on Tulagi. It was America's first assault landing since 1898. The Japanese commander, seeing the size of the American task force, radioed to Rabaul:

Right: photographed from a dive-bomber of the U.S. Carrier *Dauntless*, landing craft carry Marines of Colonel Edson's Raider Battalion to the shore of Tulagi on 7th August, 1942. This was the Marines' first assault landing since 1898.

Inland from the beachhead Marine patrols (below) found the going difficult. Dense jungle interlaced with vines and creepers slowed progress to a few hundred yards per hour. Fortunately for the Marines, the Japanese found movement just a difficult.

'enemy troop strength is overwhelming. We will fight to the last man.' He was as good as his world; the heavily reinforced Raiders took three days to exterminate the garrison.

On Guadalcanal, things had gone differently. The bulk of 1st Marine Division landed on a beach two miles east of Lunga Point shortly after 9.00am, advanced southwest to the airfield and discovered that the Japanese had fled inland. This was fortunate because the landing had been even more confused than the practise run. Supplies were dumped in hopelessly mixed-up piles and men wandered around waiting for orders.

Japanese headquarters in Rabaul was at that time much more interested in their invasion of Papua, 1,000 miles to the west of Guadalcanal, than in anything that was happening on the island. They simply did not have the men to reinforce their Guadalcanal garrison substantially, nor did they take the threat seriously. Confident in the ability of their air and naval forces to cut the Marines' supply line, they decided they could deal with the Americans by only sending a 5,000 strong detachment of General Hyakutake's 17th Army, which was then based on Guam. Although they knew it would take at least ten days for the detachment to reach Guadalcanal, they were

certain that by then their navy and air force would have won the battle.

Rabaul's strategy nearly worked. Heavy Japanese air attacks during 7th and 8th August cost Admiral Fletcher twenty-one of his ninety-nine fighters, and on the night of 8th August he radioed Turner to say that he was withdrawing his carriers out of range. The loss of air support this entailed meant that Turner had no option other than to withdraw TF 62. During the evening of 8th August supplies were dumped on the beach and the task force prepared to leave. At 1.00am disaster struck. When the first news of the landing reached Rabaul a Japanese

cruiser and destroyer force had sped south. It now surprised Turner's cruisers and in a violent, thirty-minute action off Savo Island sank four.

As dawn broke on 9th August the men of 1st Marine Division knew they were completely alone on an isolated beachhead 1,000 miles from the nearest Allied base. Their supposedly imposing navy had fled, leaving only debris and the still- burning hulls of the cruisers. For many, the situation seemed very close to that which had faced MacArthur's beleaguered forces on Bataan four months earlier. A determined Japanese ground attack at this time would almost certainly have destroyed the beachhead. Instead, the Japanese confined their activities to air raids and naval shelling - unpleasant enough, but it gave Vandegrift time to construct a perimeter centred on Lunga Point, about three miles wide by three deep, which encompassed the airfield. Engineers worked feverishly to complete the runway, now named Henderson Field after a hero of Midway. On 20th August thirty-one Marine Corps aircraft flew onto the just-completed airfield - twelve Dauntless dive-bombers and nineteen Wildcat fighters - which lessened the Marines' sense of isolation and allowed them to hit back.

The Marines had also discovered that they had friends on the island. Captain Clemens and a party of Solomon Islands constabulary had emerged from the jungle with accurate intelligence on the island's topography and on Japanese positions - the first real intelligence Vandegrift had received. On 19th August one of the constables, Jacob Vouza, while patrolling to the east of the perimeter, ran into a large force of Japanese. He was tortured, bayoneted, and left for dead, yet was able to crawl back to the beachhead with the news that an attack was imminent.

Vouza had stumbled across an 800-strong advance guard of the detachment from Guam which had landed by destroyer on 18th November. Its commander, Colonel Kiyono Ichiki, was an arrogant and headstrong officer who believed that even a small number of boldly led Japanese could defeat many times their own number of white soldiers. Rather than wait for the rest of the detachment, he decided to attack. During the evening of 20th August his troops infiltrated through a coconut plantation just to the east of the Marines' perimeter and at 1.20am on 21st August they burst from the trees and charged towards the Marines' foxholes across a sandbank at the mouth of the Tenaru River. The forewarned Americans cut them down with 37mm canister shot and machine-gun fire. By dawn, counter-attacking Marines had trapped Ichiki and his men in the coconut plantation. Dauntless dive-bombers from Henderson strafed the area again and again and the Marine's Stuart tanks then rolled in, crushing the Japanese beneath their tracks. 'The rear of the tanks', Vandegrift recorded, 'looked like meat grinders'. At the end of the day, 800 Japanese and thirty-five Americans were dead.

This action, which the Americans named the Battle of Tenaru, finally convinced Japanese headquarters that substantial reinforcements would have to be diverted to Guadalcanal. The American High Command, too, realized that 1st Marine Division was going to need large reinforcements if it was to retain to its precarious beachhead. Guadalcanal now became a vortex, sucking in all available Japanese and American manpower and material in the South Pacific - a gruelling battle of attrition was in prospect. As the Americans held Henderson Field (by 30th August more than sixty aircraft were operating from it), they could control the waters around Guadalcanal by day and provide cover for their own supply convoys. The Japanese were obliged to reinforce at night. From 22nd August onwards the fast transports and destroyers of Admiral Raizo Tanaka's 'Tokyo Express' made the nightly dash down through the straits of the Solomons to deposit men and supplies on open beaches. In order to cut each other's

Below: a Marine Stuart tank rolls towards the coconut plantation on the Ilu River late on 21st August, 1942. Nearly 800 Japanese had already been killed in the plantation, many being crushed by the tanks.

Facing page top: Major General A.A. Vandegrift (left) and his Chief of Staff Colonel Gerald Thomas (centre) confer with Colonel Merritt Edson in early September. Vandegrift had transferred Edson's crack Raiders from Tulagi to Guadalcanal just in time for them to play a decisive role in defeating a Japanese assault on 12th September.

Facing page bottom: Bloody Ridge, 14th September, 1942. Standing near the site of Vandegrift's HQ, a Marine of Edson's Raiders surveys the ridge to the south where 600 Japanese had been killed. By the time the photograph was taken the Marines had cleared the Japanese bodies from the ridge and incinerated them.

Japanese stragglers who missed the last evacuation barges of 7th February, 1943 and were captured by the Americans two weeks later. Emaciated and sick, they received much better treatment at the hands of the Americans than did the few Marines who had the misfortune to fall into Japanese hands.

these troops to the island, however, ended in the disastrous naval battle of Guadalcanal, described by Admiral Richmond Kelly Turner as 'the fiercest naval battle ever fought'. Battleships blazed away at point-blank range, but the issue was decided by Henderson's aircraft, which tipped the balance in America's favour. The convoy carrying 38th Division was all but destroyed, only some 2,000 troops making it to the island. Worse still for the Japanese, the battle had given the Americans control over the waters of the southern Solomons by both day and night. The Japanese now realised that they had 30,000 men on a tropical island whom they could not keep adequately supplied. Tanaka's destroyers still raced along the coast at night, but they could no longer risk stopping to unload supplies – instead they threw supplies, sealed in drums, overboard in the hope that some would drift ashore. Almost incessant rain heralded the onset of malaria, a disease soon supplemented by dengue fever and amoebic dysentery. By early December malnutrition, too, was widespread and by mid-December the Japanese were beginning to die in large numbers.

The Marines had also been suffering, but they did so on relatively full stomachs, and their malaria had been held in check, to some extent, by the new drug atabrine. A major difference was that sick Marines could be evacuated by air – of the 8,580 Americans who had been hospitalized since the beginning of the campaign, 3,919 had been flown to New Caledonia by the end of November. In early December entire 1st Marine Division was evacuated by sea – about one third were considered medically unfit for duty – and were replaced by 2nd Marine Division and the American Division, formed from U.S. Army units which had been garrisoning New Caledonia. An exhausted Vandegrift also left, handing over command to an Army officer, Lieutenant General Patch. Japanese intelligence had informed the High Command of these changes, and Tokyo knew that their own emaciated forces were no match for the fresh Americans. On 31st December an Imperial conference took the only decision possible: even though it was extremely hazardous, the entire force was to be evacuated at night.

By the beginning of January, 1943, Patch's fresh divisions were driving the Japanese steadily westwards towards Cape Esperance. Even on their last legs, the Japanese put up tenacious resistance, but as they intended to evacuate from this cape, they fell back before the Americans. On seven consecutive nights, from 1st to 7th February, fast destroyer convoys rescued 13,000 survivors from open beaches – the most skilful evacuation since the British left Gallipoli twenty-six years earlier. But the Japanese had left 25,000 dead behind. The Americans had lost 1,592 killed and 4,300 wounded. No amount of rationalization by the Japanese could disguise the fact that they had suffered a major defeat.

Unlike the freakish American victory at Midway, the gruelling attritional struggle for Guadalcanal tested not just the American and Japanese armed forces, but the economies and societies which sustained them. It was precisely this sort of battle which Yamamoto had hoped the Pearl Harbor attack would obviate, for he knew that in any contest of brute force, America was bound to win. And so it proved. In the immediate aftermath of Savo Island, the Japanese could have destroyed the beachhead had they thrown substantial forces at it. The delay gave the Americans time to prepare defences – thereafter Japanese attacks battered themselves to pieces on an ever-stronger perimeter. The capture of Guadalcanal was the key to the reconquest of the Solomons, which, in turn, made possible the isolation of Rabaul and the eventual reconquest of the Philippines. From 7th February, 1943, the initiative in the Pacific War was clearly with the Americans.

STALINGRAD–THE TURNING POINT

After their failure to win their Russian war outright in 1941, the Germans hoped that a fresh effort in the summer of 1942 would finally see them victorious. Their plan was admittedly a little less ambitious than that of the previous year, having only two main spearheads – from Kharkov to Stalingrad and from the Crimea to the Caucasus – rather than the three in 1941 that had been halted before Leningrad, Moscow and Sebastopol respectively. Nevertheless, the new eastwards push was still very grandiose and ambitious in its way, since it included some seventy-eight Axis divisions – a total of almost two million men. Its purpose was to shut down Stalin's vital supply lines through the Caucasus and along the Don and Volga rivers, thereby effectively cutting him off both from the Caucasian oilfields and from Western 'Lend Lease' aid coming in through Persia. If these targets had been achieved, the result would surely have been an utterly decisive victory, since the Russians would have had little option but to sue for an early peace.

When the Nazis failed to reach their objectives, they were no less decisively introduced to the hitherto unthinkable idea that they might not win the war. Their crack 6th Army of 300,000 men was entirely destroyed in Stalingrad itself, with enormous additional casualties being suffered by its many supporting formations. The Reich went into mourning, and for the first time came to accept that its economy had to be put on a full war footing. Dr Goebbels' propaganda adopted a newly sombre tone, while in the front line it became plain that the despised Red Army actually did know a thing or two about the art of modern warfare, after all.

All these truly momentous implications emerged from what history remembers as just 'one single battle' at Stalingrad. However, it would probably be nearer the truth to think of the event as rather 'a very protracted period of intense campaigning at the very height of the war, spread across most of the active sectors of the Russian front'. The operations covered a circular area of more than 500 miles in diameter; from Voronezh in the north to Sebastopol and Rostov in the south, and from Kharkov in the west to Grozny in the east – and they lasted nearly an entire year. In essence, German plans had been complete on 28th March, 1942, and fighting was already approaching the Stalingrad area by 17th July: yet 6th Army's final surrender wasn't to come until the following 2nd February, and it would be 24th March before the spring thaw closed down the related flank and rear operations. The whole event added up to the biggest and most important clash of armies in the whole of the Second World War, so it would be quite misleading to dismiss it simply as 'just another battle'.

Initially, the main German objective had not been Stalingrad, but the maximum destruction of Soviet forces, followed by the seizure of Caucasian oilfields and communication routes. Stalingrad itself had originally been no more than a tertiary objective, although it became increasingly more important as events unfolded. Hitler gradually developed a personal obsession with the city, which was, of course, Stalin's city, whence Stalin had personally launched a brilliant offensive down to the mouth of the Don in 1920. Hitler was also under acute stress in this period, to the point where he would permit no avoidance or by-passing of the city, nor any retreat from it once it had been entered. As the strategic reports became successively worse, Hitler withdrew into his shell, refusing to take any decisions that might imply a change in the operational layout – indeed, he appeared to equate change with defeat. It is significant that between 7th and 23rd November, 1942, – at precisely the peak of the 'Torch'-Stalingrad crisis, when conceptual innovation was surely needed most of all – he deliberately removed himself from his main headquarters in order to 'rest' at his country retreat at Berchtesgaden.

Hitler was a brilliant, inspirational leader, capable of successfully cutting through the traditional formats of war, but he had never received technical training in the vital skill of managing multiple, simultaneous international crises – least of all when a superior enemy was persistently daring to fight back. Hitler's inflexibility about Stalingrad illustrates his awkwardness as an international operator, and vividly explains how a year of flexible, armoured manoeuvres could come to be focused upon such a tiny area of broken concrete and rubble

Facing page top: Marshal S. K. Timoshenko near the front line in the summer of 1942. He was responsible for the failed offensive to Kharkov, then the phased retreat before Army Group B to Stalingrad. He did not, however, lose his standing in the Red Army, and was the only pre-war general to survive the war with his reputation unscathed.

Facing page bottom: General Lindemann points out some topographical features to General von Bock, commander of German Army Group B in the initial drive to Voronezh. Von Bock was replaced on 15th July due to his disagreements with Hitler.

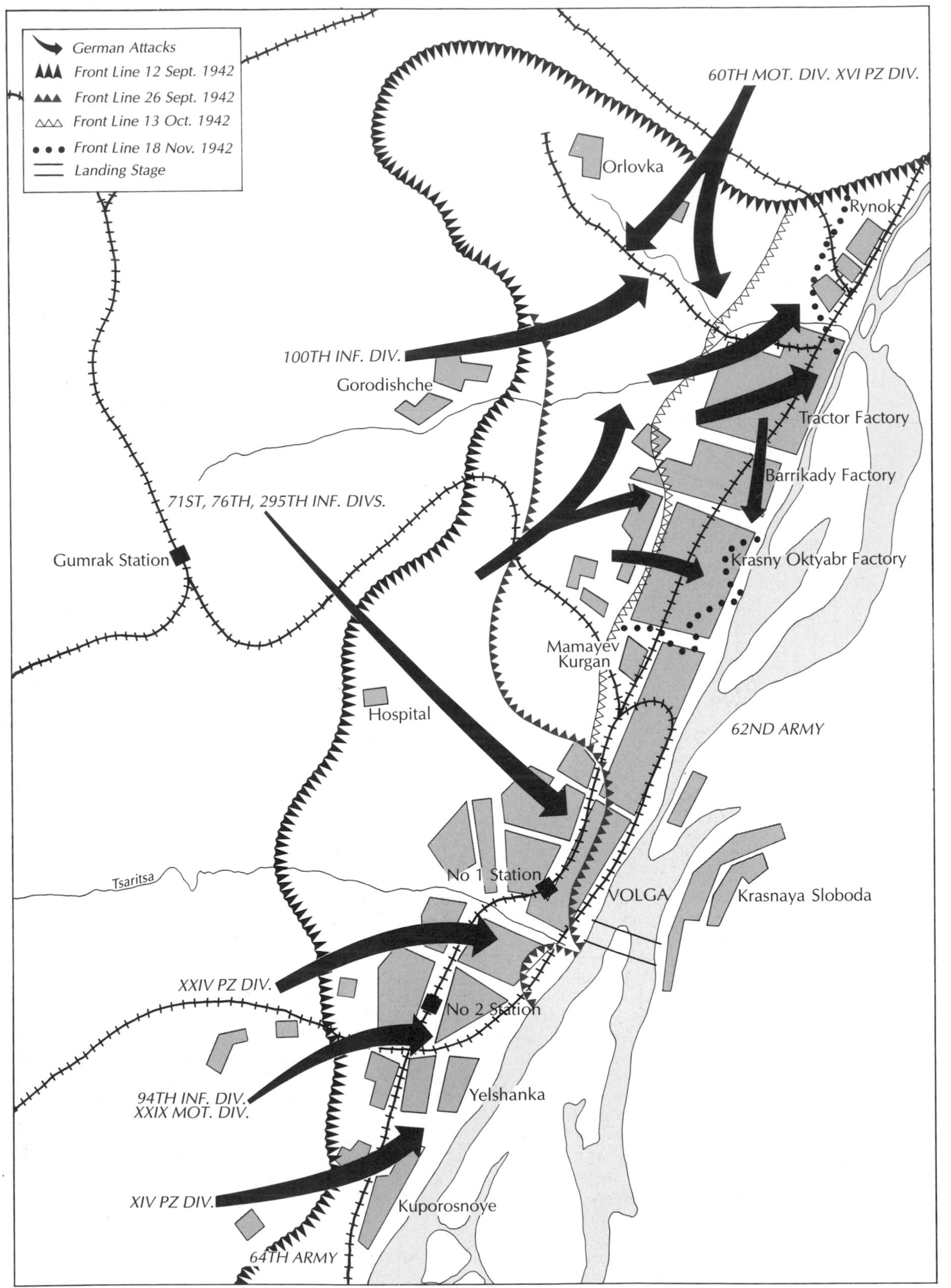

Von Paulus moves to take Stalingrad on 19th August, 1942, although he has yet to be joined by Hoth's 4th *Panzerarmee*. By 14th September, the Soviet garrison was hemmed into a narrow strip along the west bank of the River Volga. Increasingly mesmerised by Stalingrad, Hitler insisted that the city be taken, but, as the winter arrived, this task was clearly beyond von Paulus' strength.

Urban warfare in the late summer of 1942: a German platoon - bunched dangerously close together - moves up under the cover of a captured barricade.

in the centre of that city. It also explains how a merely local military reverse could turn remorselessly into a disaster of such world-shaking proportions.

Ironically, the first phase of the German 1942 operations ran even better than expected, since Stalin was obsessed with the defence of Moscow and refused to believe plentiful evidence - not excluding a captured copy of the complete plan - that the primary target would lie elsewhere. When, finally, he launched a big attack south of Kharkov from 12th May, it was quickly met and destroyed by the agile manoeuvres of *Panzer* forces. After this, the *Wehrmacht* went on to clear the Crimea of resistance, until in June the way lay open for a rapid drive towards the east, with List's Army Group A providing the main spearhead, and Bock's (later Weichs') Army Group B covering its northern flank.

Only in July did hitches and delays start to appear in the German operations. These were small in number at first, but they gradually built up to the point where a distinct sense of unease came to pervade headquarters. There were disputes over whether Voronezh should be a prime target, and then whether the bulk of the armour should be aimed along the southerly route towards the oilfields. Hitler said he wanted to advance on the broadest possible front, but this left him overstretched at every point and vulnerable to hold-ups in front of enemy centres of defence, especially in the difficult mountain terrain of the Caucasus. Nevertheless, as late as his Directive No. 45 of 23rd July, he still envisaged Stalingrad as merely a secondary objective to cover his northern flank. However, by August he began to move his centre of attention towards the city, just when the Soviet forces appeared to be breaking up under the pressure, but also when the German spearheads were encountering difficulties caused by the depletion of their supplies.

On 7th August Colonel General H. Hoth's 4th *Panzerarmee* came within thirty kilometres of Stalingrad from the south, and then Paulus'

A MG36 team in the outskirts of Stalingrad. Ultimately, German infantry tactics were based more upon the long range firepower of light machine guns (facing page) than upon the close-quarter power of assaulting riflemen, so at Stalingrad the Russians found they could fight on equal terms only if they 'hugged' enemy positions and made the battle a hand-to-hand contest.

6th Army arrived from the west to commence its main assault on 23rd August. There was a massed aerial bombardment that destroyed much of the suburbs and helped to push the Soviets back to their second – or middle – line of defence. Thanks to the German bombing, towards the centre of the city the big factories and flats had been converted into easily defensible rubble. Resistance was successfully improvised and included the widespread impressment of the city's population, as well as the diversion of many regular formations from other tasks into the city. A system was set up whereby a trickle of men and supplies could be brought in at night from the far bank of the Volga River. Energetic leadership was also provided from 23rd August by Colonel General Andrei Ivanovich Yeremenko, with the collaboration of Party Commissar, Nikita Khruschchev. Three weeks later this team would be completed with the promotion of Lieutenant General Vasily Ivanovich Chuykov as commander of 62nd Army – the army that was to bear the brunt of the close fighting in the city.

At the time of the Stalingrad battle, Soviet forces were still notoriously inefficient in co-ordinated manoeuvres and ignorant of the finer points of battle-handling. Their furiously repeated counter-attacks to push the invader out of Stalingrad achieved only negligible successes, apart from the purely sacrificial one of maintaining the pressure of attrition. Nevertheless, they did manage to hold a defensive line, and compressed the battle into a style of brutal but basic house-to-house combat in which German technology and mobility was virtually redundant. The Russians' trump card was their courage and endurance as infantry; but it was a card they could play only when – as now – the fast-moving thrust and parry of mechanized warfare on the steppe had been replaced by a slow-moving slugging match in the town.

By the end of the first week of September Hitler suffered a crisis of confidence, as he realised that his offensive was failing to cut cleanly through the enemy. It was only on 10th September that 4th *Panzerarmee* reached the Volga; and it would be 18th October before 6th Army even managed to capture the Tractor Factory. The Barricades Factory followed on 23rd September, and half the Red October Factory soon afterwards. Yet despite major pushes by the attackers on 14th October and 11th November, the dogged defence line – by then split into three isolated sections, and with the river only too close behind – was never to be reduced. The Fuehrer raged mightily, and replaced a number of his generals: but he

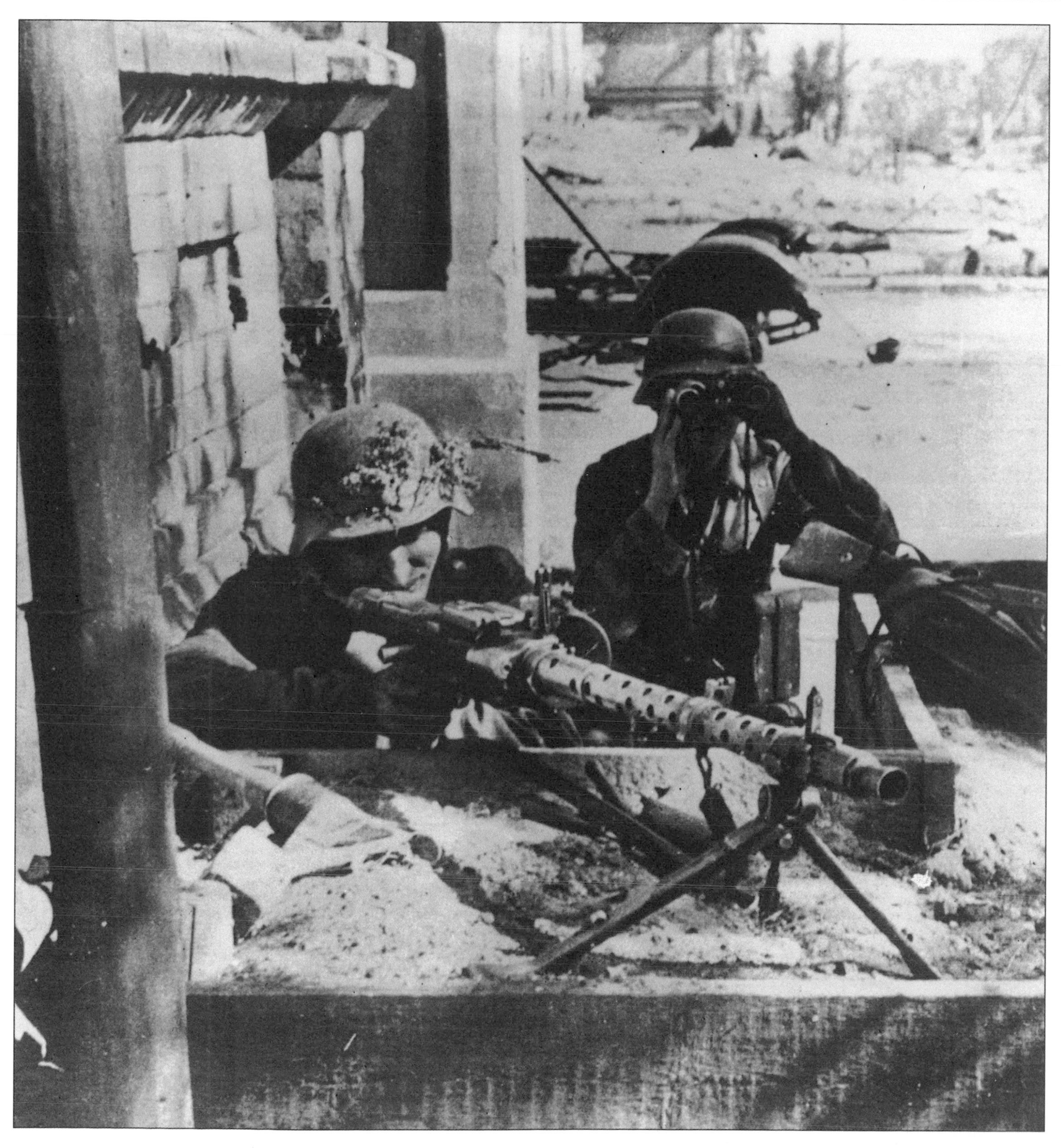

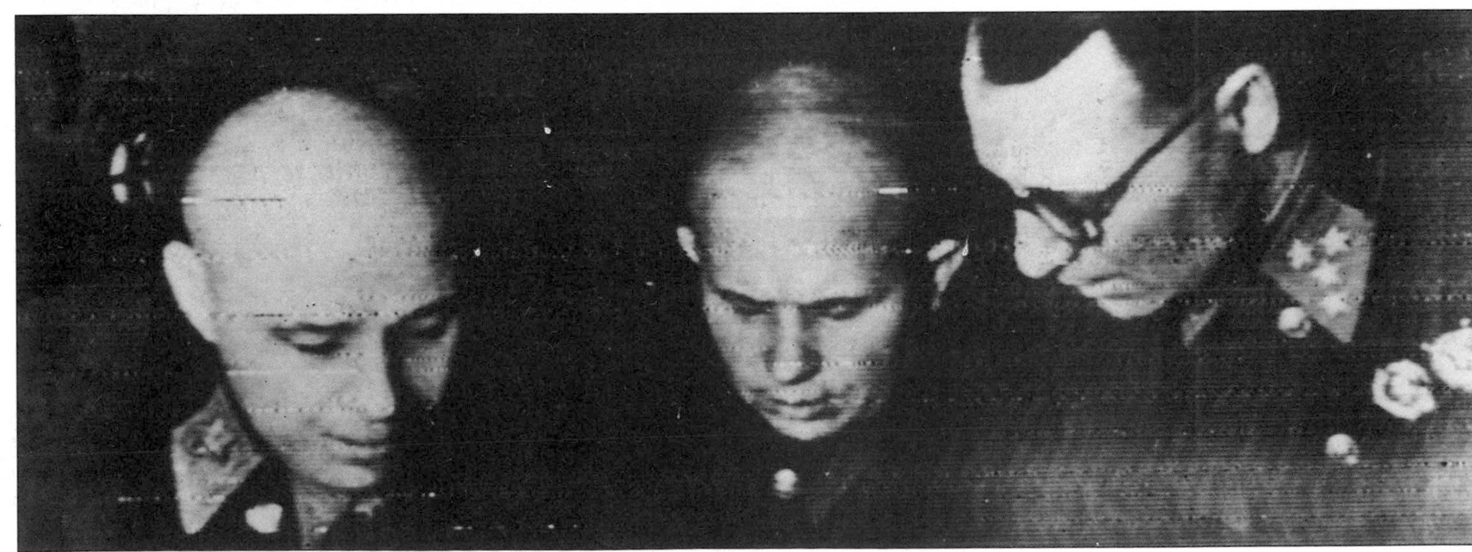

Facing page top: ammunition carriers picking their way to the front line through the charred ruins of one of the many factories that had made Stalingrad an important industrial centre. Weeks of bombardment and close fighting turned the city into heaps of rubble that were useless for anything but bitter defensive warfare.

Facing page bottom: a staff group outside Stalingrad with (left to right) Timoshenko, Khrushchev, and Timoshenko's *aide*, Colonel Cherevichenko. While Timoshenko emerged from Stalingrad as the 'grand old man' of the Red Army, Khrushchev used his energy and political authority to assert himself as a rising star of the Communist Party, eventually becoming Stalin's successor.

Below: infantry with rifles and Schmeisser SMGs advance through Stalingrad suburbs. Although snipers were often a threat to movement in the open, this area appears to have been cleared of them, since the troops betray little sense of urgency.

could do nothing to speed up the advance.

While all this was happening in the overt 'frontal' battle for Stalingrad, the Soviet staff was secretly proceeding with plans to launch a parallel 'flanking' battle – a grand double envelopment that would roll 6th Army into a vast pocket, and so bring about its complete destruction.

General Georgi Zhukov and Colonel General Alexander Vasilevsky had already visited the front on 2nd September, with instructions to examine the wider possibilities for a counter-offensive. As Stalin now knew he was free to release his large reserves from the Moscow area, he was in a position to contemplate operations a great deal more ambitious than the Germans at this stage believed possible. His two generals were especially interested to find that the Don River line on either side of Stalingrad was secured by Axis allies of dubious quality, who would probably not fight as stoutly as the Germans in the city itself. To the north of Stalingrad lay the Hungarian 2nd, the Italian 8th and the Roumanian 4th armies; and to the south the Roumanian 3rd Army. In the event none of these formations were strengthened with the stiffening of German elements that several commanders had wanted. Zhukov and Vasilevsky did not therefore take long to realise that well-prepared assaults against these weak links at the extremities of the enemy's chain might mortally ensnare the stronger ones at its heart. A secret and complex build-up began to be conceived, codenamed 'Uranus'.

Nazi over-confidence in Russia received its final comeuppance through the total success of this silent Soviet concentration comprising a million men, 1,500 tanks, 6,000 guns and 10,000 mortars. Using the series of deception, disinformation and security techniques that are known collectively as *Maskirovka,* Stalin's generals managed to emplace five armies of the Southwest Front and Don Front to the north of the city, and two armies of the Stalingrad Front to the south, without raising any major alarm at Hitler's headquarters. The Roumanians themselves knew that something big was brewing locally for them; but their warnings were dismissed higher up as 'exaggerated'. When the storm finally broke on 19th November, however, even the Roumanians were found to have underestimated the full danger.

The two Roumanian armies that were initially attacked were both swept away almost instantaneously, leaving wide gaps in the Axis line on either side of Paulus' army. The German XLVIII *Panzer Korps* put up some resistance in the north, as did 24th Motor Division in the south, but on 23rd November – after 'five days that won the war' – the two attacking spearheads were able to join hands at the Kalach Bridge and complete 6th Army's encirclement. In the ensuing days they worked

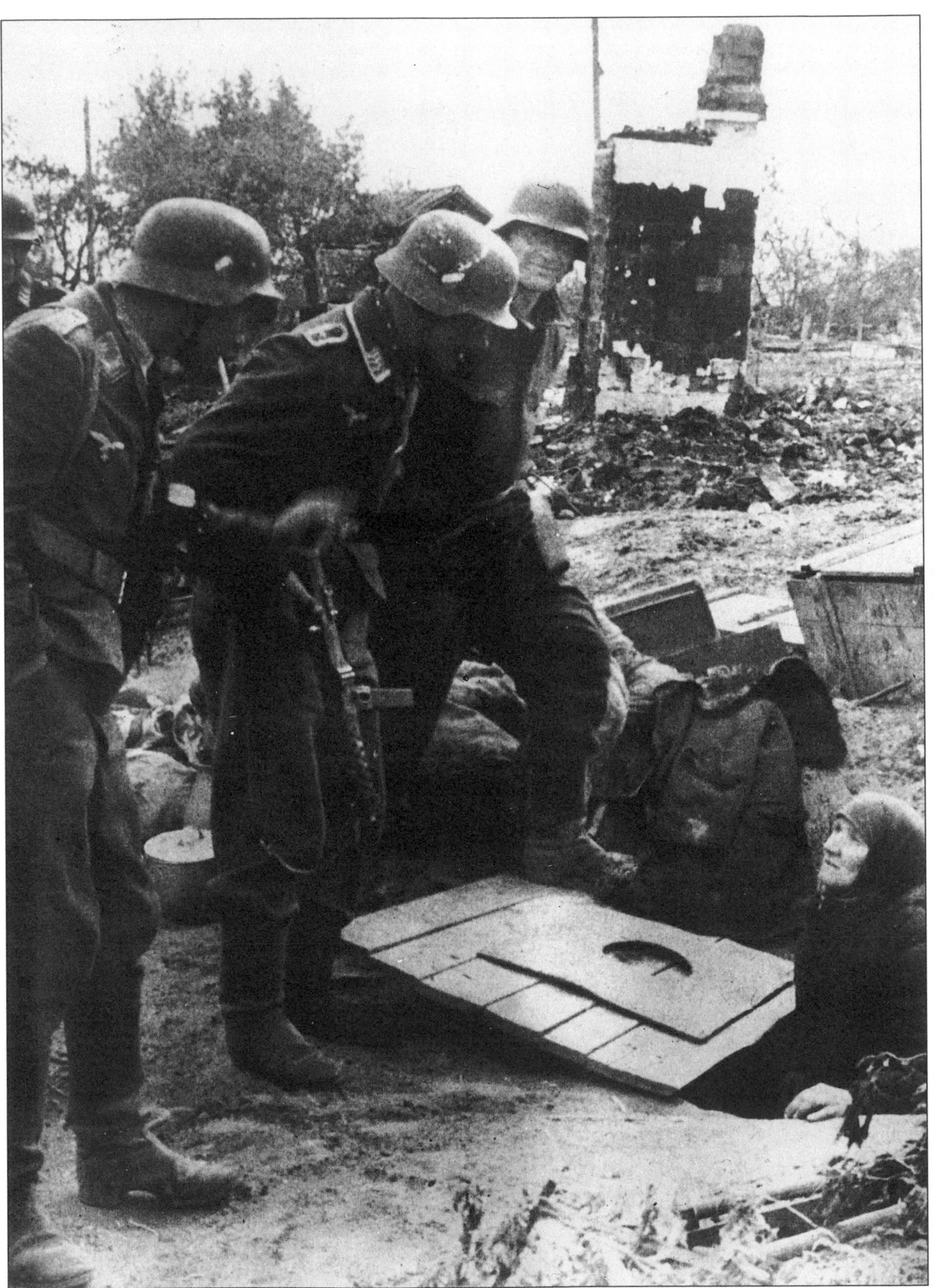

Luftwaffe field troops, carrying the ageing Steyr-Solothurn S100 sub-machine gun and smoking casually, flush a Stalingrad inhabitant from her air-raid shelter. Although the scene looks outwardly relaxed, her chances of survival must have been slim indeed.

Facing page top left: Joseph Stalin, General Secretary of the Communist Party of the Soviet Union and Commander in Chief of her forces, in his marshal's uniform, March, 1943.

Facing page top right: Field Marshal Erich von Manstein poring over a map with his advisers - an activity that came to occupy him almost round the clock. Manstein, an aristocratic officer of the old school, rarely left his headquarters to visit the front, yet his operational decision-making was unsurpassed.

Facing page bottom: Red Army infantry counterattack in a photograph that was probably posed. Note the padded jackets, thick boots and fur hats for winter warfare, and the mass-produced PPSh SMG for close-quarter fighting. The man in the right foreground carries a captured Schmeisser.

OPERATION TORCH

Propaganda headlines announcing the North African landings claim them as the long-awaited 'Second Front' to help USSR. The newspaper emphasizes the American contribution since this was the first action in the West in which U.S. troops were seriously engaged.

'Torch' was the final codename for the Allied landings in French Morocco and Algeria on 8th November, 1942. It had originated a year earlier as an all-British operation known as 'Gymnast' and then, when American participation was added, as 'Super Gymnast'. In the event it constituted a grandiose – almost global – undertaking, with over 670 ships and 1,000 landing craft sailing from two different continents to land in a third. Participating units came from bases as far distant as Malta and Alexandria in the Mediterranean; the Gambia and Sierra Leone in West Africa; Glasgow in Scotland; and Norfolk in Virginia. At the time it was the largest amphibious operation that had ever been mounted, with an attack frontage no less than 900 miles long; a landing strength of 65,000 troops, and a planned build up to some 1,700 aircraft. In many ways it was the major dress rehearsal for D-Day eighteen months later, and certainly much larger and more important than the costly Dieppe raid of August, 1942.

'Torch' was doubly impressive since it was the first time the Anglo-American alliance had operated together on such a large scale. Despite some early disagreements about strategy, and a very short time for tactical training, the two nations managed to work in close harmony. So successful was the deception plan, furthermore, that almost complete surprise was achieved. This allowed opposition to be kept to a minimum, and casualties light.

Despite all these remarkable achievements, however, two great question marks had hung over 'Torch' ever since it had first been mooted. The first of these uncertainties concerned the political attitudes of the French and Spanish, upon which much would turn. In the absence of hard intelligence, the expedition naturally had to prepare for the 'worst case' of sustained heavy fighting; and this made it a far larger and more cumbersome affair than it actually needed to be. When comparatively little French resistance was encountered, and Spain did not become involved at all, the planners were seen to have excessively over-insured. This lost them several valuable opportunities elsewhere.

The second uncertainty arose from the central question of just how Torch was supposed

"All the News That's Fit to Print."

The New York Times.

LATE CITY EDITION

Section 1

NEW YORK, SUNDAY, NOVEMBER 8, 1942

AMERICAN FORCES LAND IN FRENCH AFRICA; BRITISH NAVAL, AIR UNITS ASSISTING THEM; EFFECTIVE SECOND FRONT, ROOSEVELT SAYS

U.S. DRIVES ON BUNA

American Troops Flown to Area Closing In on Big Japanese Base

PAPUA IS OVERRUN

All Except Beachhead of Buna-Gona Seized in New Guinea Push

LEADS IN AFRICA

Lieut. Gen. Dwight Eisenhower

R.A.F. ROCKS GENOA; U.S. RAID ON BREST

Bombers From Britain Pound North Italy 2 Nights in Row —Hit Nazis on Coast

NAZIS NEAR LIBYA

British Drive Out to Bar New Stand by Enemy or Reinforcements

FOE BOMBED ALL NIGHT

Pursuers Reported to Be Within 40 Miles of Halfaya Pass

SHOCK TROOPS LEAD

Simultaneous Landings Made Before Dawn at Numerous Points

PLANES GUARD SKIES

An Armada Pours Men on the Beaches—Early Actions Satisfactory

WHERE THE UNITED STATES PREPARES FOR NEW FRONT

U.S. MEETS 'THREAT'

Big Expeditions Invade North and West Africa to Forestall Axis

EISENHOWER AT HEAD

President Urges French to Help, Calls Move Aid to Russia

LANDING PLAN KEPT SECRET BY WRITERS

President's Statement

War News Summarized

Major Sports Yesterday

Blow to Knock Italy Out of the War Called Goal of American Invasion

to achieve grand strategic results. There was a widespread suspicion that the Allies had painstakingly provided a large tactical hat, only to draw from it a diminutive strategic rabbit.

Many Americans had hoped for an operation – codenamed 'Sledgehammer' – that would directly attack the Germans through the Cherbourg peninsula in France. They thought of the French as friends to be liberated, not enemies to be invaded. The Soviets were even more insistent that a major second front should be opened as early as possible, especially in view of the very difficult battle that was just beginning at Stalingrad. Thus, when instead the British demanded an 'indirect approach' against the French in North Africa, they were greeted with considerable incredulity from all sides. North Africa seemed a sideshow of little relevance to the main operations, and there was suspicion that Churchill was playing a deep imperial game to win back southeast Europe, using American lives and efforts merely to score postwar points against the Russians in the Mediterranean and the Balkans.

Against all this the British replied that the

military record of assault landings within Europe – which ranged from Gallipoli and Narvik to the very recent Dieppe disaster – was far from reassuring. The necessary landing craft and logistics for a D-Day in France were not yet ready; nor were the troops yet 'blooded', or Allied command structures tested. The mere threat of invasion was already enough to divert a quarter of the German field forces and half of the *Luftwaffe* to the West; but much of this would be free to return to Russia if 'Sledgehammer' should be defeated. Besides, there would be a big potential saving in shipping mileage, for if the armies in North Africa could be supplied directly through the Straits of Gibraltar instead of around the Cape, they would become a 'local' theatre to Britain, rather than the strenuously 'far distant' theatre that they had been since 1940. This could release huge shipping resources for more

important tasks, such as the sea bridge between Britain and the U.S.A. – or even the U.S.S.R. In the end, the Americans reluctantly bowed to these arguments and agreed to go ahead with 'Torch', although the closer they came to embarking upon the operation the more pessimistic their planning staff seemed to become. At one point the operation was given less than a fifty per cent chance of success.

The command team assembled for 'Torch' constituted a veritable galaxy of stars, notable among whom was Lieutenant General Dwight D. Eisenhower, the sagacious and – in the best sense – diplomatic Commander in Chief. He was seconded by Major General Mark W. Clark, who before the operation made some risky personal visits to meet Vichy moderates within Algeria itself. At a slightly less exalted level, Major General George S. Patton was to command the main U.S. assault in Morocco – his first step in a dashing 'glory ride' that would take him through Africa and Italy to France and finally the Reich. For the USAAF the command fell to yet another hero, Brigadier General James H. Doolittle, who had bombed Tokyo in April, 1942.

On the British side there was a scarcely less distinguished cast of characters, with Admiral Sir Andrew Cunningham – victor of Matapan, Taranto and many a Malta convoy – commanding the naval forces. He was supported by Vice-Admiral Sir Bertram Ramsay, who had masterminded the miracle of the little ships at Dunkirk, and who would one day preside over the D-Day landings themselves. Perhaps the British ground forces lacked an equivalently prestigious commander, since it was the relatively unknown Lieutenant General Kenneth Anderson who took command of the nascent 1st Army. He was only third choice for the appointment, however, after Alexander and Montgomery. Alas, it would also be his misfortune to be overshadowed in the history books, not entirely deservedly, by the more spectacular achievements of those two men.

The 'Torch' plan called for 24,500 American troops with 250 tanks to sail direct from the U.S.A. and land through the surf on the beaches around Casablanca. Meanwhile 18,500 more with 180 tanks would sail from Britain via Gibraltar into the more sheltered Mediterranean and land around Oran. These

Below: American generals at a North African airfield. From left to right: Major General Lloyd R. Fredendall, commander of the U.S. Central Task Force, who was later to be criticised for his role in the Kasserine battle; Lieutenant General Mark W. Clark, Eisenhower's Second in Command, who would one day liberate Rome; and Brigadier General James Doolittle, the Allied air force commander who had shaken the Japanese by bombing Tokyo.

Facing page top: Lieutenant General George S. 'Blood and Guts' Patton, photographed in Tunisia at the start of his two-and-a-half year 'glory ride'.

Facing page bottom: assault landing craft leaving their parent troop transports for the 'Torch' landings. The journey from the transports to the beaches was planned to be between six and eight miles - but 800 troops from one torpedoed transport had to sail some 150 miles in their landing craft!

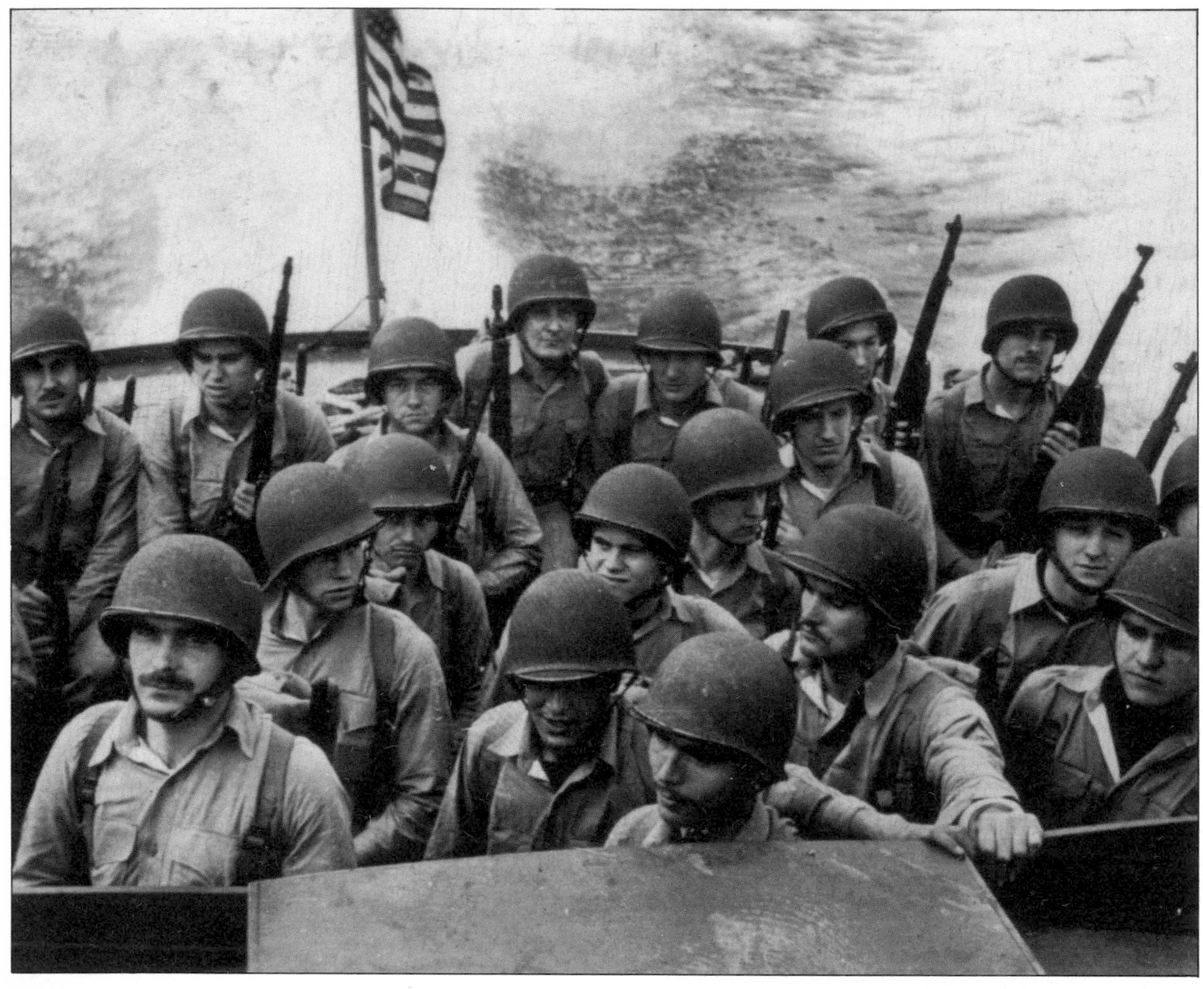

U.S. infantry in the 'Torch' landings, apparently relaxed and therefore not under fire while this photograph was taken.

two U.S. forces would then combine as 5th Army and take up a defensive posture against any intervention from Spanish Morocco. A joint U.S. and British force of 20,000 men would simultaneously arrive from Britain to secure the area of Algiers. As 1st Army it would then move eastwards as rapidly as possible to capture the four key ports of Bône and Philippeville in Algeria, and Bizerta and Tunis itself in Tunisia. These ports were not deemed suitable for direct landings because they were beyond the range of Gibraltar's air cover, and too near to Axis air forces in Sicily. However, the British, at least, always believed they were really the most vital targets of all, and did not share American pessimism about venturing so far to the east.

Against such a powerful Allied assault, what was the measure of the opposition? On the French side there was plenty of infantry, some 120,000 in all, but they lacked modern equipment and their 500 aircraft were obsolete. On the other hand, they had good coastal batteries and a very powerful Navy, based at Toulon, but with a battleship in both Casablanca and Dakar, and many smaller warships in Algerian ports. Allied planning also had to take into account the possible threat from the garrison of Spanish Morocco – some 130,000 strong – and the possibilities that the *Luftwaffe* might be invited to operate from southern Spain, or that the huge Italian battle fleet might intervene.

In their command structure the French appeared strong, and were all known to despise de Gaulle; but in reality they suffered from political divisions. Admiral Jean François Darlan commanded North Africa in the strongly anti-British spirit with which he had fought against them at Mers el Kebir in 1940. It was hoped that he would be absent at the time of the 'Torch' landings and his subordinates would be in control. Such men as General Alphonse Juin,

Riflemen filing inland from their landing craft over open beaches near Casablanca, supported by White half tracks and 'DUKWS'. Smoke in the background is from supporting naval gunfire.

and still more Major Generals Béthouart and Charles Mast, were known to be more amenable to the Allied cause, and had even been made partly aware of the plan. The last two mobilized the patriotic youth in Casablanca and Algiers to support the invasion, managing to prevent leaks to the Vichy authorities until as late as 6th November. For good measure, the Allies also hoped to use the popular General Henri Giraud, who had escaped from imprisonment in a German fortress, but in the event his inexperience and lack of formal hierarchical position in Algeria entirely negated his influence. Darlan actually turned the tables on both him and the Allied planners by chancing to return to North Africa at the crucial moment. Receiving no clear guidelines from Pétain, he seized control of negotiations – although as a secondary surprise he proved to be considerably more flexible and less hostile than had been expected. It was largely due to his influence that a general ceasefire could be arranged within three days of the landings. Nevertheless, by his clever political footwork he continued to block the influence of de Gaulle, and to be lukewarm in active support for the Allies.

Even if peace were to be made quickly with the French, that still did not disarm the Germans. They were not initially deployed in any of the

territories under attack – nor in either Tunisia or the south of France – but they had got some inkling of the landings as early as 15th October, and were ready to move swiftly. Once the fact of the landings had become clear, from 9th November they rushed through Operation 'Anton' to completely occupy the whole of the French mainland, failing only to seize the Toulon fleet, which was scuppered. They also hastily sent troops by air to Tunisia, where a ground defence was improvised by General Walther Nehring, a tough soldier whom Hitler had just relieved of command of the *Afrika Korps*. The brilliant *Luftwaffe* Field Marshal Albert Kesselring became the overall German commander in this area and, despite some clashes with Rommel over allocations of equipment between the two North African fronts, his administrative genius went far towards consolidating Tunisia and preventing the Allies breaking out to the east.

The German reaction, although fast, was nevertheless not fast enough to prevent the Allied landings themselves. The gigantic plan swung smoothly into operation from 2nd October onwards, when the first supply convoys left Britain to begin stockpiling equipment and aircraft in Gibraltar. By the night of 7th to 8th November the attack armadas had all been assembled and were silently approaching their designated beaches. An intense reconnaissance effort and U-boat attack was mounted throughout the Mediterranean and the Central Atlantic, and the Germans were deceived into thinking that the shipping movement was nothing more than another routine convoy for Malta – or possibly an assault on Tripoli. Even when chance encounters led to sinkings by U-boats and Axis bombers, they failed to alert the German High Command that this was actually the expected invasion of French North Africa.

On arrival close to the beaches, however, a strong westerly swell disorganised and dispersed several of the assault groups. Landing was made difficult by heavy surf around Algiers and Casablanca, and many of the coastal batteries were found to be fully alert. The French navy was especially active in defence of their port at Mers el Kebir, which had already been surprised by the British in 1940, and they inflicted very heavy casualties upon U.S. *coup de main* parties trying to seize the docks at both Algiers and Oran. Allied naval gunfire had to be widely used to suppress the shore defences and to sink several French destroyers that tried to come out and fight. Air attacks destroyed at least seventy French aircraft on the ground at the two key fields around Oran, although some of the defenders did manage to take off and shoot down Allied planes. A parachute drop designed to seize these airfields also became dispersed by bad weather in the Bay of Biscay, and failed to find its objectives. One of the airfields held out for forty hours, while the port of Oran could not be occupied before its defenders had sunk blockships to deny its use.

Even more difficult was the battle for the beaches around Casablanca, where the infantry made no progress from the shoreline until some of Patton's tanks could be landed. In this battle, the defenders' ground fire and air attacks were the heaviest of all and the weather least favourable. Some 216 out of 629 landing craft had to be written off, as compared with only 106 out of 400 at Algiers and Oran combined. Over half the 1,404 American land and air casualties suffered in the whole operation were on this front, whereas the British Army and RAF at Algiers suffered just eighty-

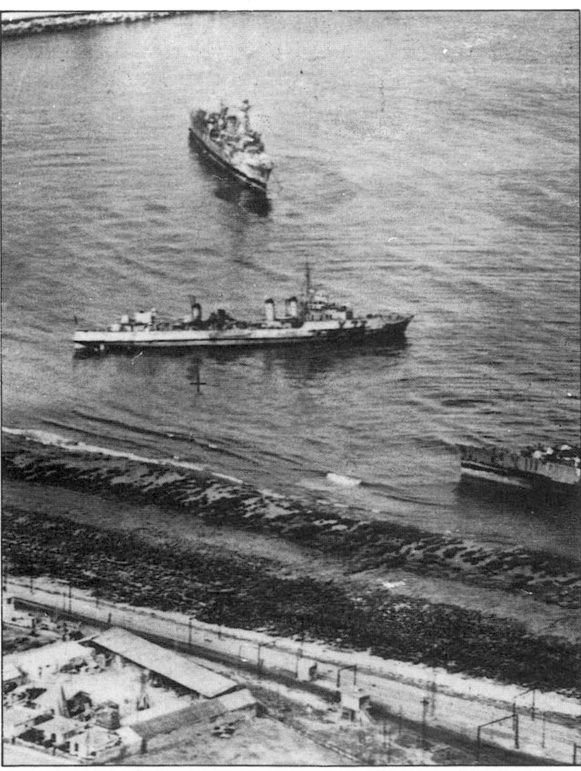

Below: two seriously damaged French destroyers and a light cruiser - probably *Milan*, *Albatros* and *Primauguet*, respectively - beached at Casablanca after vainly resisting the U.S. landings. At least five other French warships were badly damaged or sunk in the Casablanca battle.

Facing page top: an Algiers beach with a two-and-a-half-ton prime mover pulling a 105mm howitzer -the gun that was to remain the mainstay of U.S. field artillery from World War Two through the war in Vietnam.

Facing page bottom: a 'Priest' self-propelled M7 105mm howitzer on a Grant chassis. This was one of the earliest examples of true SP artillery, which initially suffered from mechanical unreliability.

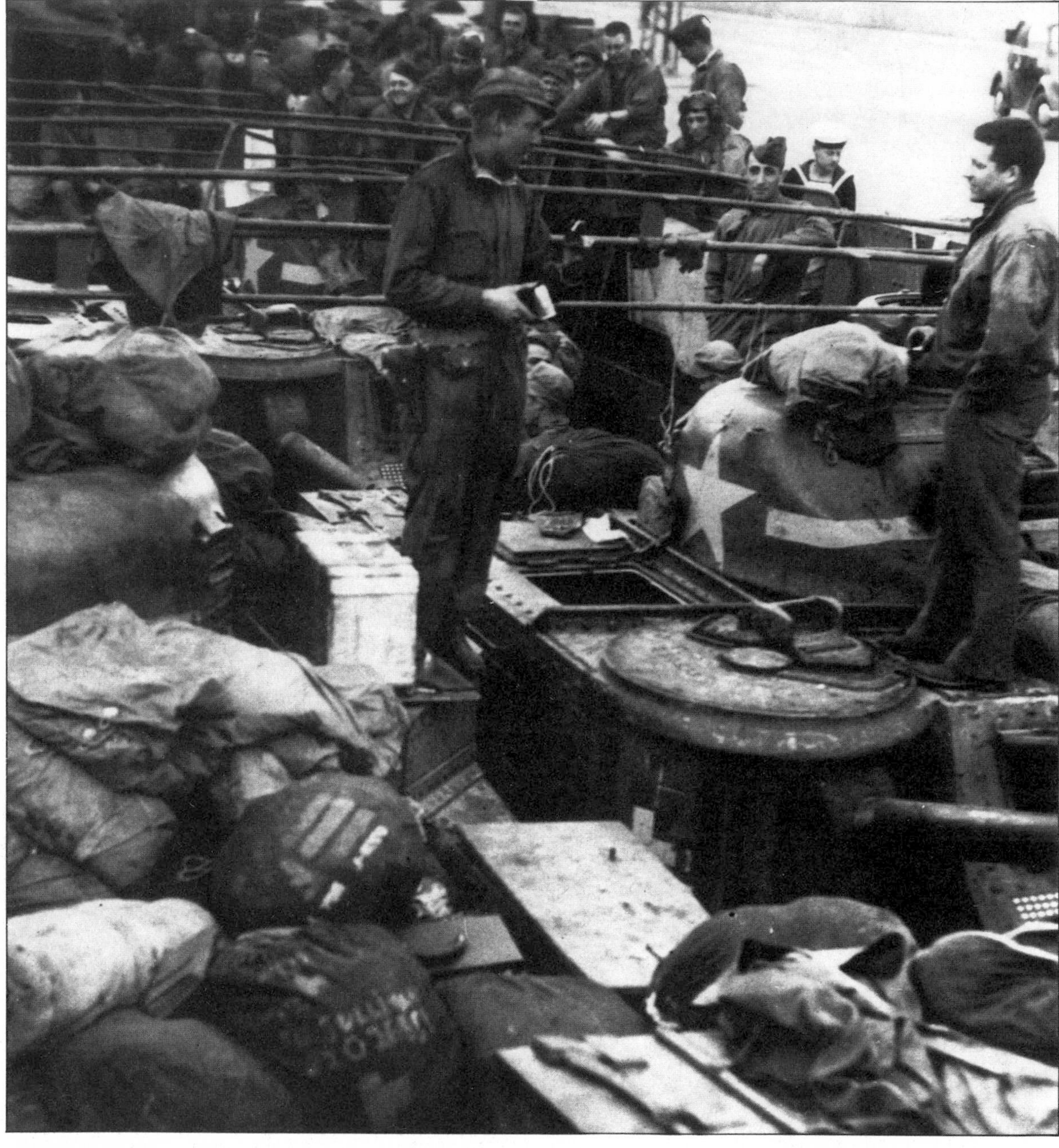

General Lee tanks and other American equipment *en route* for Algiers in December, 1942. President Roosevelt had generously sent all supplies of the more advanced Grant tanks to the British 8th Army, leaving the growing 1st Army with the earlier, more cramped Lee.

nine losses. However, there were 662 British, 117 Dutch but only seventy U.S. naval casualties. French losses are unknown, but they must have been at least comparable in scale. A total of fifty-four Allied aircraft were lost, and perhaps a dozen ships, but in return the Allies ensured that the Vichy Navy and Air Force were no longer factors in the war, as well as destroying seven German submarines.

Despite their setbacks, by the morning of 10th November the Allies had won positions from which they were poised to make final assaults to clear all three of their main objectives. Ceasefire negotiations were already under way, however, so in most areas hostilities died down and the vital targets were secured before a final attack needed to be made. The French were satisfied that they had defended their military honour against overwhelming odds; while the Allies were relieved to have finished their long and dangerous voyage without having to face the much heavier level

German paratroops were not slow in occupying the ruins of the Cassino Monastery once the dust settled. Allied action had effectively turned it into an even strónger position to defend; it was to be three long months before the Poles at last became masters of the position on 18th May, 1944.

Line to come to a halt at the River Garigliano. Past Cassino lay the road to Rome.

Both sides had carried through a series of command changes. On 6th November Hitler had appointed Kesselring as Supreme Commander Italy, creating Army Group 'C', comprising the German 10th Army and General von Mackensen's German 14th Army. Rommel and Army Group 'B' were transferred to northwest Europe and given responsibility for the preparation of defences against the Allied invasion, when and wherever it came. The Allies created 15th Army Group in southern Italy under Alexander, but recalled both the Supreme Commander, General Dwight D. Eisenhower, and General Montgomery to England to prepare for 'Overlord'. General Maitland 'Jumbo' Wilson assumed supreme command, while Lieutenant General Sir Oliver Leese took over 8th Army. It was also firmly decreed at the 'Big Three' conference held at Teheran in early December, 1943, that operational requirements in Italy were to take second place to the preparations for mounting 'Overlord' and the associated 'Anvil' landings in the south of France later in 1944. Once and for all, this removed any prospect of penetrating the eastern Alps towards Vienna. It was, however, recognised that the capture of Rome was highly desirable for Allied propaganda purposes, and it was operationally important to tie down as many German resources as possible in Italy, and thus prevent transfers to either the Eastern Front, where critical fighting was taking place west of Kiev and in the Crimea, or to northwest Europe. Such was the strategic background in Europe against which the four bitter battles for Cassino were to be fought.

The central and western sectors of the Germans' Gustav Line were forbidding indeed, the region's geography being as daunting as the defenders. Three rivers dominated the approaches. First, there was the River Rapido, flowing from the east – a once-narrow waterway made much larger by flooding north of Cassino; second, was the River Liri, flowing from the northwest to join the Rapido southwest of Cassino; and thirdly there was the River Garigliano and its tributary, the Ausente, flowing into the Mediterranean.

Then there were the mountains. By mid-January, 1944, the Allies had made themselves masters of the Monte Pile massif south of the Rapido, the neighbouring Monte Arcalone range and, nearest to Cassino, the towering Monte Trocchio on the inland and central sectors of the region. The Germans were firmly placed, however, on the western half of the Gustav Line. Firstly, they still held Monte Cairo and its inland neighbour, Monte Santa Croce, linking with the main inland mountain chain. Secondly, there was Monte Cassino itself, standing at 435 metres high on a spur south of Monte Cairo and Monte Castellone, which overlooked Cassino town and the Rapido-Liri confluence, and was backed by higher ground, including Snake's Head Ridge, Point 593, and two other eminences, Points 569 and 445. Further to the west stood the Arunci Mountains, a separate chain overlooking the River Garigliano.

Four roads were of importance. Route 6, the old Roman *Via Casilina*, which was the main Rome-Naples highway, ran through Cassino town and along the northern side of the Liri valley, while Route 7, the ancient Appian Way, linked Rome to the coast by way of Minturno. The third and fourth roads ran laterally, the western route running from west of Minturno to

of fighting they had feared as their 'worst case'.

By landing in French North Africa the Allies had indeed shortened their sea voyage to the desert theatre, and had brought the whole northern shore of the Mediterranean under threat. Despite some tactical fumbles in the landings, they had won a vast swathe of territory at relatively trivial cost and, at the same time, laid the foundations for a close, fruitful alliance with French forces. They had also unwittingly planted some fast-growing seeds of doubt in Hitler's mind that would greatly distract him – and many extra Axis resources – away from the crucial Stalingrad battle. Spain had not and would not enter the fighting, and Anglo-American co-operation in battle had been very firmly cemented. A real step forward had thus been made in preparing for D-Day, even though it was not yet known that this would take place in 1944, rather than 1943.

One of the reasons why D-Day would be delayed was that Allied exploitation immediately after 'Torch' remained incomplete. The German footholds in Bizerta and Tunis had not been quickly stamped out by the Allied pursuit from Algiers – in the event this took almost two weeks to develop into serious tactical contact. By then it was too late to break through, and the assault soon bogged down into a wet and miserable winter

A U.S. troop transport enters Algiers harbour, some time after the initial fighting has died down. Note the denseness of the buildings in the city, every block of which could have become a fearsome fortress had Algiers been stalwartly defended by the French.

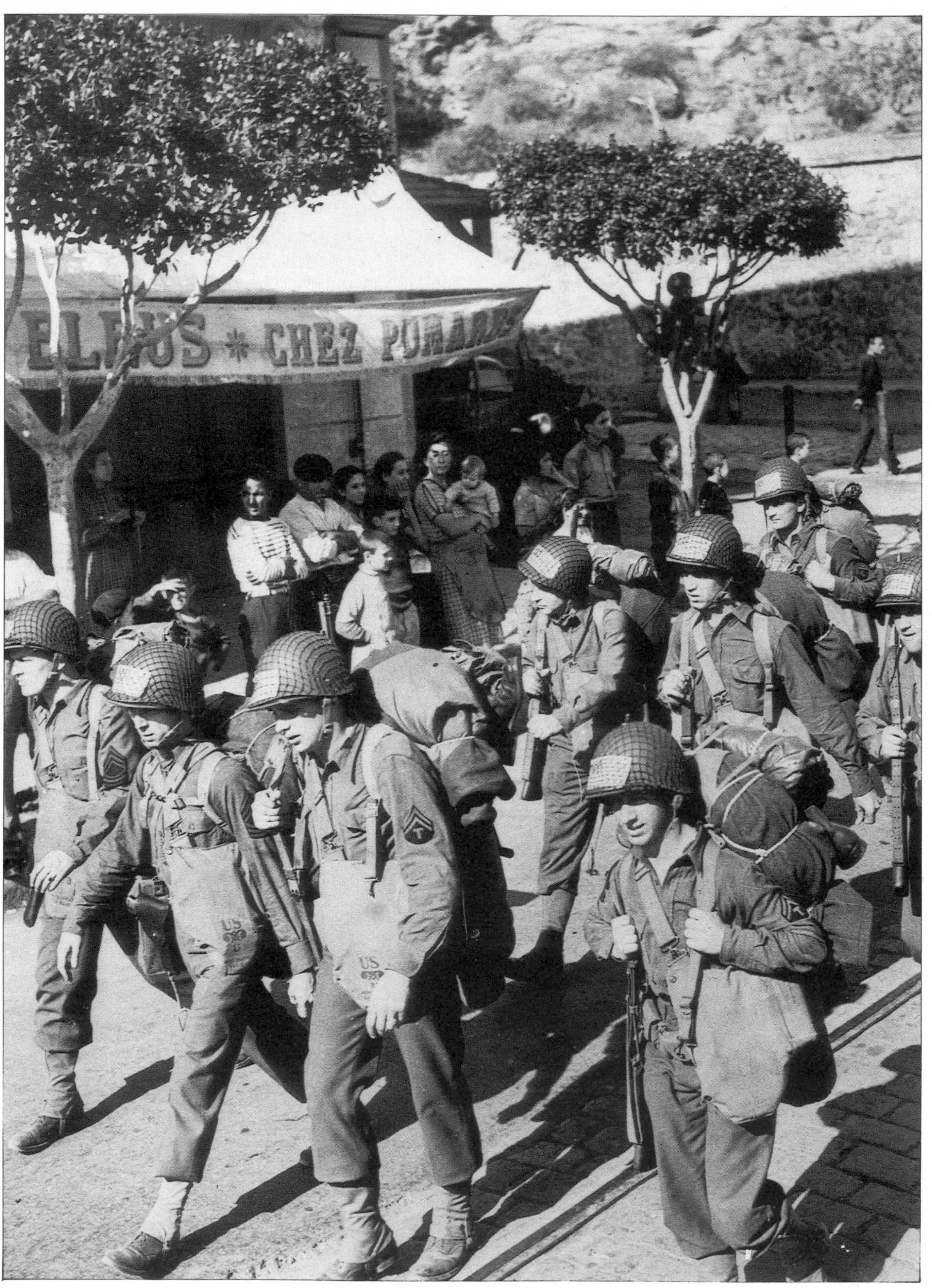

Facing page: U.S. weapon carriers and 37mm anti-tank guns advance through Algeria. The western half of the North African coastline had far more trees and greenery than had most of Libya and Egypt, and could not truly be called 'desert'.

Left: U.S. infantry 'showing the flag' in Oran as they march to the front - or at least as far as their motor transport. Note the 'very French' cafe life in the background.

After advancing into Tunisia, the Americans captured this Italian 75mm cannon, which they adopted for their own use in an anti-tank role.

campaign in which the defender held all the trumps. As the 'Torch' landings had been prudently designed to cope with the 'worst case' that could be imagined, the Allies found themselves unable to switch quickly to the mobile and opportunistic form of warfare that was demanded by the actual situation. The loss of a vital week in mid-November, 1942, meant the capture of Tunisia was delayed for no less than six full months until mid-May, 1943; and this in turn threw back the timetable for the Normandy landings by a complete year. It was by no means the first occasion in the history of warfare that a great opportunity had been lost 'for the want of a nail' – but it must surely rank as one of the most striking.

KURSK–THE CLASH OF STEEL

Colonel General Hermann Hoth, the commander of 4th *Panzerarmee* during the Kursk offensive. Hoth had previously commanded 4th *Panzerarmee* in the Stalingrad battles. The battle between Hoth's tanks and those of Rotmistrov's 5th Guards Tank Army at Kursk was one of the classic armoured engagements of the war.

By the summer of 1943, the German Army appeared to have recovered from the destruction of Field Marshal Paulus' 6th Army at Stalingrad. Manstein's brilliant counter-offensive at Kharkov during February and March, 1943, had brought the Soviet winter offensive to a halt and stabilised the German front. German High Command then took the decision to seize the initiative by going on the offensive. On 13th March, 1943, Operation 'Order Five' was issued. This warned that the Soviets were likely to attack during the summer months, and therefore Germany would have to make a pre-emptive strike. The chosen battleground was the Kursk salient, a sizable bulge of Soviet-held territory that jutted out from the main Soviet position.

The German Army Group South was ordered to prepare to strike north from Kharkov in April and assault the southern flank of the salient. In many ways this was a sensible decision. Kursk was the natural jumping-off point for a future Soviet offensive, but the Soviets had only recently captured the area, and were still consolidating the 360-mile perimeter of the salient. Moreover, the Kursk operation, codenamed Operation 'Citadel', was not initially designed to be an 'all-or-nothing' attack. Rather, it was just one of a whole series of local attacks that would be carried out along the Eastern Front, including an offensive against Leningrad. In the event, 'Citadel' was to be subjected to months of delay. The offensive might have succeeded in the spring, but by the time the attack actually commenced on 5th July, 1943, the situation in the Kursk salient had changed dramatically.

'Citadel' was a controversial operation from its inception. Guderian, the Inspector General of Armoured Troops, opposed it, and Jodl, Chief of Staff at the German High Command, urged that reserves should be kept in hand to respond to any move by the Western Allies in the Mediterranean. However, Zeitzler of Army High Command, and Kluge, commander of Army Group Centre, were both in favour of 'Citadel'. Faced with contradictory advice, Hitler prevaricated, admitting that just thinking about the offensive gave him 'butterflies in his stomach'. As it was, the initial starting date of April came and went without action, as it became clear that the German forces were not ready to begin the offensive. Still no final decision was reached as Hitler considered carrying out two other subsidiary operations, 'Hawk' and 'Panther'. The fate of the offensive was not finally decided until 1st July, when Hitler finally gave the go-ahead for 'Citadel'.

The Soviets had not wasted the breathing space granted through German indecision. Stalin was receiving high-grade intelligence concerning the forthcoming German offensive at Kursk from a number of sources. 'Lucy', a Soviet spy with access to the deliberations of the German decision-making elite, forwarded invaluable information to Moscow. For some time the British had been reading German signals sent by the supposedly safe Enigma cipher machine, and Churchill passed on these 'Ultra' decrypts to the Soviets, although they were disguised as 'information from a trusted agent'. In addition, the Soviets had had an intelligence windfall by gaining possession of Enigma machines themselves. The Soviets were in much the same position as their enemies –

aware that they were about to be attacked, and forced to make a decision whether to pull back, launch a pre-emptive strike, or stand and fight. Finally, they decided on the latter course. In Zhukov's words, the Red Army would 'wear down the enemy on our defences, knock out his tanks, then bring in fresh reserves and finish off his main grouping with a general offensive'. Thus, like the Germans on the Somme in 1916, the Soviets intended to convert an enemy offensive into a defensive battle of attrition. Unlike the Germans in the earlier war, the Soviets possessed the resources to launch a major counter-offensive once the enemy's impetus had been spent.

The success of the Soviet plan depended upon the Red Army being able to absorb the German blow without allowing the *Panzers* to make a significant penetration into Soviet positions. The Soviet answer to a German *Blitzkrieg* was to build positional defences in great depth – up to 110 miles deep in places. Some 300,000 civilians were put to work on such defences, which consisted of six belts of what the Germans called 'pakfronts' – strongpoints bristling with anti-tank guns,

A spectacular aerial view of a head-on clash between Soviet and German armour. Clouds of smoke can be observed issuing from burning vehicles. The Soviets relied mainly on the T-34 during the Kursk battle, while the Germans used five different types, including the Panther, which was probably the most effective German tank of the war.

Operation 'Citadel' attempted to 'pinch out' the Kursk salient with assaults by 9th Army in the north and 4th *Panzerarmee* in the south. The former advanced only six miles at great loss, while the latter was initially more successful, yet still only managed a distance of some twenty-five miles before it was fought to a standstill.

mortars and artillery. Interspersed between each belt were minefields. Beyond the main defences were the positions of Koniev's Steppe Front, the formation which was intended to deliver the *coup de grâce* to the German attackers, and some reserve positions along the bank of the River Don. The southern shoulder of the salient was held by Vatutin's Voronezh Front, the northern by Rokossovsky's Central Front, while the Southwest Front covered the southern flank of the salient, and Popov's Bryansk Front the northern. Estimates of Soviet strength at the Battle of Kursk vary. Zhukov claimed a total of 1,330,000 men and 3,600 tanks; in addition, the Soviets probably had 2,500 aircraft, while the two main fronts alone had 13,000 guns, 6,000 anti-tank guns and 1,000 rocket-launchers.

The German plan was to snip off the salient in classic fashion by simultaneously attacking the flanks. This was far from being the limited offensive which had originally been envisaged. Hitler committed a high proportion of the German Army's armour to the battle. In the words of the British military theorist and historian, Basil Liddell Hart, 'Hitler was gambling for high stakes'. Manstein's Army Group South was to use Hoth's 4th *Panzerarmee* to advance north from Belgorod against the southern flank, supported by Army Detachment Kempf. Manstein's forces consisted of six *Panzer*, five *Panzergrenadier* and eleven infantry divisions, with about 1,500 tanks and assault guns. The northern attack was to be delivered by Kluge's Army Group Centre. Model's 9th Army – which had about 900 tanks organised into six *Panzer* and one *Panzergrenadier* divisions, and fourteen infantry divisions – was to make the attack. Thus the attackers were significantly outnumbered by the defending forces.

The attack began inauspiciously for the Germans, when, forewarned by a captured German soldier of the time of the attack, Soviet guns opened up in the early hours of 5th July. At 3.30am Model's forces began their attack. As heavy rain fell on the battlefield, three *Panzer Korps* succeeded in advancing four miles. In the process they had broken through the first belt of Central Front's defences on a frontage of thirty-five miles, and had begun to make inroads into the second line of defences. Manstein's men also experienced some success – 2nd *SS Panzer Korps* and 48th *Panzer Korps*

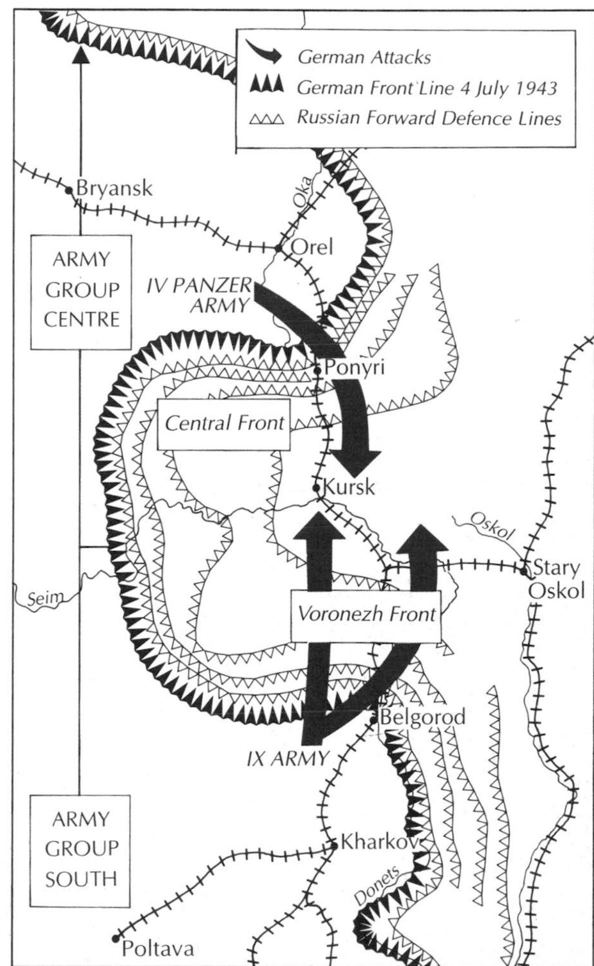

smashed through the first line of Soviet defences, forcing Vatutin to commit his reserves and to withdraw to the second line. The German assault was covered by an air umbrella of Stuka dive-bombers and fighter aircraft. The Soviets were faced with enemy formations consisting of hundreds of armoured vehicles. The new Tiger tanks and Ferdinand self-propelled guns, in which Hitler had placed so much faith, were in the vanguard, followed by Panthers, and the old workhorses of the *Panzerdivisions, Panzer* IIIs and IVs. The Soviets replied in kind; one German divisional commander later commented 'The Russians used aircraft in numbers as we had never yet seen in the East'. By the end of the day approximately 4,000 Soviet Armoured Fighting Vehicles (AFVs) were either engaged in the battle or preparing to join in. Both sides had suffered heavy losses of men and material, but the while the Soviets could afford to absorb

Facing page top: the price of defeat: a German tank, knocked out during the 'Citadel' offensive. While the Soviets also suffered heavy losses in their armoured formations, they, unlike the Germans, were able to replace them with relative ease.

Facing page bottom left: Stalin's 'God of War' - a Red Army mortar crew advance under fire to take up a new position. Throughout history, Russian forces have placed great emphasis on artillery, and the defenders of the Kursk salient were able to bring a massive volume of firepower to bear on the Nazi attackers.

Facing page bottom right: Soviet automatic riflemen in action. Although not as skilled as their German counterparts, the Soviet infantry were capable of performing extraordinary feats of endurance and played a major role in the Soviet victory.

Right: German troops snatch a brief rest. The German infantryman was probably the best trained and most effective soldier of the war. Each soldier was taught to be a leader, with the result that German units were still able to operate effectively even if most their officers and NCOs were killed or captured.

such losses in the long run, the Germans could not.

The struggle between Model and Rokossovsky continued on 6th July. The Soviets threw in an unsuccessful counterattack at dawn, only to see the German 9th Army continue to grind their way forward throughout the day. Rokossovsky changed his tactics, switching his tanks from an aggressive to a defensive role. The striking force of 4th *Panzerarmee*, 48th *Panzer Korps* and 2nd *SS Panzer Korps* continued to push forward, with two fresh *Panzerdivisions* also being thrown into the battle. 2nd *SS Panzer Korps* succeeded in advancing twenty-five miles. The Soviet 7th Guards Army was forced to give ground, although they repulsed twelve separate German attacks and claimed to have destroyed 332 tanks. The following day, 7th July, was a success for 4th *Panzerarmee*, who forced the Soviets to feed in yet more reserves in an attempt to blunt the German advance. On the southern flank of the salient, 1st Tank Army was badly mauled by an attack spearheaded by 400 *Panzers*. Furthermore, Vatutin's plans for a counterblow were largely stillborn; the crisis developing on the front of 1st Tank Army and neighbouring 6th Guards Army forced him to send men and machines to stiffen the line. Army Detachment Kempf also began to make progress, although it lagged behind the two *Panzer Korps*.

Manstein's advance continued on 8th and 9th July, until by the evening of the latter the prize of the town of Oboyan, a key position in the Soviet defences, appeared within reach. But 4th *Panzerarmee*'s situation was not as healthy as it might have appeared. The impetus of the German advance was beginning to flag, and human and mechanical casualties

Far left: a tank commander's view of battle. Kursk was the largest armoured battle in history; the Soviets claimed after the war that the Germans deployed 2,000 tanks against their 3,600. A new type of German tank, the Porsche Ferdinand, proved to be unsuccessful because it lacked the secondary armament needed to keep infantrymen at bay.

Left: the infantryman's view of battle. A German soldier watches a Soviet tank from a foxhole. Infantry were not entirely defenceless against armoured vehicles; large numbers were destroyed by foot soldiers armed with bazooka-type weapons, mines and even hollow-charge grenades. Tanks were sometimes coated with anti-magnetic paste as a protection against such devices.

had been heavy. One *SS* division, which had started the battle with 300 tanks, was reduced to only eighty, and the new types of tank were not performing well. The Panther was prone to mechanical breakdown, and the Elefant, which lacked machine guns, was vulnerable to determined infantry attacks. Worse still, Model's 9th Army was ninety miles away, and the Germans had not yet broken through the Soviet defences, which were being tenaciously and skilfully defended. Finally, the strong showing of the Soviet Air Force deflected the *Luftwaffe's* attention away from the role of ground support – the role which had been so important in the German *Blitzkrieg* offensives of the early years of the war.

By 9th July Model's advance against Rokossovsky had ground to a halt. On the previous day, 9th Army had begun to crash its way through the Soviet defences on the Olkhovatka Ridge, an area of great tactical importance. The Soviet defenders fought ferociously. The Soviet 3rd Anti-Tank Brigade was almost entirely destroyed when it was attacked by a force of 300 *Panzers*, which it engaged at ranges as small as 700 yards. On the evening of 8th July, Model, whose forces had so far lost 10,000 men, ordered the attacks to cease. In sharp contrast to the *Blitzkrieg* advances of previous campaigns, on this sector the *Panzers* had been halted within two days of the assault beginning. Two more days of attritional fighting, on 10th and 11th July, also failed to achieve a breakthrough.

On 11th July Army Group South once more renewed their offensive. The previous two days had seen both the Germans and the Red Army regroup their forces, and a furious battle develop around the town of Prokhorovka, which lies about thirty miles from Oboyan. Army Detachment Kempf advanced from the south, while the main assault was launched by three *SS* divisions (*Adolf Hitler*, *Totenkopf* and *Das Reich*) from the northeast. The Germans once again battered their way forward against tough opposition, and by the end of the day the Soviets were aware that the battle had reached its crisis. On 12th July Rotmistrov's 5th Guards Tank Army counterattacked and the greatest armoured battle in history began. About 1,500

A German Focke-Wulf 190 aircraft in action. Although at the beginning of the 'Citadel' offensive the *Luftwaffe* could put some 1,800 aircraft into the air, by the end of the battle the Red Air Force had gained air superiority. A trail of burning vehicles was the testimony to the Soviet success in the air.

AFVs – 900 Soviet, 600 German – were locked in close-range battle around Prokhorovka in area little bigger than that of a Napoleonic battlefield. By nightfall, in John Erickson's words, 'more than 300 German tanks ... 88 guns and 300 lorries (lay) wrecked on the steppe: more than half the Soviet 5th Guards Tank Army lay shattered in the same area'. The battle in the Prokhorovka area continued until 15th July, but by then it was clear that Army Group South's offensive had failed.

Even before the battle for Prokhorovka had ended, Hitler had decided to bring the operation to a halt. The Anglo-American landings in Sicily on 10th July clearly influenced Hitler's decision, but other factors played their part as well. On 12th July the Soviet West Front and Bryansk Front had attacked 2nd *Panzerarmee*, which was defending the Orel area where a large German salient thrust out into Soviet-held territory. This, in turn, threatened the rear of 9th Army, which was forced to divert troops to face this new threat, and on 17th July, Model began to pull back from hard-won positions in the Kursk salient, thus nullifying the gains made in the south. The Soviets were now taking the initiative, attacking to the south as well as in the salient itself. The subsequent Soviet offensives were to carry them 250 miles from Kursk to Kiev and the River Dneiper. The fruits of Manstein's counter-offensive of March were thrown away; never again was the German army able to carry out a major offensive operation on the Eastern Front. Kursk had cost the Germans more than the initiative. They had lost about 1,000 tanks, compared with Soviets losses of about 1,500, but these lost German AFVs were virtually irreplaceable. The German *Blitzkrieg* successes of 1939-42 had been based on surprise, speed and rapid exploitation. Faced with the formidable Soviet defences in the Kursk salient, the Germans discovered that their magic formula was no longer effective.

Soviet troops advance past a group of Russian T-34 tanks. The T-34 had features such as wide tracks, which enabled it to keep going through mud and snow, and sloping armour. Vast numbers of T-34s were built - many were used by Arab armies in the post-1948 wars with Israel.

THE BATTLES FOR MONTE CASSINO

RAF Baltimore medium bombers fly over the Appenines in Central Italy. The vaunted German-held 'Gustav Line' stretched from coast to coast of the peninsula through mountain ranges. The four battles for Cassino - the town that was the key to the whole area since it guarded the main road to Rome -were fought over terrain such as this.

'It is my duty', signalled General Alexander to Churchill on 13th May, 1943, 'to report that the Tunis campaign is over. All enemy resistance has ceased. We are masters of the North African shores'. The final expulsion of Axis forces from Bizerta and Tunis posed the Allies with something of a dilemma. With a full year to go before Operation 'Overlord' could be launched against *Festung Europa* in northwestern Europe, the question arose as to how best to employ the victorious Allied forces in the Mediterranean region.

Although they distrusted Churchill's enthusiasm for an all-out attack against the 'soft under-belly of Europe', with its possible expansion to include a major blow past Trieste and through the Lubianja Gap to link with Tito's Yugoslav partisans and thence invade Austria, the Americans expressed agreement at various top-level conferences for, first, an invasion of Sicily and then an extension of the campaign into southern Italy. The rapid capture of Sicily, between 10th July and 17th August, and the subsequent successful invasions of Calabria through the 'toe' of Italy, with the associated landings at Salerno and Taranto in early September, served to bring down the Fascist regime of Benito Mussolini as early as 25th July. Any hopes that the subsequent Italian surrender (announced on 8th September) would lead to a rapid capture of Rome were abruptly dashed when the Germans efficiently took over all positions from their former allies and began to mount a tough defensive campaign under the command of Field Marshal Kesselring. Rommel was appointed to command Army Group 'B' in the north of Italy, whilst General von Vietinghoff took the brunt of the early fighting with a reinforced German 10th Army in the south. The Germans made the most of the mountainous terrain of the Appenines to delay further Allied advances northwards. In response, 8th Army under Montgomery took the east coast route past Termoli and the River Sangro, which was crossed on 20th November, while General Mark Clark adopted the west coast route in command of the U.S. 5th Army.

Every kilometre had to be stubbornly fought for against the Germans' skilful demolition of bridges and determined rearguard actions. Eventually von Vietinghoff fell steadily back upon his main position, the Gustav Line. This was a series of strong defences running from the Mediterranean coast east of Gaeta, past the massif of Monte Cassino dominating the River Liri valley and thence over the mountainous spine of central Italy to the Adriatic coast near Ortona. Montgomery successfully breached the northern end of the Gustav Line in late November, capturing Ortona after a tough fight on 27th December, but then he lost momentum as a hard winter set in. Meanwhile, the Americans and the Free French forced a crossing over the Volturno and fought their way through the outlying Bernhard

Below: the ancient Cistercian Monastery of Monte Cassino was bombed by 254 Allied aircraft on 15th February, 1944, which dropped 576 tons of bombs. This controversial act had scant military effect, but the destruction of the buildings raised Allied morale as the monastery had overlooked all their positions.

Left: the aged abbot of ancient Cassino Monastery with unwelcome German guests. Whether the Germans were in occupation of the huge stone buildings when the monastery was bombed on 15th February, 1944, is still disputed, but they most certainly occupied the ruins after the raid was over.

On 14th March, 1944, it was the turn of Cassino town (facing page top) to receive the dire attentions of Allied air power. Saturation bombing preceded General Freyburg's attack with the New Zealand Corps. But so much damage had been caused that tanks could not cross the rubble, and the German defence was bitter. The Third Battle of Cassino petered out on 22nd March.

Facing page bottom: Allied medical units edge their way into the town to seek the wounded after Cassino has been visited by Allied bombers. The German resistance - particularly that of their 'Green Devil' paratroop units - remained staunch, and Highway Six to Rome remained unopened.

Cassino by way of Ausonia and San Giorgio, and the eastern extending from Cassino to Sant'Elia and distant Attina. The Rome-Naples railway also ran through Cassino and up the Liri valley. Besides Cassino itself, on the central sector of the front, were the towns of Sant'Angelo on the west bank of the Rapido, Aquino, ten miles west of Cassino on the railway line, and Cairo, which nestled below a massif of the same name west of the Rapido and about four miles north of Cassino.

The military significance of these features were clear. Monastery Hill, or Point 435, was topped by a vast Cistercian monastery, famed as a seat of learning and as a bastion of Western Christianity, which completely dominated the Rapido and Liri valleys. This hill also controlled access along Route 6 towards Rome. The only approach to gain the monastery was along a zigzag road past points 165, 236 and Hangman's Hill. The town of Cassino was overlooked by Castle Hill, 300 metres high, while a railway station dominated the west bank of the Rapido and the 'short-cut' approach to the key highway, Route 6.

For three months, General von Senger Etterline had been preparing defences, which in mid-January were held by 14th *Panzer Korps*, comprising 5th Mountain Division on Monte Belvedere, 44th Infantry Division around Cassino itself, together with *Schultzgruppe* (1st Paratrooper Regiment and parts of 3rd). Deployed in the centre to link with 71st and 94th infantry divisions were 15th *Panzergrenadiers*, and finally, in reserve, were 90th and 29th *Panzergrenadiers* and part of the *Herman Goering Panzerdivision* – making about 100,000 men in all.

The Allied plan called for a series of heavy attacks on all sectors leading to Monte Cassino. Land assaults were prefaced in early January by 3,000 RAF and USAAF bomber sorties against German communications. Then, on 15th January, the U.S. II Corps drove the German 44th Division from Monte Trocchio, gaining an excellent observation post thereby. From then on, all preparations were dominated by the need to open the main offensive on 17th January – five days before what was intended to be the *coup de grâce* – namely the landing of Major General John Lucas' 50,000 men of U.S. VI Corps at Anzio in an amphibious operation code-named 'Shingle'. Already the effects of the Teheran decisions were making themselves felt: naval heavy units and, above all, LSTs (Landing Ships Tank) were required to leave the theatre soon to prepare for Operation 'Overlord'. As a result all planning had to be rushed.

The offensive duly opened on 17th January at 9.00pm, when three divisions of General McCreery's British X Corps eventually achieved a crossing over the River Garigliano. As anticipated, the German reaction was robust. General Schlemm rapidly reinforced 94th Division with armour and *Panzergrenadiers*, and a hard battle raged until the end of the month, costing McCreery over 4,000 casualties. Nevertheless, the German counter-offensive was finally beaten off.

The second phase of the first battle of Cassino began on 20th January, when General Keyes' U.S. II Corps launched its 36th Division against Sant'Angelo and 34th Division against Cassino itself. The secondary attack almost reached the monastery and made important gains, but 36th Division's attacks became disasters, 1,681 casualties were lost in a single day's fighting. Vietinghoff quickly summoned reserves, and their strong counter-attacks regained Colle Sant'Angelo on 6th February, while 34th Division was halted just 300 yards short of the monastery. The Americans had shot their bolt, and 2nd New Zealand and 4th Indian divisions relieved the U.S. 36th and 34th divisions on 6th and 13th February respectively. By the latter date, the U.S. 135th and 168th regiments totalled only 840 survivors between them, out of an original 3,200 sent into battle.

Meanwhile, on 22nd January, Operation 'Shingle' had begun successfully enough, but Lucas failed to exploit his advantage to press inland, and very soon found himself hemmed in by the German 14th Army under Mackensen. As Churchill was to describe it: 'We had hoped to hurl ashore a spitting wildcat; instead we found ourselves with a stranded whale'. A major break-out attempt by the Allies on 31st January was frustrated by the six available German divisions, and although three more infantry divisions and part of U.S. 1st Armoured were sent to double Lucas' force, a stalemate soon developed which would last until 22nd May. Over-hasty planning and a lack of initiative had ruined a bold plan.

Back on the Cassino front, the French

Facing page: an Italian 194mm railway gun pounding German positions from a range of over ten miles. It proved a redoubtable weapon, the equivalent on land of a battleship's main 16-inch armament.

The fighting in the mountains of the 'Gustav' Line was as much against geography as against the German enemy. Sometimes the front on the narrow paths of the mountain sides was just two men wide; in such instances, all ammunition and supplies had to be manhandled up goat-tracks by soldiers (right). Somehow, however, Allied pressure upon the German positions was maintained.

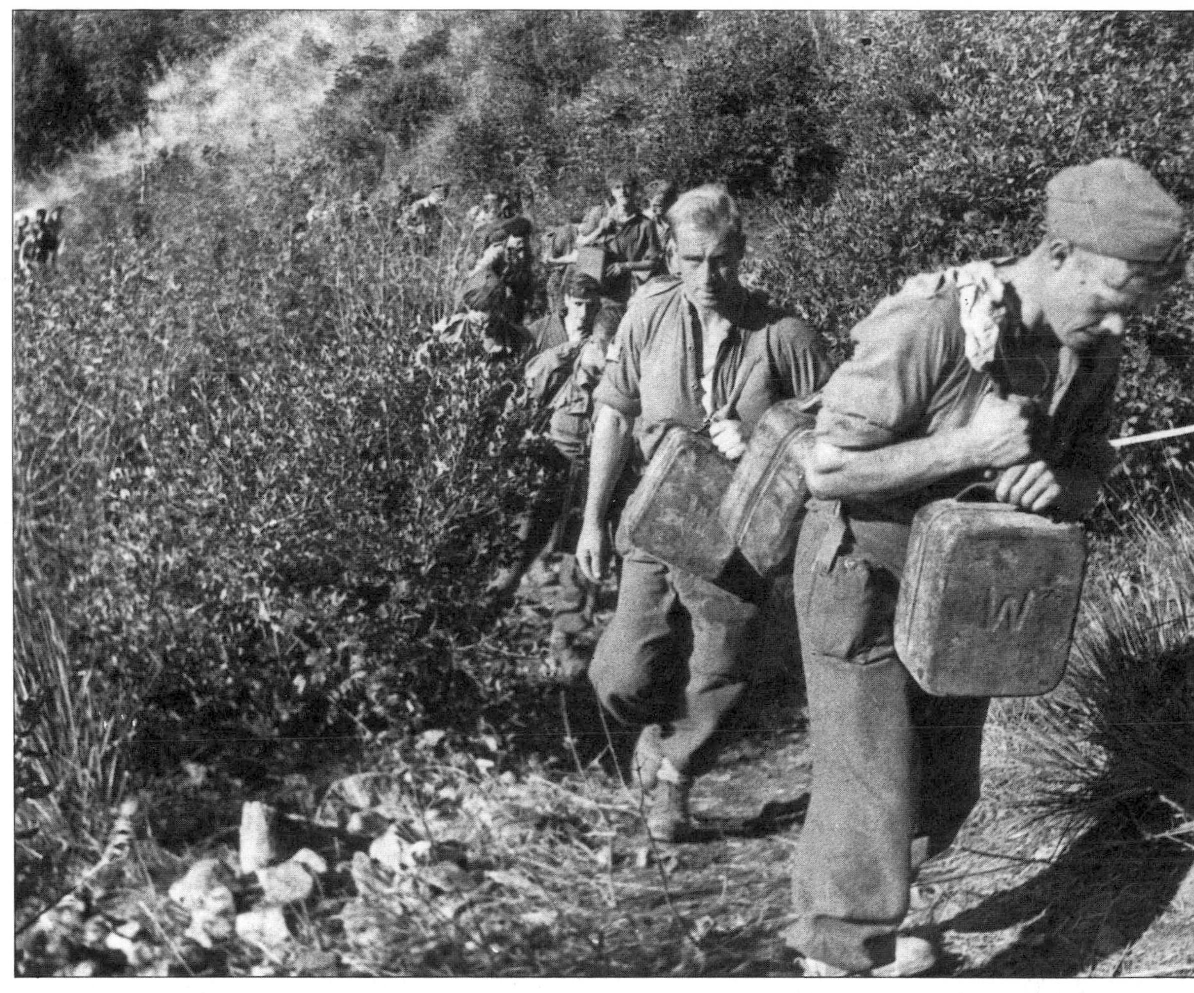

Expeditionary Corps under General Juin had swung into full action on 24th January on the interior sector. Great gains were made – 3rd Algerian Division took Sant'Elia, Colle Belvedere and Monte Castellone in turn, but its main thrust was halted on 27th January. In due course 2nd Moroccan Division similarly captured Monte Santa Croce, creating a threat to Atina. In all, the outcome was a mixed one, comprising considerable Allied achievements on the flanks, but failure on the critical sector, the centre. A furore broke out in the U.S.A., leading to a Congressional enquiry into the failure by U.S. 36th Division. So ended what has become known as the First Battle of Cassino.

The Second Battle was destined to be short and another failure. Lieutenant General Freyburg's New Zealand Corps from 8th Army was placed under General Mark Clark's command from 3rd February, and relieved U.S. II Corps. Far from being able to exploit an American break-in as had been hoped, Freyburg found himself having to re-fight for most of the ground. His aims were to capture Point 593 and the monastery with General Tuker's Indian Division, while General Parkinson's 2nd New Zealand Division, aided by a part of U.S. 1st Armoured, penetrated Cassino town as far as the dominating railway station. These attacks were scheduled for 16th February, and were preceded on 15th February by 254 bombers dropping 576 tons of bombs on the ancient monastery in the mistaken belief that it was being fortified by the Germans. This act led to an international outcry – and, ironically, the ruins of the buildings proved far more defensible. When 4th Indian Division (which had received many 'stray' bombs in its forming-up area) attacked on the next day, the Royal Sussex Regiment and 7th Brigade made little progress on Snakeshead Ridge. Although 2nd New Zealand Division made more ground and actually reached its objective, they then pulled back, lacking the anti-tank guns needed to repel the German armour-supported counter-attack by 15th *Panzergrenadierdivision*. During 17th February the famous 78th (Battleaxe) Division joined the New Zealand Corps, but this did not prevent the battle being called off the following day. So a second major effort had ended abortively, although three artillery batteries had fired off the equivalent of one three-ton load of HE ammunition every eight minutes on 17th February. Once again hurried preparation and a failure to coordinate stunning bombing with a ground attack had ended in costly disappointment. The containment of the Anzio landings had permitted the Germans to switch reinforcements back to the Rapido. By this time, 44th and 5th mountain divisions had been joined by *Gruppe-Schultz* and 90th *Panzergrenadiers*, backed by large elements of 15th *Panzergrenadiers* and 94th Infantry Division, with 71st Infantry and 29th *Panzergrenadier* divisions in reserve.

The 'Third' Battle of Cassino is sometimes considered as a continuation of the Second as it largely involved Freyburg's New Zealanders once more. More usually, however, it is regarded as a major engagement in its own right. General Keightley's 78th Division was added to the left flank of the New Zealand Corps on the Rapido. The Germans had also made adjustments to their order of battle. Two divisions – 5th Mountain and 44th Infantry – were holding the sector north of Cassino; General Heidrich's tough 1st Parachute Division had taken over from the exhausted 90th *Panzergrenadiers*; 15th *Panzergrenadiers* and 94th Infantry Division were now fully committed; and the Arunci sector was entrusted to 71st Infantry Division.

The Allied plan was to attack Cassino town on a 1,000-yard front after heavy bombing. To open the land battle, 78th Division was to cross the Liri near Sant'Angelo as a diversion for 2nd New Zealand Division's assault on the German 3rd Parachute Regiment, and make itself master of Cassino and Castle Hill; this achieved, Tuker was to move from Castle Hill to take Hangman's Hill on the right and then there would be a general advance towards Route 6. Unfortunately, bad weather caused a three-week delay which had a lowering effect on morale. It was only on 14th March that preliminary operations began.

That day, covert local withdrawals were put into effect to reduce the danger of bombs hitting friendly troops. At 8.00am on 15th March, a four-and-a-half hour bombing raid reduced Cassino town to rubble, and this was followed by a three-hour artillery bombardment by 748 guns – 200,000 shells were fired in ten hours. The German garrison took severe casualties, but

General Heidrich (left) and Field Marshal Kesselring (right), German Supreme Commander Southern Europe, discussing the situation on the Cassino front in 1944. On 16th May, accepting that the battle was lost, Kesselring ordered the German forces to abandon Monte Cassino and retire northwards.

German paratroopers, nicknamed 'Green Devils' for their determined fighting skills, take cover during Allied shelling. They were the toughest defenders of Monte Cassino, and fought fanatically, earning the grudging respect of their opponents. Cassino proved the hardest battle of the war in southern Europe.

some were well-sheltered in caves. When Parkinson's infantry advanced at 3.30pm they were able to occupy most of the town, as well as Point 193 (or Castle Hill), but so clogged were the streets that the Allied tanks could not get through them. Now it was the turn of the pre-registered German artillery to wreak havoc, but this notwithstanding the Indian troops managed to take Point 165 that night. Further progress proved impossible, and for six days a desperate attritional battle raged. German counter-attacks against Castle Hill were beaten off on 19th March, but the tough paratroopers conceded nothing. At last, on 22nd March, this battle was called-off in its turn. The exhausted remnants of Freyburg's New Zealand Corps had to be reallocated to other formations. Much of Cassino town was now in Allied hands – but no breakthrough had yet been achieved, and the daunting monastery dominated the scene.

For what was to prove the last Battle of Cassino, massive preparations were put in hand. Leaving only British V Corps to hold most of the line all the way to Ortona, the rest of 8th Army secretly moved to the Cassino sector – namely the X and XIII British Corps, Canadian I and General Anders' II Polish corps. These, added to U.S. 5th Army's U.S. II and the French corps, amounted to 300,000 men in three armoured and thirteen infantry divisions. Further troops were also fed into the Anzio bridgehead (now commanded by General Truscott), where a state of stalemate existed from 3rd March after the repulse of the last serious German attack against the perimeter by General Mackensen's 14th Army. At Cassino itself, the Allies now faced only six German divisions – a mere 80,000 men – but so serious did the Allied High Command consider the overall situation in Italy that it was agreed to postpone Operation 'Anvil' against Marseilles and Toulon in southern France to allow Operation 'Diadem' full priority.

The new battle opened early on 12th May. The Poles made some initial gains, but failed to take the monastery. On the left, the French Expeditionary Corps, supported by U.S. II Corps, made great progress through the Arunci Mountains, dominating them by 14th May, but XIII Corps made only limited advances. Field Marshal Kesselring considered the French success critical and, on 15th May, ordered his forces to conduct a general withdrawal to the

rearward 'Adolf Hitler' or 'Dora' Line. By this time, the German 94th and 71st divisions were all but gone.

On 17th May, British XIII Corps at last reached Route 6, while the gallant Poles renewed their attack on Monastery Hill, only to earn another bloody repulse by the German rearguard. Nevertheless, at 8.30am on 18th May a third assault found the foe had gone overnight. Monte Cassino was at last in Allied hands. The price of success had been high. The German defenders had inflicted 115,000 casualties on the Allies at Cassino and another 40,000 at Anzio. The Germans had lost some 60,000 around Cassino and 35,000 more containing Operation 'Shingle'. It had been one of the costliest battles of the war.

To the victors, however, went the spoils. On 19th May, U.S. II Corps captured Gaeta on the coast, having breached the 'Dora Line'. By 22nd May, the French had reached Pico and British XIII and Canadian I Corps had also smashed their way though the incomplete German positions. The German 10th Army fell back steadily. Then, on 23rd May, General Truscott at last broke out from Anzio, and after a last fight in the Alban Hills, Rome was occupied by American troops on 5th June. But even this proved something of an anticlimax, for early on 6th June the world awoke to even more dramatic news: Operation 'Overlord' had begun.

BURMA – FROM IMPHAL TO KOHIMA

Troops of Lieutenant General Motozo Yanagida's 33rd Division pass through a Burmese village on their way to the Chindwin in February, 1944. The Japanese were still confident of victory, while the Burmese, who less than two years earlier had greeted the Japanese as liberators, were now disillusioned and apathetic.

At the beginning of 1944 the war on the Indian-Burmese frontier was at a stalemate. Neither the British on the Arakan and Assam fronts, or their American and Chinese allies to the north, had been able to launch a successful offensive. For their part, the Japanese had been content to remain on the defensive, holding the line their invading forces had first reached in May, 1942. But the stagnation which had characterised this 'forgotten' war was about to come to an end. Since the autumn of 1943 new spirit had been breathed into British Far Eastern forces: a new command headed by Lord Louis Mountbatten – South East Asia Command (SEAC) – had been established and a brilliant trainer and logistics expert, General George 'Pop' Giffard, had been appointed to command SEAC's land forces. The 'forgotten' Far Eastern army also received a new commander – Lieutenant General William ('Uncle Bill') Slim – and, reinforced, retrained and rebuilt, had been reborn as 14th Army.

Since October 1943, 5th and 7th Indian divisions of 14th Army's XV Corps had been advancing slowly and methodically down the Arakan Front against increasing Japanese resistance. In the far north another offensive was in preparation – a glider-borne assault by five brigades of Major General Orde Wingate's Chindits, designed to support a drive southward by General 'Vinegar Joe' Stilwell's Sino-American forces. But for Slim these operations were diversions from where he intended to fight the main battle and launch his offensive for the reconquest of Burma. Forty miles west of the Japanese front on the Chindwin River, beyond the jungle-clad mountains along which ran the Indian-Burmese border, lay a 700-square-mile plain. At its centre was Imphal, a small town which served as the capital of the Indian border district of Manipur. A single road linked Imphal with the outside world. It meandered eighty miles north through mountains to the hill station of Kohima, from where it swung fifty miles northwest to a railhead at Dimapur. Throughout 1943, troops and supplies had poured in through this railhead from India – Slim had concentrated the three

Moving secretly on Kohima, heavily laden troops of the Japanese 33rd Division, accompanied by pack animals and bullocks, ford a tributary of the Chindwin at Marcy in 1944. Supply lines in this area were so bad that once these troops had consumed the supplies they carried with them they starved.

Despite the thick jungle and rough terrain the Japanese 14th Tank Regiment was able to get a number of tanks (below) through the Kebaw Valley and onto the Imphal-Tiddim Road in an attempt to cut off the retreat of 17th Indian Division. The effort was unsuccessful - on the night of 22nd March six of these tanks were destroyed by British mines.

divisions of 14th Army's IV Corps on this plain, and had transformed it into a springboard for his offensive. It now contained 100,000 troops, 50,000 Indian labourers, six airfields and several vast depots, the largest of which, at Dimapur, was a mile wide and eleven miles long.

In preparation for the offensive, two roads had been built from Imphal to the Chindwin River. One ran seventy miles southwest via the villages of Palel and Tamu to the river at Sittaung, and here IV Corps' commander Lieutenant General Geoffrey Scoones had deployed Major General Douglas Gracey's 20th Indian Division. The other ran 130 miles directly south to Tiddim, before swinging west to Fort White and the Chindwin at Kalewa. Here Scoones had positioned Major General 'Punch' Cowan's 17th Indian Division. The remaining division, 23rd Indian, he held in reserve at Imphal. Scoone's deployments were designed for the offensive. During January,

however, British intelligence began piecing together indications that the Japanese were preparing to launch their own offensive towards Imphal. Slim hoped very much that such was the case – it would be much easier to destroy the Japanese in a battle on the Imphal Plain, where British superiority in armour and air power could be brought to bear, than to fight them beyond the Chindwin.

The Japanese were indeed preparing to attack, but in numbers much greater than the British believed possible. Burma Area commander Lieutenant General Masakazu Kawabe believed a successful assault on Imphal would have a profound effect on Japan's strategic situation. Not only would it disrupt Slim's preparations for the reconquest of Burma, but if Dimapur were taken, the Sino-American and Chindit operations, supplied almost entirely from this depot, would be seriously inconvenienced and Stilwell's efforts to reopen a land route to China would end forever. Moreover, there remained a possibility that a successful Japanese invasion of India – albeit an invasion of a remote border territory – would spark off an explosion of anti-British nationalism throughout the sub-continent, with incalculable consequences for the Allied cause in the Far East.

To ensure the success of 'U-Go' – the Japanese codename for the offensive – Kawabe planned to divert Slim's attention. On 4th February, 54th and 55th divisions struck into the Arakan where, by 12th February, they had surrounded XV Corps. The situation was serious, but Slim refused to take Kawabe's bait; instead he ordered XV Corps to stand firm, and supplied it by air. Kawabe had not yet fought against a general of Slim's calibre and assumed that his deception had been successful. On the night of 6th March he set the first stage of 'U-Go' in motion. Lieutenant General Renya Mutaguchi, commander of 15th Army, now in operational control, sent his 33rd Division across the Chindwin near Kalew. Avoiding contact with British patrols, the Division infiltrated through the Chin Hills. It then split into two columns. The bulk of the Division under Lieutenant General Motozo Yanagida marched due west and, by 12th March, established roadblocks on the Imphal-Tiddim road, which cut 17th Indian Division off from its base. Meanwhile, a powerful detached column, including a regiment of light tanks under Major General Tsunoru Yamamoto, moved due north to cut the Imphal-Sittaung road and isolate 20th Indian Division. Mutaguchi made his next move on the night of 15th March, when Lieutenant General Masafumi Yamauchi's 15th Division crossed the Chindwin River at a point a hundred miles north of Kalewa. They then struck northwest for Sangshak, a small town thirty miles northeast of Imphal, from where Yamauchi intended to drive due west and cut the Imphal-Kohima road. Further upriver on the same night Lieutenant General Kotoku Sato's 31st Division crossed at two points forty miles apart and moved in three columns towards Kohima, its ultimate objective being the huge supply depot at Dimapur.

In all, Mutaguchi had sent 100,000 men across the Chindwin, a force so large that he estimated the conquest of Manipur would take only three weeks. It had to. The logistics of 15th Army were primitive in the extreme – large herds of cattle were driven in the wake of the advancing columns, but even with these Mutaguchi knew that his army could not be fed much after the beginning of April unless it captured British supply depots. Another factor also loomed large in his calculations. His meteorologists had forecast that the monsoon would break early in May, which would turn the dirt roads and tracks of Manipur to quagmires and reduce resupply to a trickle. Against a determined enemy an operation of this sort would have been folly, but Mutaguchi had fought Eastern Army before and held it in profound contempt. He did not know of the transformation Giffard and Slim had effected.

Having been warned well in advance of Operation 'U-Go', Slim and Scoones had prepared a defence plan; rather than resisting the Japanese when they crossed the Chindwin, 17th and 20th Indian divisions were to fall back and form a tight defensive perimeter around Imphal. Unfortunately, Slim's intelligence had been inaccurate in one crucial detail. The predicted date for the attack was 15th March, nine days later than 33rd Division's actual crossing of the Chindwin. It was not just the timing of the attack which surprised the British commanders, but also its sheer scale. Cowan's 17th Indian Division, its 16,000 men, 2,500 vehicles and 3,000 mules strung out along twenty miles of highway, did not begin its withdrawal until late on the afternoon of 14th March. A few hours later, Yanagida's troops were pressing all along Cowan's right flank, and in many places Japanese battalions managed to position themselves between the widely spaced British units. The withdrawal slowed to a crawl, Cowan's men fighting a series of desperate clearing operations.

Realizing he was presiding over a disaster,

Winding like a giant white snake through the jungle, the Imphal-Tiddim Road was the scene of 17th Indian Division's epic struggle with the Japanese 33rd Division.

Right: 'Uncle Bill' Slim at work. The general later calculated that he spent about one third of his time visiting units and talking to soldiers in an effort to raise morale. It was through such encounters that he transformed the defeated Eastern Army into the victorious 14th Army.

Below: a Sikh signaller in a command post in thick jungle west of Bishenpur calls mortar fire onto a Japanese position. The fighting in this area reached its height in late May. The dense jungle made the manouvering of large forces impossible and most actions took place between platoons.

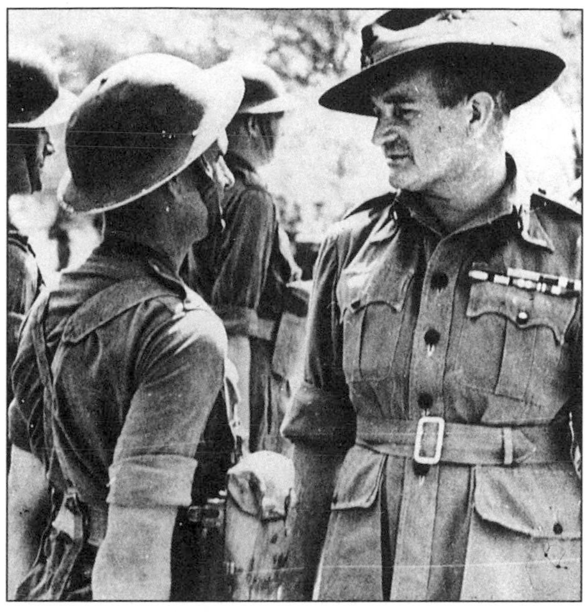

Scoones rushed two brigades of 23rd Division south. These struck Yanagida's troops in the rear and enabled 17th Indian Division to fight free of the Japanese grip. On 26th March the British and Indians reached Bishenpur, twenty miles south of Imphal, and turned to face their enemy. Meanwhile, Yamamoto's force was approaching the Palel-Sittaung road and threatening 20th Indian Division's communications. After reluctantly destroying his depots, Gracey ordered a withdrawal to a line of hills, the Shenan Saddle, some ten miles to the east of Palel. With the completion of these withdrawals, the perimeter around Imphal was secure. Slim had acted just in time, for on 29th March, Yamauchi's 15th Division reached a point only fifteen miles north of Imphal on the Imphal-Kohima road and IV Corps was now cut off.

Although the attack was both heavier and more rapid than expected, Slim and Scoones were still confident, as thus far Japanese moves had more or less conformed with intelligence appreciations. But on 27th March 14th Army HQ received news of a potential catastrophe. Six days earlier, 50th Indian Paratroop Brigade had been attacked by a strong Japanese force (part of 31st Division) at Sangshak thirty miles northeast of Imphal. The paratroopers were quickly surrounded, but after a week long battle had been able to fight their way back to Imphal. They had discovered on a dead Japanese officer a map which showed clearly that an entire division was advancing towards undefended Dimapur. Slim now moved rapidly and decisively. By 2nd April he had appointed Lieutenant General Montagu Stopford to the command of a new formation, XXXIII Corps, tasked specifically with the defence of the railhead. Already the first elements of 7th Indian Division had been flown in from the Arakan, followed closely by the highly trained and well-equipped 2nd British Division. For Slim, Dimapur was all important – a scratch garrison of 1,500 commanded by a Chindit officer, Colonel Richards, already in Kohima, was ordered to hold for as long as possible, while Stopford prepared for a defensive battle around Dimapur.

But there was to be no Battle of Dimapur, for against all expectations Richards' men held Kohima. The odds were incredible. By 5th April 12,000 of Sato's men had surrounded the garrison and moved in for the kill. From their dugouts on Kohima Ridge – a series of hogs' backs and hills a mile long and a half mile wide that dominated the road to Dimapur – Richards' men bloodily repulsed assault after assault. By sheer weight of numbers, the Japanese gradually inched forward and on 17th April stormed Garrison Hill, a feature in the centre of the ridge, which cut Richards' force into two pockets. At dawn on 18th April few amongst the garrison believed they would live to see the sun set.

In fact help was close at hand. Since 5th April 7th Division's 161st Brigade had been fighting its way to the garrison, but had itself been surrounded by Jotsoma, a few miles west of Kohima. By 11th April the airlift of troops had transformed the situation at Dimapur, and

Facing page top: men of 2nd Battalion Dorsetshire Regiment drag a dead Japanese from a foxhole on Kohima Ridge, 13th May, 1944. The Dorset's capture of the ridge marked the turning point of the battle, although the Japanese fought on from other positions for nearly another two months.

Facing page bottom: British soldiers advance cautiously through elephant grass towards the Chindwin in July, 1944. Although the Japanese were ill and emaciated by this time, their rearguards put up tenacious resistance and delayed the British advance in hundreds of small actions.

While the major battles raged around Imphal and Kohima, 'Vinegar Joe' Stilwell's Sino-American forces (right), supported by British Chindits, closed on Myitkyna in northern Burma. Despite being greatly outnumbered, the Japanese held on until 3rd August.

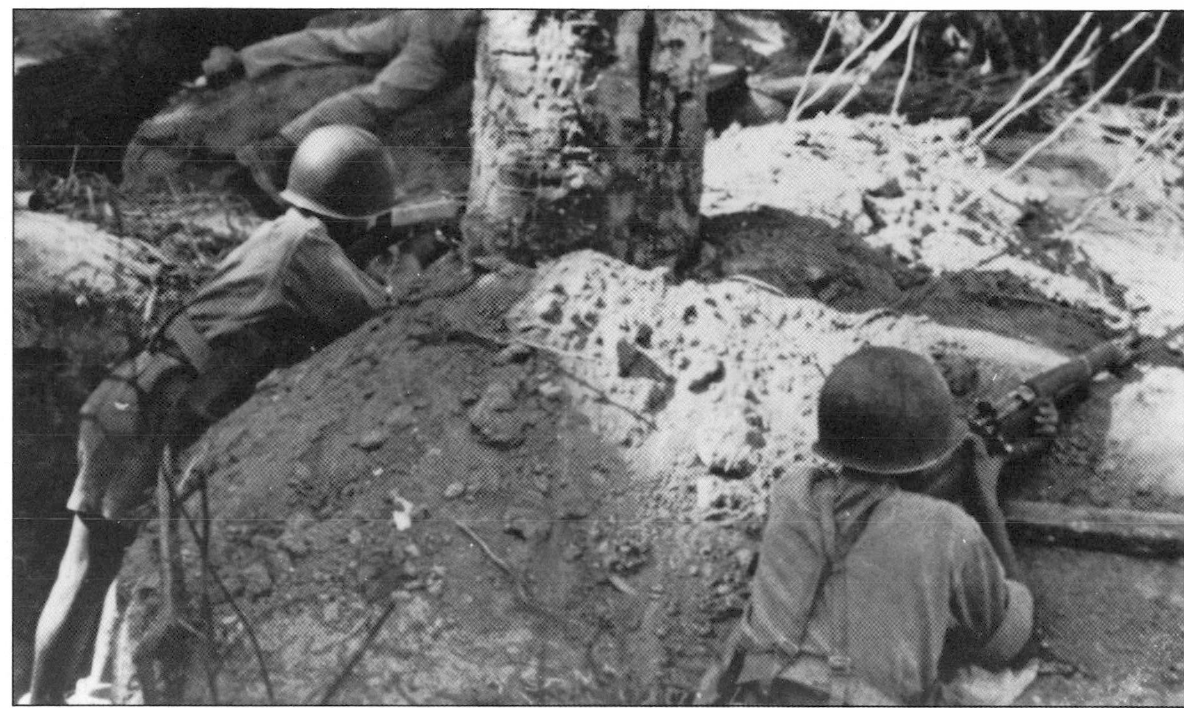

Stopford now ordered 2nd British Division to strike towards Kohima. Seven days later, with the garrison on its last legs, 1st Royal Berkshires, 2nd Division's spearhead, broke through the Japanese cordon.

Slim now received another piece of valuable intelligence. A signal had been found on the body of a Japanese sergeant major ordering Sato to send one third of his troops to support the attack on Imphal. Slim knew that this move had to be prevented at all costs and ordered 2nd Division to keep up the pressure on the Japanese. Major General J.H. Grover, 2nd Division's commander, was reluctant to put in costly frontal attacks on the now heavily entrenched Japanese positions on Kohima Ridge and the surrounding hills. Attempting to outflank Sato, he sent two of his brigades to strike the Japanese simultaneously from the north and south, but progress was slow and casualties heavy. The battle dragged on into May, the British and Japanese hammering away at each other from positions which were often only a few yards apart. Fighting was most furious in Kohima village itself, where a tennis court in front of the Japanese-held District Commissioner's bungalow had become the front line, over which the opposing sides lobbed showers of grenades. Slowly, British material superiority began to tell. By 13th May 2nd Division's artillery had pumped 11,500 round into Japanese positions, and under cover of this fire bulldozers had cleared a precipitous track to the tennis court, up which engineers now winched a Lee-Grant tank. At dawn on 13th May it rolled forward to the edge of a terrace overlooking the tennis court, and hurtled down an almost sheer slope. Miraculously the tank landed upright in the middle of the court, its crew shaken but uninjured. The gunner traversed the turret and fired at point-blank range through the weapons slits in the Japanese bunkers. Then 2nd Battalion Dorsetshire Regiment charged forward, and within minutes the last Japanese position on Kohima Ridge was in British hands.

Meanwhile, a much larger battle was raging around besieged Imphal. Yamauchi's 15th Division had taken Nungshigum Hill only ten miles north of Imphal on 6th April. A week later, under the cover of RAF dive-bombers, British tanks rolled up a narrow ridge in single file to Nungshigum's summit. Yamauchi had thought an armoured attack impossible, and his division had no anti-tank guns. Even so, the Japanese fought back desperately with small arms and mountain guns. The Lee-Grants and their supporting infantry pulverised the defenders, but at an enormous cost – every British officer was either killed or wounded. To the west, Yamamoto's force, reinforced by units of the Indian National Army, struck at 20th Indian Division's positions on the Shenan Saddle. The Japanese captured a key feature (which both British and Japanese were to name Nippon Hill) on 8th April. Two days later, the Gurkhas put in a counterattack and were cut to pieces. On 11th April swarms of Hurribombers and the concentrated fire of 20th Indian Division's artillery turned the once jungle-clad summit into a ploughed field. After storming up Nippon's slopes, 1st Battalion Devonshires wiped out the dazed survivors. But the following day the Japanese counterattacked and, securing the eastern side of the hill, dug in only yards from the British.

And so it went on – day after day. To the south, Yanigida's 33rd Division took Torbung and struck north to Bishenpur. Infiltrating through thick jungle, Japanese units clashed bloodily with the defenders in scores of platoon-size actions. By the end of April Yanagida's attack had broken down – the once-despised British and Indians had proved themselves the equals of the Japanese in jungle fighting. Mutaguchi's three-week offensive had turned into an attritional struggle in which the side best able to feed the battle was bound to win. This was the British. As early as 18th March SEAC commander, Lord Louis Mountbatten, had diverted American transport aircraft from their supply operation to China, and together the USAAF and RAF flew in 18,000 tons of supplies, one million gallons of fuel and the entire 5th Indian Division from Arakan, as well as evacuating 13,000 wounded and 43,000 non-combatants. As Slim's army waxed, Mutaguchi's waned. The monsoon broke on 27th April, earlier than Japanese meteorologists had forecast, and from that time forth an already inadequate flow of supplies dwindled to a trickle. Weak with starvation and riddled with disease, nevertheless the Japanese fought on. A desperate Mutaguchi began blaming his generals for the failure – he sacked Yanagida from command of 33rd Division, but the new commander, Major General Nobuo Tanaka, could do no better. On 2nd June, two weeks after he had taken over, he confided to his diary: 'The officers and men look dreadful. They've let their hair and beards grow and look just like wild men of the mountains. More than a hundred days have passed since the operation began and in all that time there's been almost nothing to eat and there's not an ounce of fat left on any of them. They all look pale and skinny from undernourishment.'

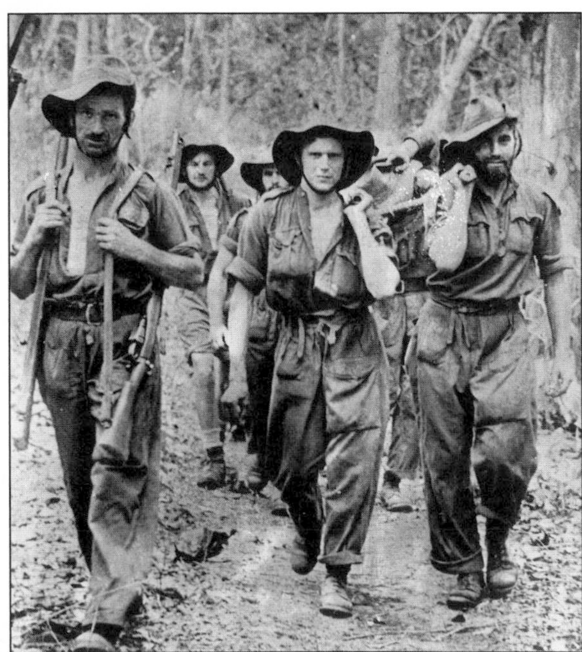

Showing the strain of months of continuous combat a Chindit column withdraws to India in August, 1944. Slim had deep misgivings about their operation but the Chindits countered, claiming that they had held down two Japanese divisions which otherwise would have been sent to Imphal-Kohima.

To the north at Kohima, Sato's men were in an even worse condition. By 31st May Sato had had enough. He ignored instructions from Mutaguchi to stay put and fell back with the remnant of his division towards Imphal. The British harried them all the way. On 22nd June, the eighty-eighth day of the siege, XXXIII Corps' troops broke through the last remaining Japanese roadblock and reached Imphal. Mutaguchi tried to cling on for a few more weeks, but on 8th July he, too, broke and so began the dreadful retreat to the Chindwin. A Japanese historian has summarised what now took place: '15th Army, once released from battle, was no longer a body of soldiers, but a herd of exhausted men.' Weeks later the pathetic survivors crossed the Chindwin – they had left 65,000 dead behind. The total British and Indian casualties, 18,000, had not been light, but of these only 5,000 had been killed. Thanks to rapid aerial evacuation, the majority of the wounded would live to fight again. It could not be denied that 14th Army had won a great defensive battle – the road to the reconquest of Burma was now open.

D-DAY–THE ALLIED INVASION OF EUROP

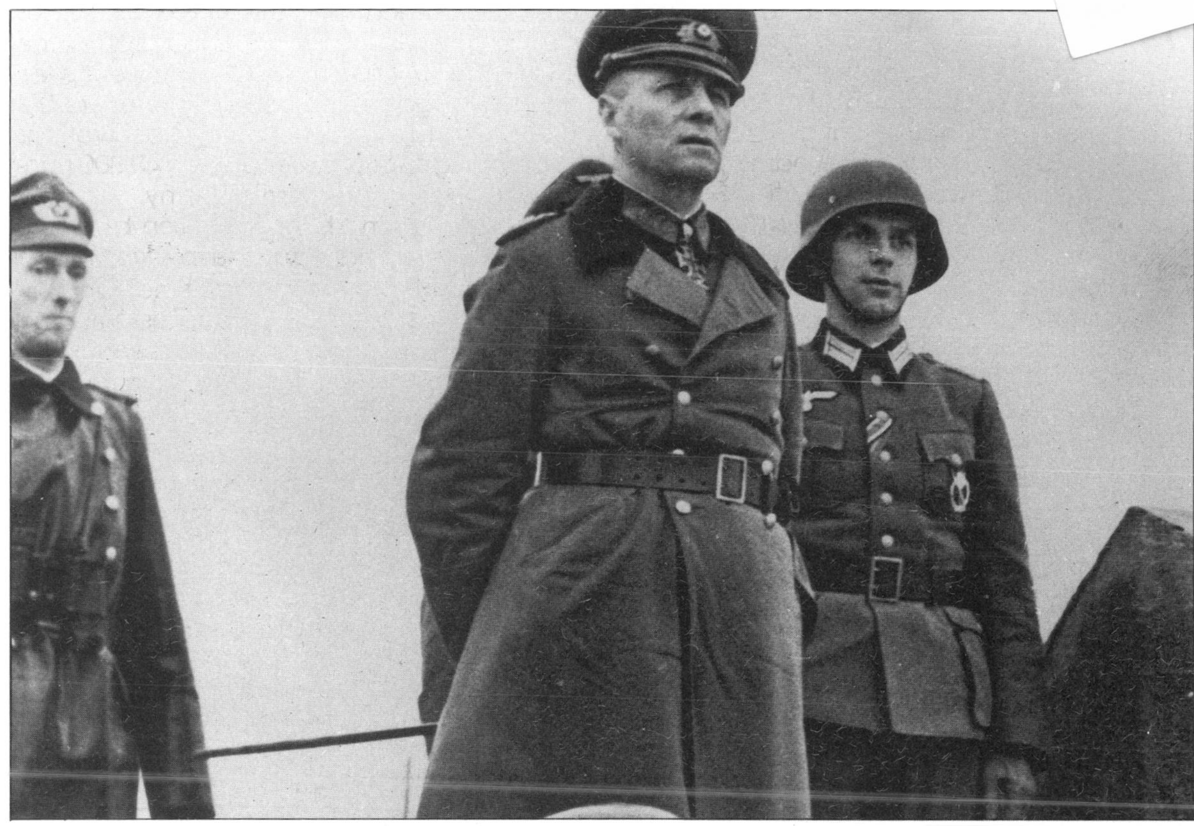

General Field Marshal Erwin Rommel with his staff inspecting the 'Atlantic Wall', the German defences against Allied invasion which stretched from the Netherlands to the Spanish border. Despite Rommel's efforts, this Wall was not complete by the time of the D-Day invasion, and was weak at the Normandy coast.

There is probably no date in the Second World War as famous as D-Day. On 6th June, 1944, the Allies returned to the continent of Europe in Operation 'Overlord', the greatest amphibious invasion ever mounted – 156,000 American, British and Canadian troops went ashore in twenty-four hours, the precursors of an army of over two million men. It was the decisive moment for which both the Allies and the Germans had long prepared. The man entrusted by Adolf Hitler with stopping the invasion, Field Marshal Erwin Rommel, believed that his only hope of success was to defeat the Allies on the beaches on D-Day itself. As early as April, Rommel observed, in a phrase that became history, that 'for the Allies, as well as for Germany, it will be the longest day'.

Rommel's command of Army Group B consisted of 15th Army, defending the Pas de Calais and Belgium, and 7th Army under Colonel General Friedrich Dollmann, defending Normandy and Brittany. Rommel had direct access to Hitler over the head of his immediate superior, Field Marshal Gerd von Rundstedt commanding OB West, but Hitler gave neither of them complete control over his crucial reserve of armoured divisions in France, *Panzergruppe West.* Rommel wanted this armour as close to the beaches as possible, while von Rundstedt wanted it held back to counterattack the Allies as they came inland. The result was a compromise which pleased neither. Yet Hitler, von Rundstedt and Rommel all believed the Pas de Calais area to be the probable invasion site, a belief encouraged by the Allies with their deception plan, Operation 'Fortitude', which created the illusion of strong American forces in southeast England opposite the German 15th Army.

The Allied Supreme Commander for Operation 'Overlord' was General Dwight D. Eisenhower, whose staff at SHAEF (Supreme Headquarters Allied Expeditionary Force) devised the landing plan for D-Day. Since not all the Allied troops could land at once, however, the commander for the invasion was General Bernard Montgomery, commanding 21st Army Group (U.S. 1st Army and British 2nd

Army). This was the first time in history that a defended coastal position like the German Atlantic Wall had been stormed from the seaward side, and in order to succeed, the Allies needed both air superiority over northern France, which had been achieved by D-Day, and the element of surprise, which they obtained through Operation 'Fortitude' and through attacking in bad weather. They were so successful that, although the Germans received some warnings of the invasion, on D-Day itself both Rommel and Dollmann were away from their headquarters.

The first American and British paratroopers landed in Normandy at about 12.20am on D-Day. Montgomery had elected to assault on a five-division front along the sandy, shelving beaches of the Normandy resorts, from the base of the Cotentin peninsula eastwards to the regional capital of Caen and the River Orne. The Americans took the two western landing beaches, codenamed 'Utah' and 'Omaha', and the British and Canadians the eastern beaches, codenamed 'Gold', 'Juno' and 'Sword'. To secure the flanks of these landings, the American 82nd Airborne Division and 101st Airborne Division were dropped inland west of 'Utah' Beach, and British 6th Airborne Division east of the River Orne, capturing the vital river crossings. The surprise of mounting a parachute assault by night was offset by the wild scattering of all three divisions in the dark, contributing to their 3,000 casualties.

The invasion area was defended by German 7th Army's LXXXIV *Panzer Korps* under General Erich Marcks, with 709th Static Division opposite the American landing beaches and 716th Static Division opposite the British beaches. These static divisions had no transport, were weak in numbers and of poor fighting quality. The Allies had, however, failed to locate the veteran 352nd Division opposite 'Omaha'

General Montgomery ashore from an amphibious DUKW craft in Normandy on D-Day Plus One, 7th June, to set up his 21st Army Group headquarters. Although responsible for the planning beforehand, Montgomery, like all senior commanders, had little direct role in the events of D-Day.

Operation 'Overlord'. Going ashore on D-Day from the sea were 57,500 American and over 75,000 British and Canadian troops, plus 900 armoured vehicles and 600 guns. Omaha Beach met with the stiffest opposition - nearly 4,000 men were casualties there by the end of the 'longest day'.

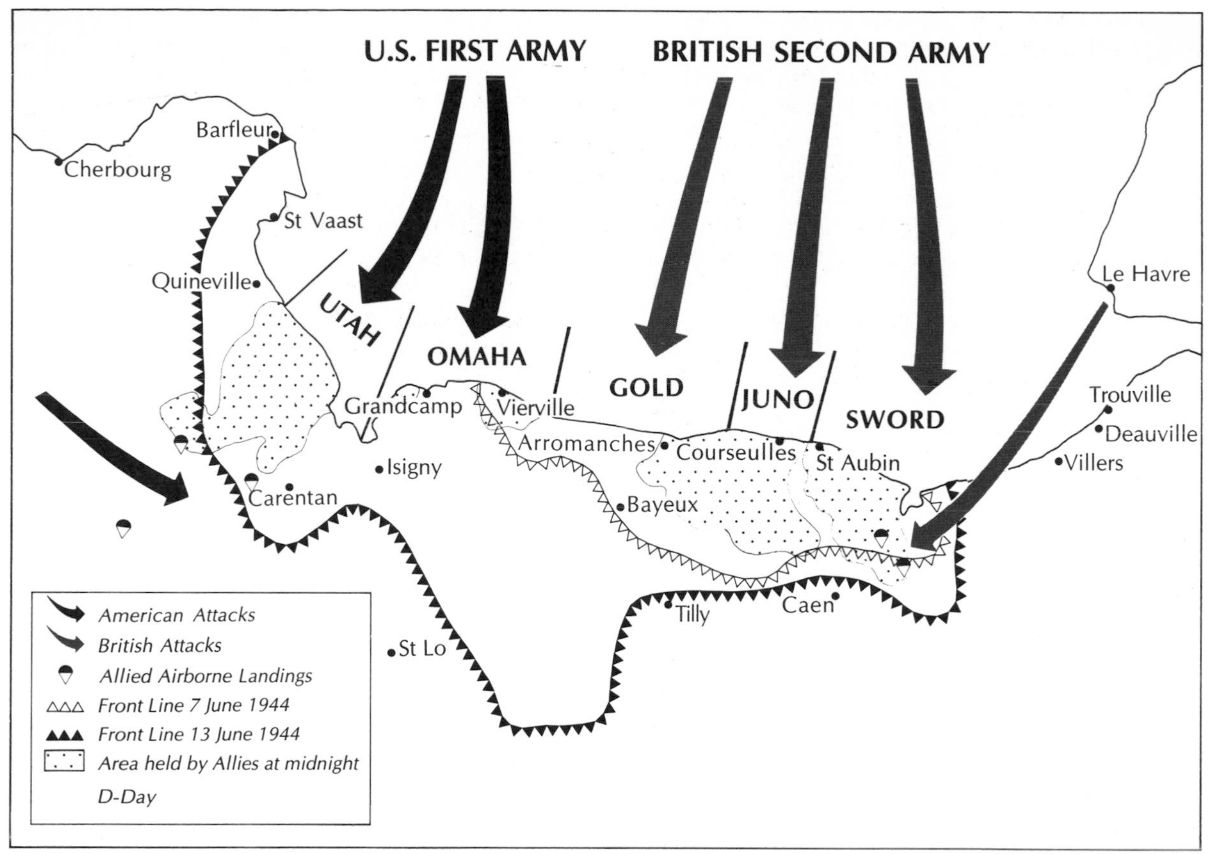

Beach and 21st *Panzerdivision*, part of the German armoured reserve, just south of Caen itself. By 2.15am 7th Army was on the alert, ready for the invasion.

At about 3.00am, as the parachutists were securing their objectives, the first of the Allied warships began to arrive off the Normandy coast. About 2,000 medium and heavy bombers joined with battleships, cruisers, and lighter vessels in a bombardment of the German positions. Before dawn, at 5.00am, von Rundstedt's headquarters ordered two armoured divisions held in reserve near Paris, 12th *SS Panzer* and *Panzer 'Lehr'*, towards Normandy, and sent a formal request to Hitler's headquarters at Berchtesgaden in southern Bavaria for their release. However, no-one was willing to wake Hitler with the still-confused news of the fighting, and the order to move the divisions was revoked until 4.00pm. Both divisions lost heavily to Allied ground-attack aircraft in moving up, and neither reached the battlefields before the end of D-Day. Rommel, also in southern Germany, was not told of the invasion until about 10.15am. Driving flat out, the German commander reached Army Group B headquarters that evening.

U.S. 1st Army opted to land an hour before the British, taking advantage of the higher tide. At 6.30am, with supporting fire from the ships out to sea, the first American troops reached their beaches. The assault was made by three specially trained Regimental Combat Teams, or RCTs, each made up of a regiment of three battalions of infantry, plus supporting armour, artillery and engineers, and which amounted to no more than 9,000 men in total. The rough weather chosen for the assault meant that tides were higher and beaches narrower than had been expected. Landing craft and amphibious tanks were swamped in the two-hour trip from the Allied ships to the shore. At 'Utah', 8th Regimental Combat Team of 4th Division landed almost quietly to discover that, in the confusion, it had come ashore on the wrong beach, about 2,000 yards south of where it should have been and away from the main German defences. Rather than move position, the landing force linked up with the paratroopers inland and waited while the rest

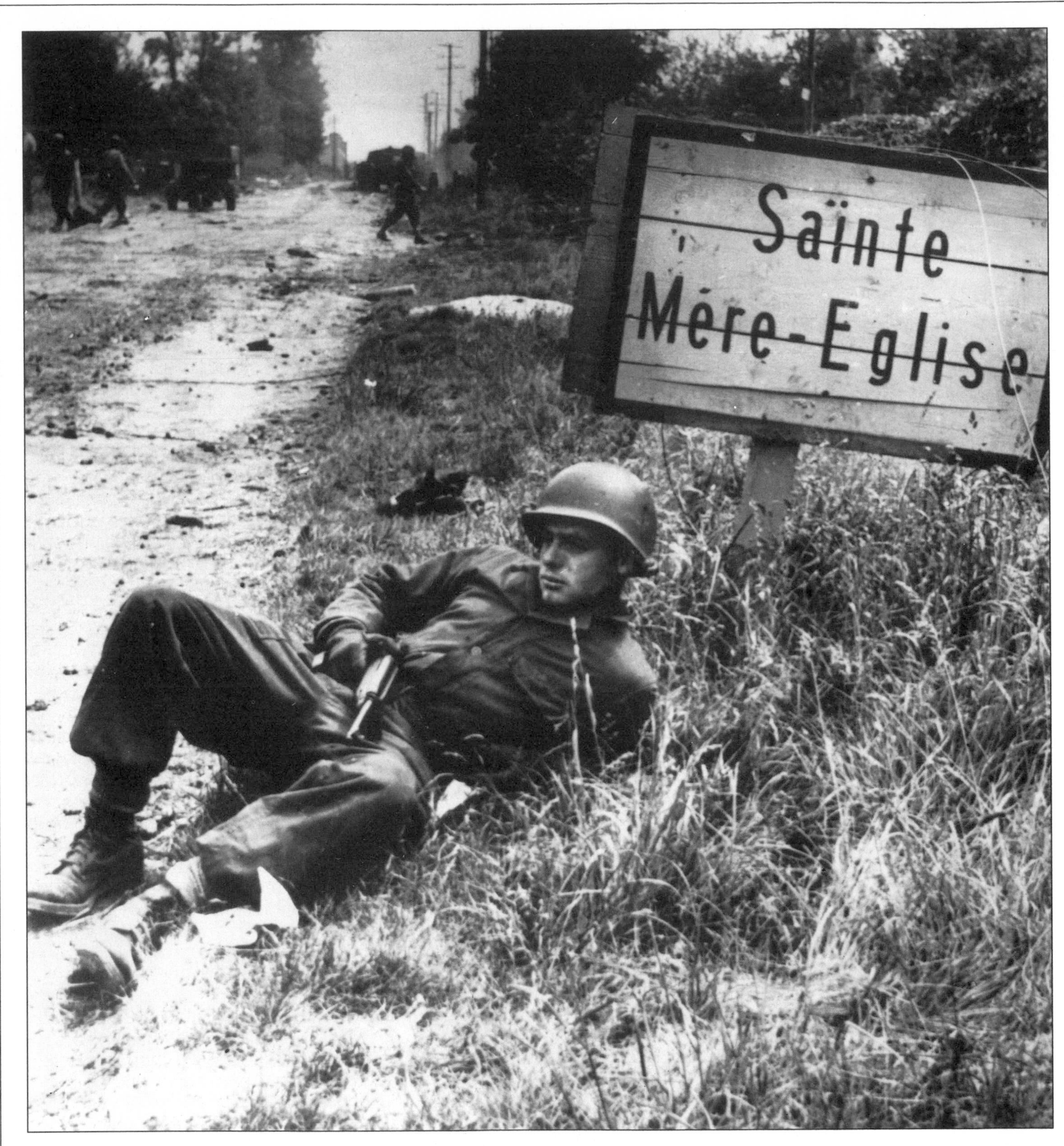
Sainte
Mére-Eglise

Facing page: an American paratrooper of 82nd Airborne Division resting beside the signpost of Saint Mere-Eglise, scene for his division of some of the strongest resistance during the night airborne assault at the start of the D-Day invasion. The village was eventually captured by the Americans after heavy fighting.

Below: American troops of 1st Infantry Division in their landing craft approaching 'Omaha' Beach on the morning of D-Day. The line of the 'Omaha' bluff can be seen rising up from the beach, already under fire from naval support gunnery out at sea.

of the Division arrived. Meanwhile, east of 'Utah' across the estuary of the River Vire, men of 2nd U.S. Rangers scaled sheer cliffs at Pointe du Hoc in order to capture a crucial German battery. This bold exploit became an anticlimax when the battery turned out to have no mounted guns.

The force allotted to 'Omaha' Beach was 16th RCT of 1st Division – the famous 'Big Red One' division – and 116th RCT of 29th Division, under 1st Division command for the assault. Almost from the start, this landing went wrong. Of the thirty-two amphibious tanks launched in support of 16th RCT, only two reached the beach, the rest being swamped in rough seas. Underwater obstacles, concealed by the high tide, ripped the bottoms out of landing craft. Once ashore, the Americans were confronted with a high bluff dominating the beach about 2,000 yards inland, fiercely held by the unexpected 352nd Division. Within minutes of landing, the two RCTs were pinned down and taking heavy casualties. It took the whole day for 1st Division and 29th Division to fight their way off the beaches and onto the bluff, leaving 2,500 casualties behind them on 'Bloody Omaha'. Apart from the airborne divisions, total American casualties for the day were about 4,000 men.

The British landings began at 7.25am, subjecting the defenders to an extra hour's bombardment from the warships. Like the Americans, British 2nd Army based its assaulting forces on units of three battalions, but under the British system these came from different regiments and combined into brigades, not regiments. The addition of engineers,

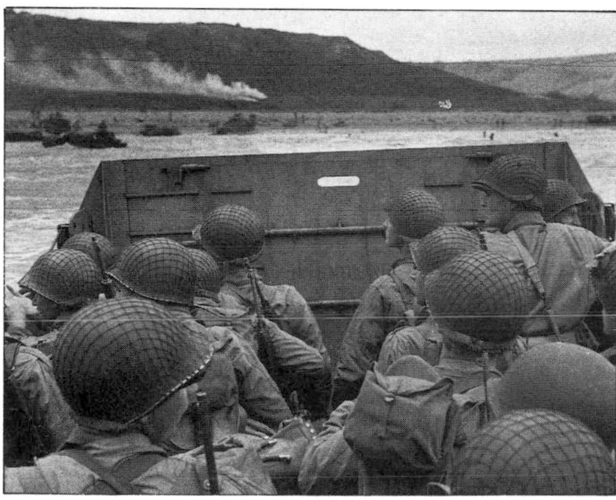

amphibious tanks and artillery made these into brigade groups, of which the British supplied three and the Canadians two. Wide use was made of the 'funnies', specially designed armoured assault vehicles supplied by 79th Armoured Division. In addition, two brigades of Commandos also came ashore with the first wave.

In the centre at 'Gold' Beach, the landing force was 231st Brigade Group and 69th Brigade Group of 50th (Northumbrian) Division, attacking with two battalions leading and one in support. The westernmost edge of the British landing overlapped with 352nd Division's easternmost defences, and like the Americans on 'Omaha', 231st Brigade Group took the rest of the day to chop its way through. In the centre, though, the British and Canadians were facing only 716th Static Division, which could not hold them. The landing of 7th Brigade Group and 8th Brigade Group of 3rd Canadian Division on 'Juno' Beach at 7.35am made steady progress inland and secured its D-Day objectives by mid-morning. Late in the day the first elements of 51st (Highland) Division and 7th Armoured Division ('The Desert Rats') were able to land in Normandy.

The most ambitious of the D-Day objectives was given to 8th Brigade Group of British 3rd Division on 'Sword' Beach, opposite the city of Caen itself. With 1st Special Service (Commando) Brigade covering its flank and linking up with 6th Airborne Division, this force of about 3,000 men was to spearhead the advance ten miles inland and secure the whole of Caen within the first day, to prevent the Germans using the city as a defensive strongpoint. Like the Americans at 'Omaha,' nothing went right for the British at 'Sword'. Unsupported infantry could not overcome the German strongpoints, while the narrow beaches and wild seas delayed or prevented the landing of heavier equipment. When they did manage to advance, 3rd Division ran into the arriving tanks and infantry of 21st *Panzerdivision*, and could make no further progress. On the credit side, they also stopped the crucial attempt by the German armour late in the day to drive them back to the beaches. On 'Gold', 'Juno' and 'Sword', the British and Canadians suffered about 3,500 casualties, bringing the Allied total to about 10,000. Under the battering that they had

LCIL 299

Facing page top left: American troops descending a scrambling net into a landing craft. In the heavy seas off Normandy the trip from ship to shore in the landing craft could take as long as three hours, and many troops drowned when their crafts were swamped or hit underwater obstacles.

Facing page top right: British troops of 3rd Division coming ashore on Sword Beach early on D-Day. The soldiers in the foreground are members of the Beach Party, a specialist group set up to control movement and landing on the beach, which is still under fire from German troops.

Facing page bottom: men of 3rd Canadian Division coming ashore at 'Juno' Beach, at the holiday resort of Besnieres, during the late morning of D-Day. The very narrow strips of beach, due to the high tide resulting from bad weather, caused considerable landing problems for all the Allies. As the day drew on and the beaches were secured, more Allied troops were able to land unhindered.

Right: American troops are able to walk ashore the short distance from their landing craft to the beach. After D-Day, the Allied victory in Normandy was never seriously in doubt.

received, 709th Static Division, 716th Static Division and 352nd Division were reduced to almost battalion strength, although as the day ended, 91st Air-Landing Division arrived from the West to support them. Estimates of German losses reach as high as 9,000 men.

Inevitably, more thought had been spent by the Allies on making their landings a success than on deciding what was to happen afterwards. On 7th June, Montgomery came ashore from his floating headquarters to take command of the land battle. All five beaches were securely held, and the Germans had lost their first chance to push the Allies back into the sea. The crucial 'longest day' was over and won by the Allies. It would take until 12th June, however, before the five beaches were linked together into a defensive perimeter. In this period the Germans came to realise the impossibility of conducting offensive operations in the face of Allied air power and artillery, including the warships still out at sea. The longer the fighting in Normandy lasted, the more Rommel's assessment that the Germans' only chance was to win in the first twenty-four hours appeared correct.

Also on 7th June the first elements of 12th *SS Panzerdivision* joined 21st *Panzerdivision* in front of Caen. Although the British and Canadians held off the German armour's attempts to break through to the beaches, the presence of these powerful armoured divisions ruled out the early capture of the city. Instead, Montgomery played brilliantly on the German fears for Caen by threatening to envelop it with his British forces, pulling more and more of the German armour towards Caen and away from U.S. 1st Army. The city finally fell to the Canadians on 18th July. On the previous day, Rommel was wounded when attacked in his staff car by an Allied fighter-bomber, and relieved of command of Army Group B. On 25th July, U.S. 1st Army broke through the weak German forces opposing it, and moved out of Normandy towards the interior of France. Exactly a month later, on 25th August, Army Group B had been wiped out and Paris was liberated by the Allies. With most of France recaptured and the Germans in full retreat, the end of the war was, for the first time, clearly in sight.

After a few weeks the Normandy beaches were unloading troops, tanks and vehicles at a rate that the Germans could not possibly match, making victory a certainty.

Left: landing ships unloading their cargo of tanks. Below: the city of Caen, capital of Normandy and the key British objective for D-Day, as it looked after its final capture by the Allies in mid-July, 1944.

—BAGRATION–THE SOVIET SLEDGEHAMMER—

Rescued! A child is lifted out of her underground hiding place by Soviet troops who have just liberated her hometown. The sufferings of the Soviet civilian population during the war were immense. Regarded as sub-human by the Nazis, many were sent to Germany as slave labour.

At the end of June, 1944, the attention of both Hitler and the West was focused on Normandy. On the Eastern Front, however, the Red Army was preparing to launch Operation 'Bagration', an offensive that dwarfed that of Montgomery's 21st Army Group in France. Four Soviet Fronts (army groups), totalling 1.2 million men organised into 166 divisions, with 5,200 tanks and self-propelled guns and 6,000 aircraft were to attack on a 450-mile front. In the event, Soviet forces smashed through the German Army Group Centre, commanded by Field Marshal Ernst von Busch, and all but destroyed it. It was the greatest *Blitzkrieg* in history.

The Soviets began planning for Operation 'Bagration' in April, 1944. Stalin personally chose the name of the operation to liberate Belorussia – Bagration was one of the Russian generals of the War of 1812 against Napoleon. In line with their concept of 'operational art', *Stavka* (the Soviet High Command) saw the struggle against Germany as one huge campaign. The first six months of 1944 had already seen the Red Army win significant victories. In the north, the siege of Leningrad was raised in January; in the south, an offensive in the Ukraine had ruptured the front of Army Group South in February and by the end of April the Soviets had cleared the Crimean peninsula and were rolling across the frontier into Germany's increasingly half-hearted ally, Roumania. Belorussia was chosen as the site of the next Soviet offensive, in part because it would have been dangerous to begin the advance from the Ukraine into the Balkans with Army Group Centre poised to fall across the Soviet lines of communication.

The objective of the Soviet forces was a German salient which protruded into Soviet-held territory. Busch's forces had a perimeter of some 650 miles to defend. The core of Army Group Centre's resistance was located in four areas, at Vitebsk, Orsha, Mogilev and Bobruysk. Once these positions had been eliminated, it was believed that the German defensive crust would have been broken, and the rest of the Army Group Centre could be destroyed at the Red Army's leisure. Six axes of advance were to be used. General Bagramyan's 1st Baltic Front was to attack north of Vitebsk against Reinhardt's 3rd *Panzerarmee*, and in co-operation with the northern portion of

Left: German troops manhandle munition carts bogged down in the Don Delta. The Russian climate was one of the principal problems facing German troops on the Eastern Front. Frequently, wheeled motor vehicles were unusable, and Russian horse drawn *panje* wagons or human muscle power had to be used instead.

Facing page top: Red Army artillery and tanks cross a river during the advance towards Lvov. The scale of the Soviet victory in Belorussia in the summer of 1944 is frequently underestimated by Westerners, who usually pay more attention to the Anglo-American offensive in France during the same period.

Facing page bottom: the fruits of lend-lease: Soviet motorized infantry move up in American-built vehicles. American equipment made a vital contribution to the Soviet war effort.

Chernyakhovsky's 3rd Belorussian Front, Vitebsk was to be encircled. Bagramyan's Front was then to provide a flank guard against a southward push by Army Group North, while 3rd Belorussian Front formed the northern arm of a pincer movement on Minsk; the other part of 3rd Belorussian Front was to also to drive north of Minsk, via Orcha. Zakharov's 2nd Belorussian Front was to move through Mogilev and launch a frontal pinning attack on Minsk, the most important communications centre in Belorussia. Rokossovski's 1st Belorussian Front was to surround Bobruysk, and then unite with Chernyakhovsky in destroying enemy forces in the Minsk area. Further advances were planned after the huge salient was snipped off, including an advance by 1st Belorussian Front (which had a frontage of no less than 670 kilometres) towards the extreme southwestern corner of the salient, towards Kovel, Lublin and ultimately Warsaw.

By early June, 1944, Busch was becoming increasingly disturbed by the evidence that clearly pointed towards a major enemy offensive in Belorussia. However, the Soviets had put into execution a highly successful programme of *maskirovka* – a term which literally means 'masking' and encompasses diversionary and deceptive moves – and, as a result, the Germans failed to detect the presence of three entire armies with 3rd Belorussian Front before the day of the assault. The principal victims of the *maskirovka* programme were Adolf Hitler and the German High Command, who became convinced that the Soviets would strike at German forces in Roumania. Hitler's reasoning was guided by a certain amount of logic, as the Roumanian oilfields were vital to the German war economy. Hitler thus took the decision to deploy the bulk of his reserves, which included 18th *Panzer* and *Panzergrenadier* divisions, in the south. Thus, on the eve of the Soviet offensive, Army Group Centre could field only thirty-two infantry and two *Panzerdivisions* – about 700,000 men – against the Soviet hordes.

At 4.00am on 22nd June, 1944, the third anniversary of Operation 'Barbarossa', the Russian attack began. Two hours of preliminary bombardment heralded the start of the attack. The Soviets amassed overwhelming superiority of numbers in the key break-through sectors. General Chernyakhovsky's 3rd Belorussian Front had an average of no less than 178 artillery pieces per kilometre in their attack sectors and 142nd Rifle Corps had the advantage of 166 aircraft sorties made against the Germans at the beginning of the attack. The Soviets also

had a still more precious asset: surprise. However, German formations, despite being desperately short of reserves, struggled to stem the Soviet advance. Even Rokossovsky, commander of 1st Belorussian Front, paid tribute to German tenaciousness in the defence: 'By eight o'clock in the morning the Nazis had recovered from the blows. The telephones at our observation post were ringing constantly: one army commander after another reported new counterattacks launched by tactical enemy reserves. A stubborn battle ensued for the first defence position. Here and there it turned into violent hand-to-hand fighting'.

The overwhelming numbers of Soviet troops, skilfully handled by their commanders, had broken the back of 3rd *Panzerarmee*'s resistance within forty-eight hours of the offensive's start. Busch, who shared Hitler's belief in positional, rather than mobile defence, refused to allow Reinhardt to abandon Vitebsk, and thus sacrificed 30,000 men in the defence of the town, which fell to the Soviets on 27th June. The news of Vitebsk's liberation resounded around the world. On 28th June President Roosevelt sent a message to Stalin conveying 'my congratulations to you personally and to your gallant army'.

Zakharov's 2nd and Chernyakhovsky's 3rd Belorussian fronts were also making excellent progress against German 4th Army based around Orcha and Mogilev. Orcha fell to 11th Guards and 31st Army on 27th June, although German 9th Army, covering Bobruysk, succeeded in slowing the advance of 3rd and 48th armies of 1st Belorussian Front north of the town. This ray of hope for the Germans disappeared when Rokossovsky threw 9th Tank Corps into the fray. On 27th June, six German divisions were encircled at Bobruysk. Rokossovsky did not pause to eliminate the Bobruysk pocket. To pin von Vormann's 9th Army in Bobruysk until the second echelon arrived, massive airstrikes were made by 16th Air Army on the city. By 28th June two German corps had been destroyed at Mogilev; the following day, Bobruysk was taken by the Red Army. One week after 'Bagration' started, the four key bastions of the German defence had been eliminated, and Soviet forces had driven ninety-five miles into the rear of Army Group Centre.

Gradually awakening to the full extent of the catastrophe unfolding in Belorussia, Hitler replaced Busch with Field Marshal Model on 28th June. Hitler accompanied this command change with the issue of Operational 'Order 8', which gave unrealistic orders to continue with static defence. Meanwhile, *Stavka* attempted to capitalise on their victories by using 2nd Belorussian Front and elements of 1st and 3rd Belorussian fronts to achieve a massive encirclement in the area of Minsk. On 3rd July, 5th Guards Tank, 11th Guards and 31st Army captured the ancient city. Five corps of 4th and 9th German armies were caught in a pocket east of Minsk and 33rd, 50th and 49th Soviet armies moved in to annihilate them. Although elements of 9th Army did break out, some 35,000 Germans surrendered on 12th July.

As Army Group Centre reeled under the blows delivered in Belorussia, neighbouring German formations were also coming under pressure. To the south, the Soviets attacked on

A Red Army scouting party creeps towards the German positions, grenades in hand. The Soviets made highly effective use of deception measures in the run-up to Operation 'Bagration', a factor which contributed substantially to their success.

Right: Soviet infantry advance under the covering fire of a tank. The Soviets massed their troops on selected breakthrough sectors along the length of Belorussian salient, achieving overwhelming local superiority in infantry, armour, aircraft and artillery.

Below: Soviet fighter aircraft of Third Belorussian Front. The figure in the foreground is Captain Mayorov, who was awarded the decoration of Hero of the Soviet Union. By the time of 'Bagration' the Soviets could field a formidable force of some 8,500 front-line aircraft.

13th July against Army Group North Ukraine. Although the Germans fell back to a prepared position – the 'Prinz Eugen Line' – they were outflanked, and were forced to retreat to the line of the River Bug. On 18th July Soviet tanks of Koniev's 1st Ukrainian Front surrounded and then liquidated German XIII Corps at Brody, east of the great city of Lvov. Lvov itself fell nine days later. In the Baltic states, too, Soviet forces took the offensive. The Soviets completed another major encirclement at Vilna, which fell on 13th July, and by the end of the month General Schorner's Army Group North had been isolated from both Army Group Centre and East Prussia, although the Soviets delayed a full scale assault on Army Group North until later in the year. Although Hitler agreed to evacuate part of Estonia, he would have been better advised to cut his losses entirely and use the *Kriegsmarine* to evacuate Schorner's men by sea to defend the Reich itself. On 5th October the Soviets wrenched the German positions apart. Russian tanks poured through the gap, and Army Group North was pinned against the coast.

However, the main battlefield remained Belorussia, where a further stage of the operation began on 18th July. Once again, the Soviets achieved surprise when 1st Belorussian Front attacked and drove deep into German positions. By 25th July Soviet troops had reached the River Vistula, the river that runs through Warsaw. Having advanced such vast distances since June, the Soviets were beginning to outrun their supply lines, and sharp German counterattacks further limited the Soviet advance. By the end of August, as the doomed Warsaw Uprising raged, major offensive moves had ended.

Operation 'Bagration' had destroyed most of Army Group Centre, thirty German divisions had been annihilated, and Soviet forces had moved 300 miles nearer to Germany. The Red Army had demonstrated in the most convincing way possible just how much it had learned from its mistakes in the first years of the war. The Soviet successes were not merely the product of overwhelming numbers and brute force. By

Warsaw in flames: the destruction of the Warsaw Ghetto, 1943. Similar scenes were enacted during the uprising of the Polish Home Army in the autumn of 1944. In both cases, the Nazis suppressed the insurrections with considerable savagery. In 1944, some of the worst atrocities were committed by the notorious Dirlewanger Penal Brigade.

the successful use of *maskirovka*, the Red Army had succeeded in achieving surprise on a number of levels, and had ensured that they had significant numerical superiority on the decisive axes of advance. Once they had broken into the German defences, they ruthlessly and efficiently exploited their successes, using armoured and mechanised formations to penetrate deep into the enemy rear and disrupt and disorient the German forces. Furthermore, the Soviet offensives came as a series of hammer blows; the German forces were never allowed the luxury of catching their breath. The flexibility of the Red Army stands out in sharp contrast to the rigidity of the German defenders, who were out-thought, as well as out-fought, in the summer of 1944.

There is a sad footnote to Operation 'Bagration'. As the spearheads of the Soviet 2nd Tank Army approached to within eight miles of Warsaw, the underground Polish Home Army rose to liberate their capital. Only about 30,000 of the 250,000 strong Home Army were armed. The insurrection began on 1st August. The Germans, under the command of SS General von dem Bach-Zelewski, committed tanks, artillery and aircraft to the battle in a savage attempt to crush the uprising. The Soviets gave the insurgents little help. Most of the Home Army was anti-Communist, and it would certainly have been politically inconvenient for Stalin to contend with a large, non-communist Polish force in Warsaw; memories of the Russian invasion in 1939 were still fresh. But it is also clear that Rokossovski's 1st Belorussian Front could not have attacked Warsaw in early August because of logistic problems. It would seem that, in military terms, the Uprising was launched prematurely. However, Stalin did nothing to aid the Poles in the early, critical stages of the battle. The Soviets began to advance on 10th September, but on 2nd October Bor-Komorowski capitulated. In all, 200,000 Poles had died, including 15,000 members of the Home Army. Hitler ordered Warsaw to be razed to the ground, but there was little left to destroy. Bor-Komorowski accurately described Warsaw as an empty shell of a city, where the 'dead are buried inside the ruins or alongside them.'

ARNHEM–THE BRIDGE TOO FAR

Operation 'Market-Garden' is launched on 17th September. Although they succeeded in capturing the bridge at Arnhem, ultimately 1st Airborne Division could not hold it against two *Waffen-SS Panzerdivisions.*

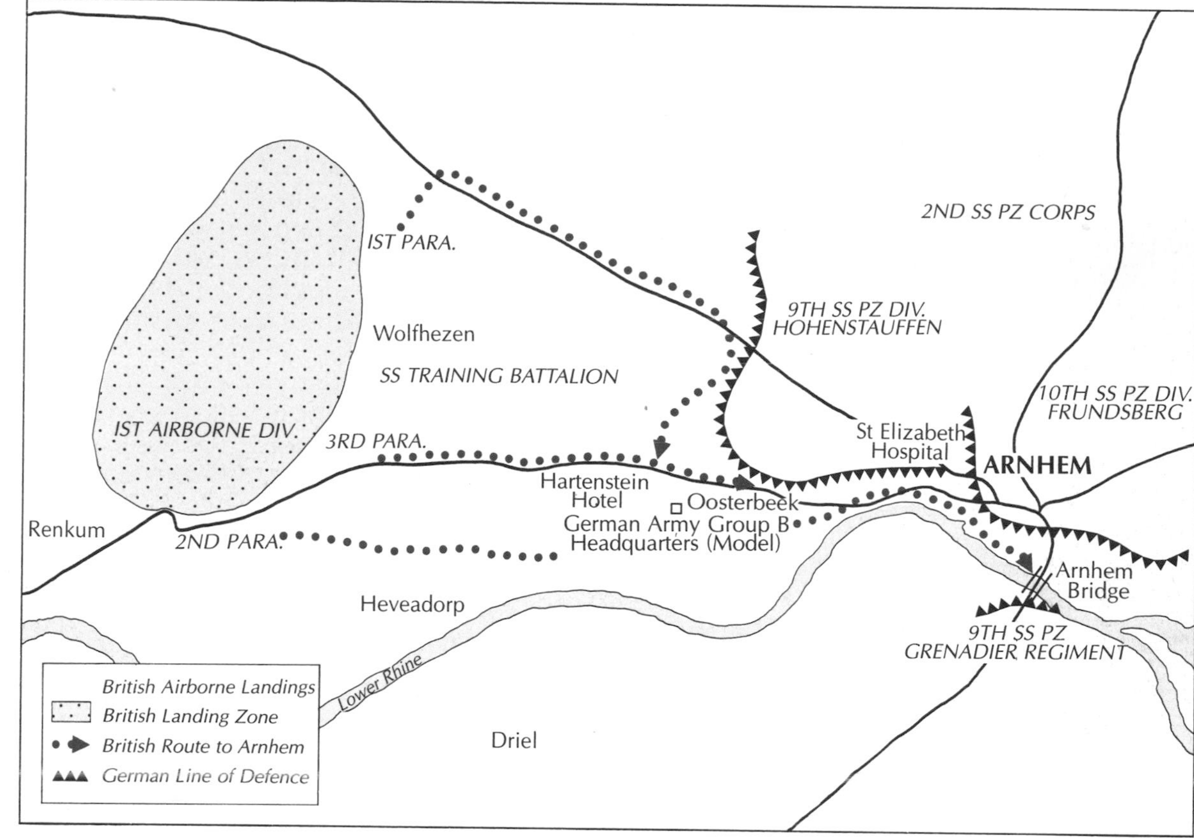

On 1st September, 1944, General Dwight D. Eisenhower, as Supreme Allied Commander, assumed direct command of the Allied land forces in Europe from General Bernard Montgomery, who reverted to the command of his own 21st Army Group and was promoted to field marshal in compensation. On that date, Montgomery's forces, together with Lieutenant General Omar Bradley's 12th Army Group and 6th Army Group under Lieutenant General Jake Devers, were driving flat out across France and the Low Countries towards the German border, with the Germans in full retreat before them. On 4th September, Adolf Hitler recalled from enforced retirement the elderly Field Marshal Gerd von Rundstedt to command all German forces on the Western Front in place of Field Marshal Walter Model, who himself reverted to command of Army Group B, covering Holland and northern Germany. The prospects for Germany were grim. After its mauling in France, Army Group B barely existed, the Western Front was wide open, and total defeat seemed only a matter of weeks. On the day von Rundstedt was appointed, British 2nd Army under General Sir Miles Dempsey, part of Montgomery's command, liberated Brussels, and, a day later, Antwerp. After coming 250 miles in five days, the British only had to advance another sixty-five miles to the River Rhine – and the German industrial heartland of the Ruhr – to end the war.

Months before the D-Day invasion, the Allied strategy for this phase of the campaign had been agreed. Canadian, British and American armies would advance on a broad front like the outspread fingers of a hand, giving the Germans no chance to counterattack in a single thrust, and letting all share equally in the glory of victory. Yet with German garrisons still holding the Channel ports and main river estuaries, all Allied supplies were coming from Normandy alone, along an ever-lengthening supply line. Eisenhower's staff advised him that such a rate of advance could not be maintained – his three army groups were simply

Major General 'Roy' Urquhart, commanding 1st British Airborne Division (standing nearest to the camera) with four members of the Glider Pilot Regiment belonging to his division. Although Urquhart lacked experience of airborne operations, he proved to be a very determined and effective leader at Arnhem.

running out of fuel and ammunition as they moved.

Montgomery's solution to Eisenhower's dilemma required a major change in Allied strategy. While Canadian 1st Army dealt with the Channel ports, British 2nd Army would drive on a narrow front northwards through Holland to the Rhine; U.S. 1st Army covering its flank. All other American forces would halt and give up their supplies to support this drive. Eisenhower, however, refused to change from the broad-front strategy, arguing that American public opinion would not stand for British troops under Montgomery appearing to win the war. Convinced he was right, although in danger of insubordination for his insistance, Montgomery continued to press Eisenhower on this point. Finally, on 10th September, Eisenhower compromised. Montgomery could try for a bridgehead over the Rhine, using Eisenhower's strategic reserve, 1st Allied Airborne Army, which had been sitting unused in Britain since its formation in July.

Below: the main road bridge over the Lower Rhine at Arnhem, the chief prize of Operation 'Market-Garden'. This view from the north shows how built-up areas ruled out any glider landing close to the bridge itself. The flat area south of the bridge was also considered unsuitable for gliders.

British paratroopers on the ground at Arnhem, with supplies still coming in. Jeeps were flown in by glider to make ground movement easier, but a plan to seize Arnhem Bridge with a sudden dash by a special jeep squadron came to nothing when the jeeps were ambushed by German troops.

The new 1st Allied Airborne Army was commanded by the American Lieutenant General Lewis Brereton, a pilot and former commander of 9th U.S. Air Force, with the British Lieutenant General Frederick 'Boy' Browning as his deputy and ground commander. Browning also commanded 1st British Airborne Corps, consisting of 1st Airborne Division and 1st Polish Parachute Brigade (6th Airborne Division was still refitting after its role in Normandy).

Lieutenant General Matthew Ridgeway commanded XVIII U.S. Airborne Corps, consisting of 82nd and 101st airborne divisions. These forces would be dropped by air to seize key bridges behind the German lines across which Lieutenant General Brian Horrocks' British XXX Corps, led by the Guards Armoured Division, would advance. The final bridge across the Rhine at Arnhem was the target of British 1st Airborne Division under Major General 'Roy' Urquhart. According to Montgomery's plan, Urquhart's Division would hold Arnhem bridge for two days before the Guards arrived and established themselves on the north bank of the Rhine. Then, 52nd (Lowland) Division, would be flown in to improvised airstrips near Arnhem and secure the bridgehead. The plan was codenamed Operation 'Market-Garden', with 1st Allied Airborne Army as 'Market' and British 2nd Army as 'Garden'. Never before had airborne forces been used to secure a deep strategic penetration in this manner. It was a considerable risk, but Montgomery was gambling to end the war before Christmas, and Browning advised him that, if necessary, 1st Airborne Division could hold Arnhem bridge for four days instead of two.

From Eisenhower's approval to the start of 'Market-Garden' was only seven days. The airborne forces, however, were well trained and had already seen seventeen plans made and cancelled at the last minute – they were anxious to get into the war before it ended. After the experience of a night drop on D-Day, their commanders agreed to go by daylight, but not even the Allied air forces had enough transport aircraft to move three and a half divisions at once. An airborne division was two parachute regiments (brigades in the British Army) and one air-landing regiment in gliders. The two American divisions opted to use all their paratroops on the first drop, with the glider regiments joining them on the following day. Major General Urquhart chose a single parachute brigade, plus his air-landing brigade with its heavier weapons. The only landing zone suitable for gliders turned out to be eight miles northwest of Arnhem bridge – a long walk for troops who relied on surprise for their success. The big problems for all airborne forces was their lack of armour and anti-armour weapons should they encounter tanks, and the difficulties of supply. Some intelligence reports suggested German armoured forces at Arnhem, but in the general rush and euphoria of battle these reports were not considered sufficient reason to cancel the operation.

At 2.00pm on Sunday, 17th September, all along the line of the planned XXX Corps advance, airborne soldiers jumped from their aircraft into battle and gliders skidded down onto their landing zones. Nearest to the British line, 101st Airborne began to secure the bridges in the area of Eindhoven. Fifteen minutes later, the Guards Armoured Division began its attack through the defences of German 15th Army to link up with the paratroops. In the centre, 82nd Airborne Division dropped near the town of Nijmegen, itself the site of one of the crucial

The British airborne forces at Arnhem soon learned that they had dropped into trouble. Facing page top left: a heavy mortar crew provides covering fire against a *Waffen-SS* assault. Lack of heavy weapons greatly limited the defence that the airborne troops could put up against German tanks.

The only heavy anti-tank weapons with the British at Arnhem were 6-pounder anti-tank guns (facing page top right), flown in by glider. A handful of these guns were to be vital in holding off the first German attacks at Arnhem Bridge, but they soon ran out of ammunition.

While 1st Airborne Division held out at Arnhem, XXX Corps fought its way towards them. Facing page bottom: a British soldier taking cover behind a knocked out *Panzer* V 'Panther' tank, a formidable machine which caused the British much difficulty in their advance over the flat terrain of Holland.

Right: British paratroopers pressing forward through the built-up areas of Arnhem, unable to reach the bridge due to the unexpected *Waffen-SS* presence. The battle brought serious destruction to the town of Arnhem, which until then had escaped the worst ravages of the war.

river bridges. Neither the Guards nor the American paratroops, however, found German resistance as light as they had expected on the flat, open heathland that characterised much of the terrain for the advance.

In just a few days, Field Marshal Model had performed miracles in putting back together formations that the Allies believed they had wiped out, and even his most improvised defence imposed a crucial delay on the Allied advance. It was also too much to hope that all the twelve bridges over the rivers and canals needed for 'Market-Garden' could be captured intact. The bridge at Son, just north of Eindhoven, was blown by the Germans just before its capture, and the main bridge at Nijmegen, in the centre of the advance, was too strongly held for the paratroops to take it. As bridging equipment and boats were rushed up behind the armoured spearhead, 'Market-Garden' began to slip badly behind schedule. None of this was known, however, at Arnhem, where Urquhart's forces had landed safely and set off for their objective – the main bridge across the Rhine in the centre of the town.

The chief reason for 1st Airborne Division's ignorance was that in the wooded, flooded and low-lying Dutch countryside, their radios would not function properly. Urquhart had no contact with higher formations, nor with his own paratroop battalions, which were being dispatched down the road to Arnhem as rapidly as possible. By mid-afternoon, frustrated at finding his Division slipping away from him, the General set off down the main route towards Arnhem to link up with his advancing men. There he found out what they had already discovered. By chance, the British Division had dropped practically next door to Field Marshal Model's headquarters at Oosterbeek, while nearby, north of Arnhem, resting and refitting from its near destruction in Normandy, was General Wilhelm Bittrich's II *SS Panzer Korps,* comprising of two *Panzerdivisions,* 9th *SS Panzerdivision 'Hohenstauffen'* and 10th *SS Panzerdivision 'Frundsberg'.* Although well below strength, these elite armoured divisions were far too strong for airborne troops to overcome. As the German pressure increased and the radios remained uncooperative, Major General Urquhart decided to stay with 1st Parachute Brigade on the road to Arnhem. He had no control over the rest of his Division, and no indication of whether his troops had reached the bridge. He would remain out of contact with the rest of his Division for the next thirty-six hours.

In fact, a single British battalion, 2nd Battalion of 1st Parachute Brigade under Lieutenant Colonel John Frost, reached Arnhem bridge on the evening of 17th September and took up defensive positions in the houses on the northern side of the bridge. So began what Lieutenant General Ridgeway would later call 'the outstanding small unit action of the war'. Arnhem bridge, the objective an entire Division was to hold for two days against light opposition, was held by Frost's battalion – with a few more troops who also made it through to the bridge, including the division's anti-tank gunners – against the tanks and infantry of 9th *SS Panzerdivision* for three days and nights. On

Left: the men who made it – members of 1st Airborne Division who swam or rowed back across the Rhine after the decision to evacuate 1st Airborne Division from Arnhem. A few have kept their famous red berets, now the international hallmark of airborne forces.

The British were surprised to find *Waffen-SS* armoured troops (below) among the first of their prisoners at Arnhem. Later it would be the turn of 1st Airborne Division's men to surrender. Treatment of prisoners on both sides was very good, each respecting the other's high fighting ability.

the morning of Wednesday, 20th September, Frost was able to speak to Urquhart by radio, only to find that the rest of the Division was itself being surrounded by the Germans. Finally, that afternoon, Frost was himself wounded and the battalion, out of food and ammunition, was overwhelmed. To their surprise, the surviving paratroops, nearly all of them wounded, found that the *Waffen-SS* men treated them well, showing respect for an enemy that had more than lived up to their own standards of bravery. It was not until midnight that night that the first tanks of XXX Corps got across Nijmegen bridge, the last obstacle before Arnhem.

The only remaining question was whether anything could be salvaged from 'Market-Garden'. Without a good bridge, armoured troops could not cross the Rhine. The rest of Urquhart's Division had arrived at Arnhem, but its supply zones had been overrun by the *Waffen-SS*, and the entire Division was fighting at Oosterbeek with its back to the river. The Polish brigade, dropped according to plan on the south side of the Rhine, was unable to help. Although the distance from Nijmegen was less than ten miles, it was across the flattest of the Dutch heathland, in the face of increasing German opposition. It took until 22nd September for the first units of the Guards Armoured Division to reach the south bank of the Rhine, to be separated by 400 yards of river from Urquhart's men. On the evening of 24th September Urquhart, now in radio communication with Browning's headquarters, reported that his Division was out of supplies and ammunition – it would either need to be supported or withdrawn. In the early hours of 26th September, after volunteers had agreed to stay with the wounded, the men of 1st Airborne Division, abandoning their equipment, piloted small boats or swam across the Rhine to safety. Horrocks then pulled his forces back towards Nijmegen. 'Market-Garden' was a failure.

Of 10,000 men of 1st Airborne Division and 1st Polish Parachute Brigade who fought at Arnhem, Major General Urquhart took 2,163 men back across the Rhine with him. The German casualties were 3,300 dead and wounded. The result was a fifty-mile salient into Holland leading nowhere. Montgomery's first gamble was also his only defeat in a major battle. Characteristically, he refused to admit this, calling 'Market-Garden' ninety per cent successful. Whether, if the operation had worked, Eisenhower would have agreed to Montgomery's change of strategy is a matter of speculation. As it was, the broad-front strategy continued and the Allied armies, all short of supplies, slowed their advance before the German frontier. The war would *not* be over by Christmas.

Some who did not make it. German soldiers and British dead in the streets of Arnhem after the battle. About 8,000 British soldiers were killed or taken prisoner in the course of the battle. Some men remained in hiding for months. After Arnhem, 1st Airborne Division was not re-formed.

BATTLE OF THE BULGE

The German offensive in the Ardennes, often called 'The Battle of the Bulge', began on 16th December, 1944, and was the last great gamble of the Third Reich. By late 1944, Soviet troops were pushing the Germans steadily back on the Eastern Front, German cities were being destroyed round the clock by the Allied strategic bombing offensive, the Italian peninsula had been liberated, and Allied ground forces were advancing virtually unopposed through France and the Low Countries – being stopped only by their own supply difficulties and the German frontier defences, the *Westwall* (known to the Allies as the Siegfried Line). On 20th July, 1944, Adolf Hitler survived an assassination attempt by members of the German Army who had hoped to negotiate peace after his death. Thereafter, Hitler relied less on the Army and more on the Nazi Party's own forces, the *Waffen-SS*, as well as upon his own increasingly erratic judgement. It seemed that nothing could save Germany from being crushed on all sides.

Hitler decided that there was one chance. The alliance between the Soviet Union, the United States and the British Empire was, he argued, inherently unstable and would collapse under a sufficient shock. As Germany moved at last to a 'total war' footing, enough troops could still be scraped together to mount one last offensive on the Western Front through the thinly held line of the Ardennes forest, towards the port of Antwerp. By attacking through the bad going of the Ardennes, in bad weather and close to Christmas, the Germans could achieve surprise and reduce the massive Allied air superiority that had so hampered their previous armoured operations. By taking Antwerp, they would cut off the main Allied supply base for the Western Front, surrounding Canadian 1st Army and British 2nd Army, as well as 9th and 1st U.S. armies, leaving them with no choice but to surrender or evacuate in another Dunkirk. The British would blame the Americans for the loss of their troops, and the Anglo-American alliance might well break down altogether. Even at worst, there could be no attack from the West for at least six months, in which time Germany would develop its 'wonder weapons' and be free to concentrate on defeating the Soviet Union.

The problem with Hitler's plan was that it needed everything to go right at once. It needed German troops to advance in fog and snow at high speed through hills and forests along dirt roads, reaching the River Meuse in two days and Antwerp in four, before the Allies could respond. It needed the British and Americans to quarrel and collapse in the face of the German offensive. It needed a small German armoured force to out-fight three or four times its own number of troops, showing a superiority over the Americans that – for a scratch force in the fifth year of the war – was scarcely to be expected. None of Hitler's generals had any faith in his plan, and only loyalty and fear compelled them to carry it out. This was very much Hitler's personal battle.

Originally codenamed 'Watch on the Rhine' but later renamed 'Autumn Mist', the German attack was made by Army Group B under Field Marshal Walter Model. Eight armoured and thirteen infantry divisions assembled in secret against the five southernmost divisions of U.S. 1st Army under Lieutenant General Courtney Hodges. At 7.30am on 16th December, after a two-hour artillery bombardment, the five infantry divisions of 6th *Panzerarmee* attacked the two southernmost divisions of U.S. V Corps positioned in front of the Elsenborn Ridge. Behind the infantry waited four powerful *Waffen-SS* armoured divisions, the force expected to reach Antwerp in four days. The remaining forces were German Army rather

Adolf Hitler at his headquarters at Rastenburg with Joseph Goebbels, his Reich Plenipotentiary for Total War, shortly after the unsuccessful bomb plot against Hitler's life. It was Goebbels who scraped together a last reserve of German troops for the Ardennes offensive.

The formidable 88mm KwK43 anti-tank gun fitted to a Jagdpanther assault gun, and also the main armament of the *Panzer* VI 'Tiger' and 'King Tiger' Although few in number and slow in movement, these 'wonder weapons' caused much trouble for the Americans during the Ardennes offensive.

than *Waffen-SS*. The original plan called for 5th *Panzerarmee* of four infantry and three armoured divisions to cover 6th *Panzerarmee's* flank and for 7th Army of four infantry divisions to secure the flank against American interference from the south. Hitler also held one armoured division in reserve. From the start, however, 6th *Panzerarmee's* attack against the veteran troops of V Corps made little progress. In contrast, U.S. VIII Corps, holding a line of more than a hundred miles with inadequate troops further south, was burst upon by 5th *Panzerarmee*, and its least experienced division totally surrounded. Even so, the rest of VIII Corps put up a tough defence. Small forces of English-speaking German troops in American uniforms, driving behind the Allied lines, produced much confusion but no major results. After two hard days' fighting, the Germans were clearly making progress too slowly, and in the wrong places. They were still nowhere in sight of the Meuse.

Lieutenant General Omar Bradley, commanding 12th Army Group, of which 1st Army was a part, assumed at first that he was facing a small German spoiling attack, but nevertheless began to move armoured divisions from the north and south in support of VIII Corps. Using the two days bought by their front-line troops, the Americans, although they had no clear picture of what was happening, secured the crucial road junctions at Saint Vith in the north and Bastogne in the south against the German advance. Short of engineers, and unable to move easily across country in the snow and mud, the Germans were heavily dependent on these roads. The only formation of 6th *Panzerarmee* making progress was '*Kampfgruppe Peiper*', a force of a hundred tanks and 4,000 infantry belonging to 1st *SS Panzerdivision*, which had broken through the Losheim Gap and was driving on, unsupported, towards the Meuse, unaware that the rest of the Division had failed to follow it. Meanwhile, on 19th December, the lead elements of 5th *Panzerarmee* reached the outskirts of Bastogne, only to find a solid defence based on newly arrived 101st Airborne Division and armoured support. Unable to take Bastogne and maintain their advance, the Germans by-passed the town, leaving it for their arriving infantry.

Despite the initial shock, the Americans recovered well from the surprise of 'Autumn Mist'. Indeed, the reaction of Allied higher commanders was the same as that of their German enemies - that the offensive could not possibly succeed. Nevertheless, on first hearing of the attack on 16th December, both Field Marshal Montgomery commanding 21st Army Group to the north, and Lieutenant General Patton, commanding U.S. 3rd Army to the south of U.S. 1st Army, ordered their staffs to draw up plans in case what appeared to be a spoiling attack was something more. On 19th December, with the picture much clearer, General Dwight D. Eisenhower called a major conference for his commanders at Verdun to decide the next move. The German attack had failed to take St Vith or Bastogne, and, although the Americans were still retreating, there was no panic and the initial surprise had now gone. Lieutenant General Hodges was to continue his defence, moving the powerful U.S. VII Corps down from the north to extend his line against *Kampfgruppe Peiper*. While this line held, the crucial counterattack would be made from the south by Patton's U.S. 3rd Army, which would relieve Bastogne and smash through the flank protection provided by 7th Army to

roll up the German line. Patton decided that his first attack would come in three days with at least three divisions.

This made two separate battles, one in the north, the other in the south. Eisenhower needed someone to co-ordinate the northern battle, and also some reserves on the line of the Meuse, just in case the Germans broke through. On the following day he telephoned 21st Army Group and, drawing a line through the centre of the battlefield, placed Montgomery in charge of all troops north of that line. Montgomery at once set British XXX Corps in motion towards the Meuse, and his presence did much to restore calm and order in the northern part of the battlefield. His actual command function, however, consisted largely in agreeing to the shape of the battle which circumstances, and his American subordinates, had already dictated.

These Allied command decisions doomed Hitler's offensive. Although the Germans were able to find another eight divisions to add to the battle, they could not match the growing Allied strength – the equivalent of thirty-five divisions before the battle ended. By 21st December repeated attempts by 6th *Panzerarmee* to break through on the Elsenborn Ridge had come to nothing. Bastogne, although surrounded and under heavy pressure, refused to surrender. On 23rd December Montgomery, reluctant to incur heavy casualties now that his line was secure, authorised an American retreat from St Vith, but so great were German traffic problems that they were at first unable to advance. Also, on 23rd December the bad weather, which the Germans had regarded as crucial, lifted and the Allies were able to deploy their full air power to attack the Germans on the ground and to supply their own troops by air. By 24th December *Kampfgruppe Peiper*, the last German hope in the north, was surrounded, cut off and out of fuel miles in front of friendly troops. Nevertheless, a few hundred of its members escaped on foot back to the German lines. Finally, after a three-day offensive, III Corps of Patton's U.S. 3rd Army broke through from the south to link up with the troops in Bastogne on 26th December.

The last German effort on 26th December produced the limit of their advance, resulting in a long, narrow salient, 'the Bulge', pointing towards the River Meuse. A few tanks of 5th *Panzerarmee* actually reached the Meuse at Dinant on Christmas Day, only to turn back after a skirmish with tanks of British XXX Corps. By this time most of the German forces were seriously low on fuel. There simply were not the troops to maintain the offensive, or even to hold position. An attempt by 5th *Panzerarmee* to secure the southern flank by capturing Bastogne on 30th December stalled against a further attack by U.S. 3rd Army. It was the end for 'Autumn Mist'. Hitler, however, would not concede defeat. He insisted that the 'Bulge' should be held as the starting point for yet another planned offensive.

Against the overwhelming land and air power that the Allies could now deploy, the

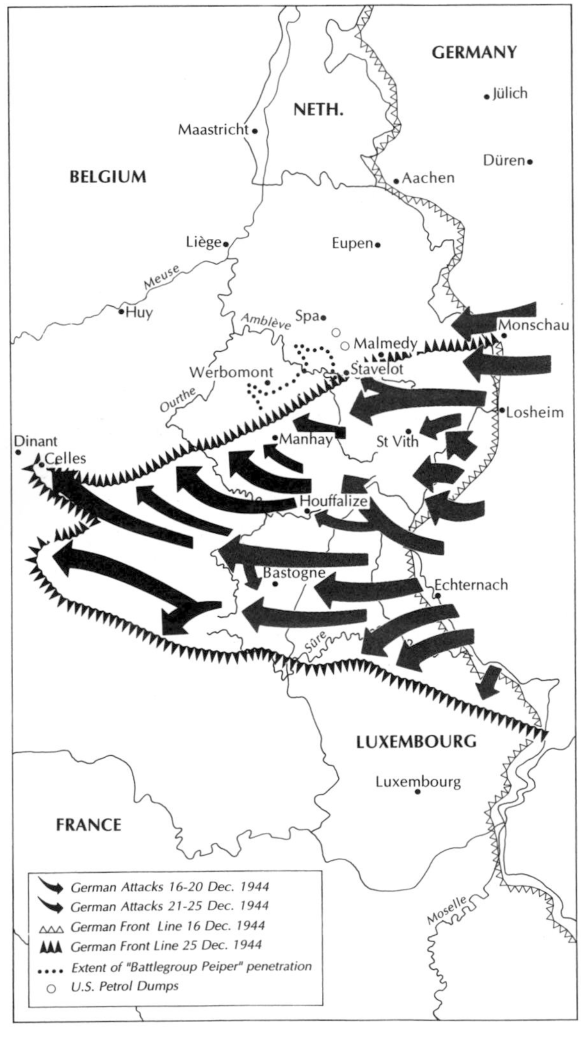

Below: Operation 'Autumn Mist', the last German offensive of the war, saw Hitler's forces push west as far as Celles. Ironically, the petrol-starved German army came within a few miles of a crucial U.S. fuel dump, but were unaware of its existence.

Facing page top left: a soldier of a *Volksgrenadier* division, which was largely made up of children, the sick, and the elderly, with little enthusiasm for the fight. Such troops were typical of the German forces in the Ardennes.

Facing page top right: twenty-nine-year old Lieutenant Colonel Joachim 'Jochen' Peiper of 1st *SS Panzerdivision*, one of the outstanding German armoured commanders of the war. A shadow was cast over his *Waffen-SS* division's achievements in the Ardennes since it was also responsible for the 'Malmedy Massacre' of nearly a hundred American prisoners.

Facing page bottom: small, improvised American ambush points like this one were crucial in slowing the German advance and buying time for the arriving reinforcements.

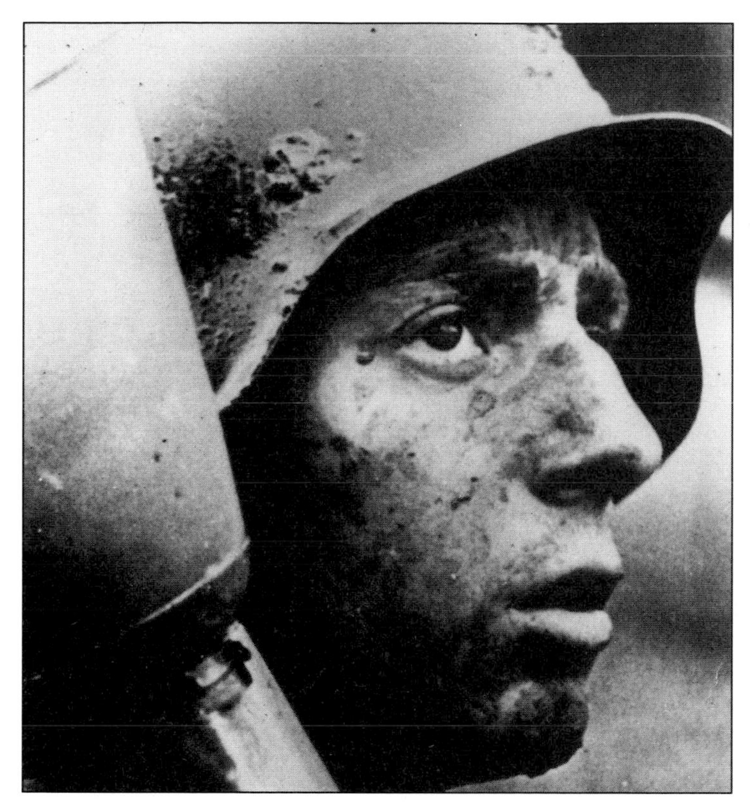

Improvisation and flexibility were the keynotes of the American defence. Facing page top: paratroopers of 82nd Airborne Division on the march in the northern part of the Bulge early in the battle. Further south at Bastogne, 101st Airborne Division played a crucial role as infantry in the defence.

Facing page bottom left: a *Panzer* V 'Panther' of an *SS Panzerdivision* knocked out in a street at Manhay, just south of Liege, on 30th December. By this time the German offensive had largely spent itself, and this tank marks one of the furthest German advances before the Allied counterattack.

Facing page bottom right: tank tracks in the snow. Once the weather improved the German columns were at the mercy of Allied aircraft. Here an advancing German force has been attacked from the air and suffered heavy casualties. Such use of air power was crucial in winning the battle.

Right: the end of Hitler's dream - American paratroopers take prisoner the first of four German soldiers hiding in a barn near Henumont, Belgium inJanuary, 1945. The losses of the Ardennes offensive left the German Army entirely without reserves.

'Bulge' could not be held. But, made cautious by the surprise that they had received from 'Autumn Mist', the Allies were content to push the Germans back slowly, having themselves the same difficulty attacking through the snow. Renewed offensives in January by Montgomery and Patton drove the Germans, harassed by aircraft, back to their starting lines, and on 28th January the Americans pronounced the battle officially over. Army Group B, not for the first time in the Second World War, had been effectively wiped out, losing between 100,000 and 120,000 men and about 1,000 of its 1,500 tanks. On 31st December Hitler launched a much smaller offensive of ten divisions, Operation 'Nordwind', against American forces in Alsace, which achieved little. Undaunted, he ordered Operation 'Bodenplatte' a day later, which was designed as a low-level attack by virtually the whole German operational strength – more than 1,000 fighters and fighter-bombers – against the Allied air forces. Its only result was their own virtual self-destruction.

The elimination of these last German reserves meant that they had nothing to stop the Soviet Vistula-Oder offensive on the Eastern Front, which began on 12th January and advanced to within fifty miles of Berlin in three weeks. American losses in 'Autumn Mist' were between 75,000 and 80,000. The British were not seriously engaged in the battle, losing fewer than 1,400 men. Although not taken lightly, these losses had little or no effect on the Allied ability to conduct offensive operations in the following spring, whereas the failure of Hitler's last offensive guaranteed the defeat of Nazi Germany.

– THE BATTLES OF MANDALAY AND MEIKTILA –

Throughout the late summer and autumn of 1944, the Allied forces of 14th Army pursued Japanese General Mutaguchi's shattered forces across the Chin Hills and down the Kebaw valley to the Chindwin River. It was a slow business. Monsoon rain sheeted down, converting the dirt roads to quagmires. Vehicles became bogged up to their axles and sometimes the army made as little as three miles a day. Mutaguchi's rearguards, although ill and starving, put up tenacious resistance – each one had to be wiped out in costly, time-consuming, small-unit actions. It was not until early December that IV Corps reached Sittaung and XXXIII Corps arrived at Mawlaik and Kalewa. Although exhausted, the British did not rest – IV Corps' engineers quickly constructed a 1,150-foot long Bailey Bridge across the Chindwin, the longest ever built. Operation 'Capital', the Allied codename for the reconquest of central Burma, could now begin.

Lieutenant General William Slim, the 14th Army commander, was convinced that the Japanese would meet his advance as close to the Chindwin as possible, probably in the Taungdan Range, a long line of rugged, jungle-clad hills that rose some twenty miles east of the Chindwin and ran parallel to it. His forces were now between a hundred and 150 miles from the railhead at Dimapur. Although 14th Army was a half million strong, he knew that even with lavish aerial resupply he would be unable to maintain more than about five divisions beyond the Chindwin. The Taungdan barrier had to be pierced as quickly as possible and the Japanese driven southeast into the flat savannah country of the Shwebo Plain, the heart of Burma's dry belt. Here conditions resembled those of the Western Desert. Slim's armoured brigades and fighter-bombers would make short work of the Japanese divisions, no matter how numerous they might be, for the latter had few tanks and virtually no air support.

On 4th December IV Corps, which since August had been commanded by Lieutenant General Frank Messervy, broke out of its bridgehead at Sittaung. With a new commander had come a reorganisation – IV Corps now comprised 7th and 19th Indian divisions and two tank brigades. In the lead was 19th Indian Division, its commander Major General 'Pete' Rees driving with the advance guard. It swept through the Taungdan Range and headed due east for Indaw, from where it was to swing south for Shwebo. Meanwhile, at Kalewa, Lieutenant General Montagu Stopford's XXXIII Corps, now comprising British 2nd Division, 20th Indian Division and 254 Tank Brigade, prepared to strike towards Japanese airfields at Yeu, seventy miles to the southeast, and at Monywa, a hundred miles due south on the Chindwin. On 15th December, only eleven days after leaving Sittaung, 19th Indian Division rolled into Indaw – it had cut through the apparently formidable Taundan Range and had encountered little resistance. The advance was going well – too well. Slim was perturbed and doubts began to crowd in.

The 14th Army commander was right to be worried. Slim had based his appreciation of Japanese strategy on what he knew about Kawabe and Mutaguchi, both tenacious but none too bright. They had demonstrated in the Imphal-Kohima battle a marked reluctance to give ground, even when the situation was hopeless. What Slim did not know was that, in

Slim's plans for the reconquest of Burma depended on maintaining complete aerial supremacy over the northern and central regions of the country. By January, 1945 British bombers ranged at will, destroying railway bridges (below) and disrupting the flow of supplies to Japanese divisions preparing for the 'Battle of the Irrawaddy Shore'.

Lieutenant General F.W. Messervy played a key role in dislodging the Japanese from their strong positions behind the Irrawaddy. Undetected by the Japanese, his IV Corps advanced 300 miles down a jungle track, and then stormed across the Irrawaddy to capture the Japanese supply depot at Meiktila.

the aftermath of the Imphal-Kohima debacle, Tokyo had instituted a thorough shake up of Burma Area Army's High Command. Kawabe had been replaced by Lieutenant General Hyotaro Kimura, a wily and intelligent soldier, who was prepared to withdraw in order to destroy his enemy. In a remarkable effort, Japanese reinforcements had poured into Burma in the autumn of 1944, and Kimura now commanded 250,000 men, organized in eleven divisions. A new commander, Lieutenant General Shihachi Katamura, had taken over 15th Army, its shattered 15th, 31st, and 33rd divisions had been rebuilt, and a new division, the 53rd, had been attached to it. Once more it was a formidable force.

Kimura had no intention of fighting a battle on the Shwebo Plain where Slim would hold all the cards. He left only light covering forces to the west of the Chindwin and ordered a general withdrawal to the eastern bank of the Irrawaddy. Here, behind the hundred-mile bend in the river that extended from Mandalay to Pakokku, Kimura instructed Katamura to deploy his 15th, 31st and 33rd divisions. It was a formidable defensive position. Along this stretch, the Irrawaddy was one-and-a-half-miles wide and banked by bluffs and cliffs, some of which were as high as the cliffs of Dover. Katamura stationed 53rd Division on the extreme left flank where it could reinforce Pakokku and cover Meiktila. The latter was the road and rail junction of central Burma, as well as the site of four airfields and a vast depot from which Japanese forces in central and northern Burma drew most of their supplies. Further south, between Meiktila and Rangoon, Kimura stationed 18th and 2nd divisions to act as a reserve. Finally, he ordered 28th Army, whose area of responsibility covered the Arakan and the Yenangyaung oilfields, to take over the defence of the area from Pakokku westwards.

Kimura had placed Katamura's 15th Army in a strong situation. If Slim wanted to take Rangoon he would have to fight his way across the Irrawaddy at the very limit of his logistic chain, whereas Katamura would be able to feed his battle from Meiktila. Kimura believed this encounter would be decisive and referred to it as the 'Battle of the Irrawaddy Shore' – in short, he intended to impose on Slim the same sort of battle that Slim had imposed on the hapless Mutaguchi and Kawabe at Imphal

and Kohima.

Kimura was a competent general – Slim was a military genius. Twenty-four hours after Rees had reached Indaw, Slim's misgivings crystalised into certainty. Reports from reconnaissance flights and documents captured during 19th Division's advance indicated a major Japanese withdrawal behind the Irrawaddy – it was clear that a gigantic trap was being prepared for 14th Army. Having divined Kimura's plan, Slim prepared to turn the tables on him. During the retreat of 1942, one of Slim's units had withdrawn through Pakokku and then along a bullock-cart track which ran due north to the west of the Chindwin all the way to Kalewa. It had served as a secure avenue for the retreat and he now intended to use this track to outflank Kimura's carefully contrived positions. Although it was 150 miles long and dirt surfaced, Slim's engineers estimated they could convert it to an all-weather road in about six weeks by laying along its length strips of bitumen coated hessian – 'bithess'. Slim proposed to send an entire corps down this road to Pakokku on Kurasaka's left flank – it would then cross the Irrawaddy and dash a further ninety miles to the southeast to capture Meiktila.

Operation 'Extended Capital', the codename Slim gave his scheme, was a design

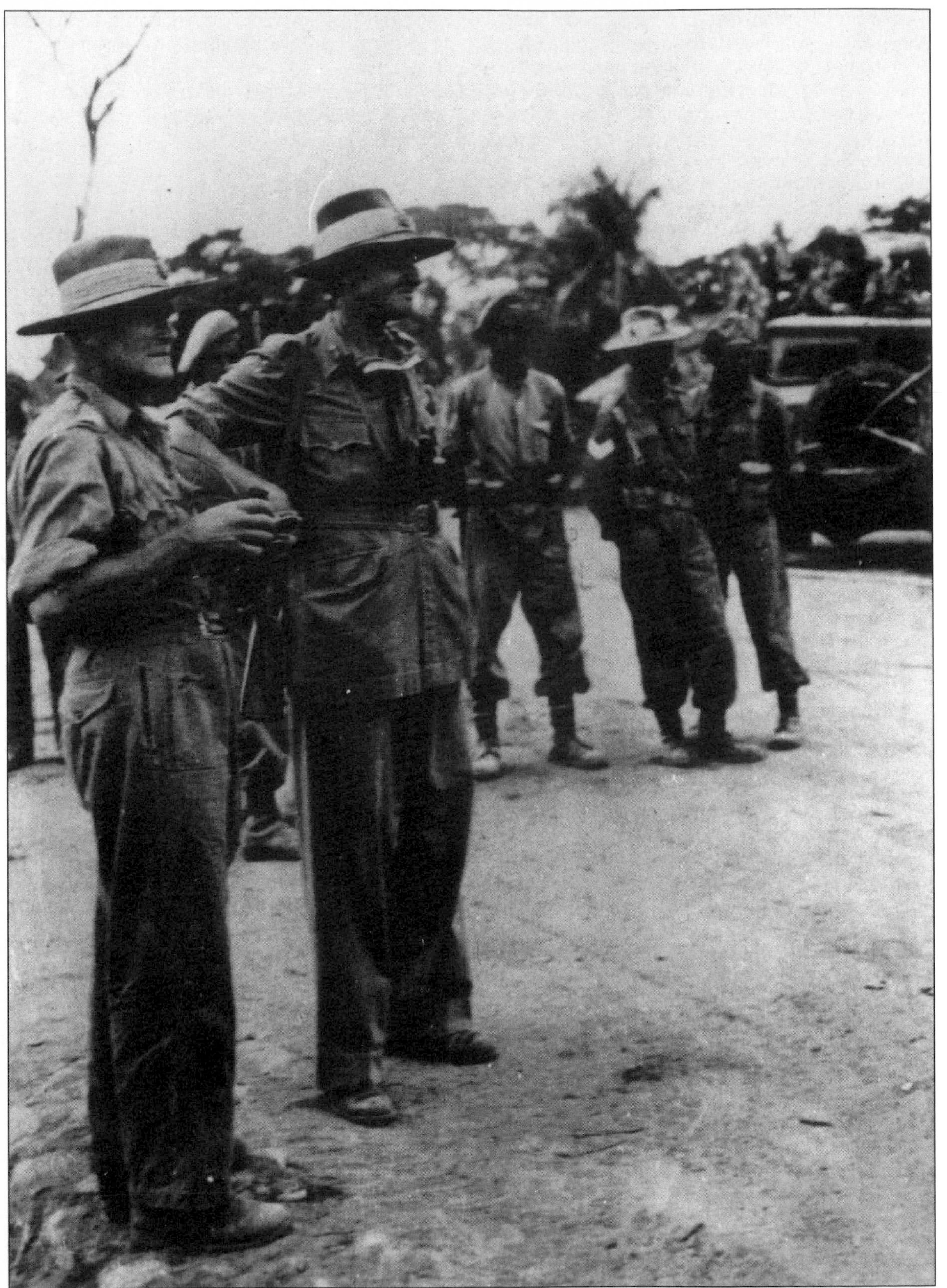

Major General 'Punch' Cowan, C.O. of 17th Indian Division, confers with Messervy before the assault on Meiktila. Cowan's division spearheaded the crossing of the Irrawaddy and played a leading role in the capture of the depot.

An Indian MP halts traffic to allow men of the 4th Battalion 4th Gurkhas to cross a Bailey bridge on their way to assault Mandalay Hill. The Gurkha's seizure of the hill cleared the way for other elements of 19th Indian Division to move on Mandalay.

worthy of Napoleon – it has never been surpassed and only rarely equalled. It involved a massive redeployment which few armies could have carried out in less than a month; Slim's army did it in twenty-four hours! Slim ordered the establishment of a dummy headquarters for IV Corps at Indaw, which he tasked with maintaining radio traffic at existing levels. Rees' 19th Indian Division was transferred to XXXIII Corps, and the 19th and 2nd British divisions were then to advance to Shwebo, after which Rees' Division would swing east and cross the Irrawaddy at a point some forty miles north of Mandalay, while British 2nd Division was to advance due south to cross the Irrawaddy twenty miles west of the city. Meanwhile, 20th Indian Division was to advance south east along the left bank of the Chindwin to Monywa, and then strike due east to the Irrawaddy, crossing the river some ten miles to the west of 2nd Division's bridgehead. Slim reasoned that these movements would so absorb Japanese attention they would fail to detect the simultaneous advance of Scoone's reconstituted IV Corps, now composed of 7th and 17th Indian divisions and two tank brigades, down the track to Pakokku. Once IV Corps had taken Meiktila, the Japanese would have no option other than to withdraw troops from their Irrawaddy defences and concentrate on recapturing their depots. The battle for Meiktila would then become a replay of Imphal-Kohima, while to the north XXXIII Corps broke through the Irrawaddy defences and captured Mandalay.

On 16th December 19th Indian Division began its advance on Shwebo. Eight days later, British 2nd Division struck southeast in a converging attack. Japanese resistance was slight, and on 5th January both divisions reached their objective. In accordance with Slim's plan, 19th Division now swung east and, between 11th and 17th January, managed to cross the Irrawaddy and establish bridgeheads at Singu and Thabeikkyin – villages between forty and fifty miles north of Mandalay. Rees' role now was to isolate Mandalay from the north and draw off the Japanese from the city and from the Irrawaddy bend. He succeeded brilliantly. An alarmed Katamura pulled 53rd Division away from Pakokku, thereby exposing Meiktila, and withdrew 15th Division from its positions on the Irrawaddy and rushed them north to nip out 19th Indian Division's bridgeheads. For the time being, Rees stayed on the defensive, allowing the Japanese to

waste themselves in desperate attacks against his perimeters.

Meanwhile, British 2nd Division had advanced slowly south from Shwebo and 20th Indian Division had struck south east from Kalewa. On 20th February both divisions reached the Irrawaddy some twenty miles west of Mandalay and launched their first assault crossings. Although Katamura's withdrawal of 15th Division had weakened the defences, the British and Indians suffered heavy casualties. In many places attempts to cross were abandoned. By 24th February small bridgeheads had been established, but it took another three weeks of bloody assaults, supported by 'cab-ranks' of fighter-bombers, to convert these scattered pockets into a secure lodgement.

Now came Slim's masterstroke. As he had surmised, Japanese attention was fully occupied by the fighting on the Irrawaddy. In mid-January Katamura received a report from a reconnaissance flight (the only one which managed to penetrate a dense RAF fighter screen) that a column of at least 2,000 tanks and trucks was moving south along the Kalewa-Pauk track. He dismissed the report as incredible – if the pilot had seen anything at all, which he very much doubted, it was probably a lightly equipped Chindit raiding column. Undetected, IV Corps' advance guard reached Pauk on 26th January. Training his binoculars to the southeast, Indian 17th Division's commander Major General 'Punch' Cowan caught his first sight of the Irrawaddy's cliffs, still some thirty miles distant. Nearly a month was to pass before the bulk of IV Corps arrived at Pauk, though the delay was in part intentional, for it allowed time for the battles to the northeast to develop. On 21st February IV Corps surged across the Irrawaddy at Nyaungu, a village twenty miles down river from Pakokku. A better place could not have been chosen – it was on the boundary between 20th Army's and 15th Army's areas of responsibility, and was lightly held by troops of the Indian National Army, who fled at the first shot.

Three days later, Brigadier Miles Smeeton's 255th Tank Brigade burst out of the bridgehead and, scattering bewildered Japanese rear area troops, raced twenty miles to Oyin. Lone Japanese, boxes of explosives strapped to their chests, hurled themselves between tank tracks, but they were too few to halt the advance. On 22nd February Smeeton's tanks rolled into Taungtha only forty-three miles from Meiktila. Even now Katamura still believed that his depot was threatened by nothing more than a raiding column which could be handled by the 4,000 soldiers in Meiktila, though they were mainly lines-of-communication troops and convalescents in the hospital. On 26th February the Deccan Horse, the leading regiment of 255th Brigade, reached Thabuktong, fifteen miles from Meiktila and overran an airstrip. Within hours, petrol, ammunition and the fresh 99th Brigade of 5th Indian Division had been flown in. Three days later, the tank brigades supported by 17th Indian Division hooked north and south of Meiktila and closed in for the kill.

It was not an easy battle. Although rear area troops, the Japanese fought desperately from hastily dug bunkers. Some squatted in foxholes, 250lbs aerial bombs clasped tightly between their knees and stones in their hands, waiting to strike the detonator when tanks passed overhead. The Gurkhas, advancing in a protective screen before the armour, killed them all. Slim, who had flown to Thabuktong to confer with Cowan, demanded to be driven to

The little village of Ywathitgyi on the Irrawady basin road. Troops of 19th Indian Division fought their way along this road into the northeastern outskirts of Mandalay in the face of fanatical Japanese resistance. The sudden emergence of this threat to Mandalay caused the Japanese to pull reserves to the northeast, thereby exposing Meiktila.

Right: an RAF bomber circles the massive walls of Fort Differin, the last major Japanese position inside Mandalay. When the fifty-foot-thick walls proved impervious to artillery fire, low flying aircraft lobbed 2,000lb bombs onto them.

Below: a 3' mortar of 17th Indian Division gives support to infantry attacking the outskirts of Meiktila. The heavily outnumbered Japanese fought desperately from hastily constructed bunkers, and each one had to be destroyed in set piece attacks.

the front, and could not resist joining his old unit, 1st Battalion 7th Gurkhas, in one bloodily resisted assault. By 3rd March Meiktila was in Cowan's hands – Indian 17th Division's soldiers counted 2,000 Japanese bodies, though many more lay buried in bunkers and tunnels.

Katamura finally realized the true nature of the threat to Meiktila on 25th February. In a frenzy, he withdrew 18th Division from northern Burma, ordered 49th Division north from Rangoon, stripped 31st Division of its heavy guns, detached regiments from 33rd and 15th divisions and ordered the lot to converge on the town. The response was vigorous but uncoordinated. A local counterattack recaptured Taungtha on 5th March, cutting Meiktila's road link to the Irrawaddy, but it would be another five days before major Japanese units could be in position to launch a full-scale assault.

For Cowan, the loss of Taungtha was a setback but not a serious one. His 17th Division had been besieged before and Cowan knew that, as long as he held even one of Meiktila's airfields, aerial resupply would suffice. Cowan did not wait for the Japanese to come to him. Leaving 99th Brigade to hold the town, he sent his armoured forces out in five directions along the roads radiating from Meiktila to intercept the Japanese advance, and by 11th March his tanks were skirmishing with the enemy on the open plains.

Since 25th February Meiktila had absorbed Katamura's attention. On 6th March, however, a new threat materialised. Rees had formed Stiletto Forces, an armoured column which burst out of 19th Division's bridgehead and headed south for Mandalay. Rees tore along with Stiletto's spearhead, behaving with the panache and ruthlessness of an *SS Panzer* commander. When a deep *chaung* (dry water course) halted the column, Rees ordered three three-ton trucks rolled into it on their sides, and the tanks rolled over them. Infantry clinging to their superstructures, the tanks pressed on through the night of 6th March, and by the following afternoon 1,000-foot high Mandalay Hill was in sight. During the night of 7th March 4th Battalion of 4th Gurkha Regiment crept up the northeastern side of the hill and at dawn stormed the summit. Within forty-eight hours 19th Division was in the northern suburbs of Mandalay – within another twenty-four hours it had fought its way to Fort Dufferin, a massive 2,000-square- yard cantonment protected by a moat seventy-five-yards wide and walls thirty-feet thick. The battle for Mandalay now resembled a mediaeval siege – 6" howitzers battered the walls from point-blank range and B-25s skipped 2,000lbs bombs into them. On 20th March the Japanese abandoned Dufferin and withdrew from the remainder of the city, their retreat impelled not only by the ferocity of 19th Division's assault, but also because British 2nd Division had broken out of its bridgehead at Ngazun eight days earlier and was now attacking Mandalay from the south.

Due to the deteriorating situation in Mandalay, on 12th March Kimura removed the conduct of the Meiktila battle from Katamura and placed it under the control of Lieutenant General Masaki Honda, commander of 23rd Army. Honda now designated the heterogeneous units closing around Meiktila the 'Army of the Decisive Battle', but it was an army in name only. The regiments from 15th Army, and 18th and 49th Divisions were all on different radio nets and used different frequencies. Instead of a massed onslaught,

the attempts to take Meiktila degenerated into a series of uncoordinated thrusts. Even so, the Japanese fought well. They managed to get within small-arms' range of one of Meiktila's airfields and fire along the runway, but the aircraft kept coming. With virtually no armour they wheeled their 75mm field guns forward and fired Ta Dam shells (an early form of shaped charge) at tanks from ranges of less than 250 yards. By 22nd March Honda's gunners had destroyed fifty British tanks for the loss of fifty guns. The 'Army of the Decisive Battle' had only twenty guns left, while the British had many more tanks – it was clear who was going to win.

Yet by this time the recapture of Meiktila had become irrelevant. Withdrawn from Mandalay, 15th Army was streaming to the southeast. Having broken out of its bridgehead on 8th March, 20th Indian Division now rampaged across 15th Army's line of retreat, cutting off and wiping out entire battalions. The object of the Army of the Decisive Battle was no longer to take Meiktila, but to prevent Cowan's force from also striking southeast and turning the withdrawal into a rout. Honda held on just long enough to allow the remnant of 15th Army to pass through Thazi, ten miles east of Meiktila, and then on 31st March he too pulled south.

Unlike the bloodbath at Imphal-Kohima, the Japanese suffered only 13,000 casualties at Mandalay-Meiktila, although the majority of these were dead. The British had fewer killed (2,300), but many wounded (15,700). The infliction of heavy casualties had not been part of Slim's plan. His skilfully handled divisions had forced a numerically superior Japanese army to abandon a formidable defensive position, and had smashed the cohesion of seven Japanese divisions, sending them fleeing south. Slim did not give them time to regroup. His armoured columns sped after them, and now the retreat became a rout. The Burma campaign was all but over.

Troops of Cowan's 17th Division enter the ruined city of Pegu, only fifty miles north of Rangoon, on 1st May, 1945. Three days of bitter fighting had delayed Cowan's advance, and the onset of the monsoon that very afternoon brought the advance to a stop. Rangoon was liberated two days later by a seaborne landing.

MANCHURIA–THE FORGOTTEN VICTORY

Red Army troops boarding the Trans-Siberian train for the Manchurian front. A massive logistical effort was needed to make the campaign possible, but despite the immensity of the build-up, the Soviets still achieved surprise.

In August, 1945, one of the least-studied but most spectacular campaigns of the war was fought in Manchuria. In just two weeks, the Soviet Red Army overwhelmed Japan's Kwantung Army and advanced up to 900 kilometres into enemy territory. Far from the popular myth of a bludgeon-like Red Army, in this campaign the Soviets demonstrated the impressive skills they had learnt fighting the *Wehrmacht*, and earned themselves a share in the spoils of the Asian victory.

The Kwantung Army had been a crack force, but by 1945 it had fallen on hard times. Over three-quarters of its troops were raw conscripts, while its 'Manchuko Empire' auxiliaries were useless. The Army's small number of tanks were merely thinly armoured vehicles with one 57mm gun, unable to successfully engage Soviet tanks in combat. Similarly, the Japanese 37mm anti-tank gun would only stop a Soviet tank in exceptional circumstances. Two divisions lacked anti-tank guns, transport or artillery and none had heavy artillery. Completing this picture of weakness, their planes were trainers with virtually no combat capability.

Despite these weaknesses, attacking Manchuria should not be dismissed as an easy task; after all, the Japanese did not have a reputation for tame surrenders. Manchuria was 1,200 kilometres from east to west, and mountains, desert and major rivers all hindered Soviet access to the region. The Japanese planned to make Manchuria's geography work for them by delaying the enemy in frontier fortifications, and then withdrawing hundreds of kilometres to the south where the pursuing, but hopefully exhausted Soviets could be counterattacked.

A tremendous logistical effort enabled Soviet

Far Eastern Command to deploy numerically superior forces against Japan. Entire armies had travelled 12,000 kilometres, over a million railway wagons had made the long journey on the Trans-Siberian and thousand of new tanks were delivered to the front. The U.S.S.R. enjoyed a qualitative advantage as well as a numerical one; Soviet guns, planes and tanks were better than anything the Japanese possessed. The Soviet 'workhorse' tank, the T34, with a 76mm or 85mm gun, was superior to Japanese tanks, while the JS2, with its 122mm gun, had no Japanese rivals.

Needing a rapid victory to establish the U.S.S.R.'s credibility as a Far Eastern victor, Stalin imposed commanders who had succeeded against the *Wehrmacht*, thus passing over men on the spot who doubted that speedy victory was possible. Far Eastern Commander Vasilevsky planned to 'fix' the Japanese with a northern attack, while reserving his main effort for two pincer movements from either side. This would be supplemented by seaborne assaults. Vasilevsky didn't just depend on numbers; an element of surprise, the appropriate concentrations of resources and a rapid exploitation would give Stalin the quick victory he required.

In 1941, the Red Army had learnt the hard way that surprise could act as a force multiplier, so for this campaign they strove to disguise the imminence and direction of their attack. Elaborate precautions were taken to hide the build-up, but knowing the Japanese had to notice something, deceptions were planned. In the Maritime Provinces, Soviet troops dug fortifications where they could be seen, civilians near the frontier were not moved, normal leave was issued and troops were sent to help with the harvest. Even forward reconnaissance was strictly controlled – it was better attacking units should be ignorant of the enemy than *maskirovka*, the Soviet term for deception and surprise, be lost.

This should not have deceived the Japanese and, indeed, revised intelligence estimates warned of an attack in September. Soviet forces were not expected earlier, as summer is a period of seasonal rains over most of Manchuria. There was also an element of wishful thinking in this Japanese calculation, since they desperately needed Soviet mediation to enable them to negotiate peace with the U.S.A.

The Red Army also achieved surprise by attacking from an unexpected direction. The attack made by 36th Army down the railway towards Hailar was a feint designed to draw attention from Trans-Baikal Front's main thrust over the Great Hingan Mountains, which were considered impassable by the Japanese. Further south, the Soviet-Mongolian Cavalry Mechanized Group achieved surprise by advancing across the Gobi Desert. In the east 1st Far Eastern Front faced fortifications, wooded hills and numerous rivers, considered by the Japanese an unlikely direction for a major attack.

Even at the tactical level the Red Army strove to achieve surprise. On 9th August many initial advances took place without prior artillery fire and where artillery was used it was in a brief, 'hurricane' bombardment. Infantry advances were small group infiltrations, not the human waves typical of the Red Army earlier in the war.

Vasilevsky expected different types of advance from each of his three fronts. Trans-Baikal Front was the key mobile thrust and consequently it received a disproportionate allocation of tanks. Facing formidable river barriers, 2nd Far Eastern Front obtained the services of the powerful Amur River Flotilla. In the east 1st Far Eastern Front had its artillery component strengthened to enable it to deal with Japanese fortifications.

The spearhead of Malinovsky's Trans-Baikal Front was elite 6th Guards Tank Army, whose experience of mountain warfare in the Carpathians was put to good use as it led the

A Red Army mortar crew prepares to fire. The Soviets had massive artillery and mortar superiority over their Japanese opponents. First Far Eastern Front, which faced the stronger Japanese fortifications, had its artillery element strengthened. They achieved tactical surprise by either dispensing with any preliminary artillery preparation or else using a brief 'hurricane' bombardment.

Red Army self-propelled guns on the move. The Japanese had nothing capable of matching the powerful Soviet mechanized forces - neither their anti-tank guns or their tanks could effectively combat Soviet armoured units. It was logistics that held back the Soviet armoured thrust over the Great Hingan mountains, not the Japanese.

advance over the Great Hingan Mountains. Attacking on a narrow front, it enjoyed a 15:1 advantage in tanks, total control of the air and glorious sunny weather. Kravchenko's tanks advanced rapidly against feeble opposition, taking the Khorokhon Pass on the evening of 10th August and gaining access to the central Manchurian plain. Here the tanks ran out of fuel but, using the 400 planes of 453rd Aviation Battalion, Malinovsky resupplied the force and the advance resumed. Deploying a powerful forward detachment, Kravchenko was able to keep the bulk of the tank army in march formation, maximising its speed – in just eleven days it covered 900 kilometres.

To the south of Kravchenko's army, 17th Combined Arms Army (CAA) reached the coast with little opposition. The 53rd CAA provided the second echelon, advancing with relative ease behind 6th Guard Tank Army. Only the 39th CAA, of all the armies of the main thrust, encountered strong opposition: Japanese resistance in the Arshaan-Wuchakou area was fierce.

The thankless task of advancing down the route that the Japanese expected Soviet forces to take was given to 36th CAA. As it crossed the northern section of the Great Hingan, Japanese opposition was heavy. Although advancing less spectacularly than the rest of the Front, 36th CAA's achievement was in enabling other armies to advance relatively unopposed.

Pliev's Cavalry-Mechanized Group made the most exotic advance in crossing the Gobi Desert. Careful logistical support enabled it to advance up to ninety kilometres a day and the only real resistance was met northwest of Kalgan. Crossing the Great Wall, Pliev met the Chinese Communist 8th Route Army and was preparing to enter Beijing when the campaign ended.

Meretskov's 1st Far Eastern Front faced Japanese fortifications in awkward terrain. Despite this his front penetrated up to 600 kilometres into Manchuria, and the southern 25th CAA reached northern Korea.

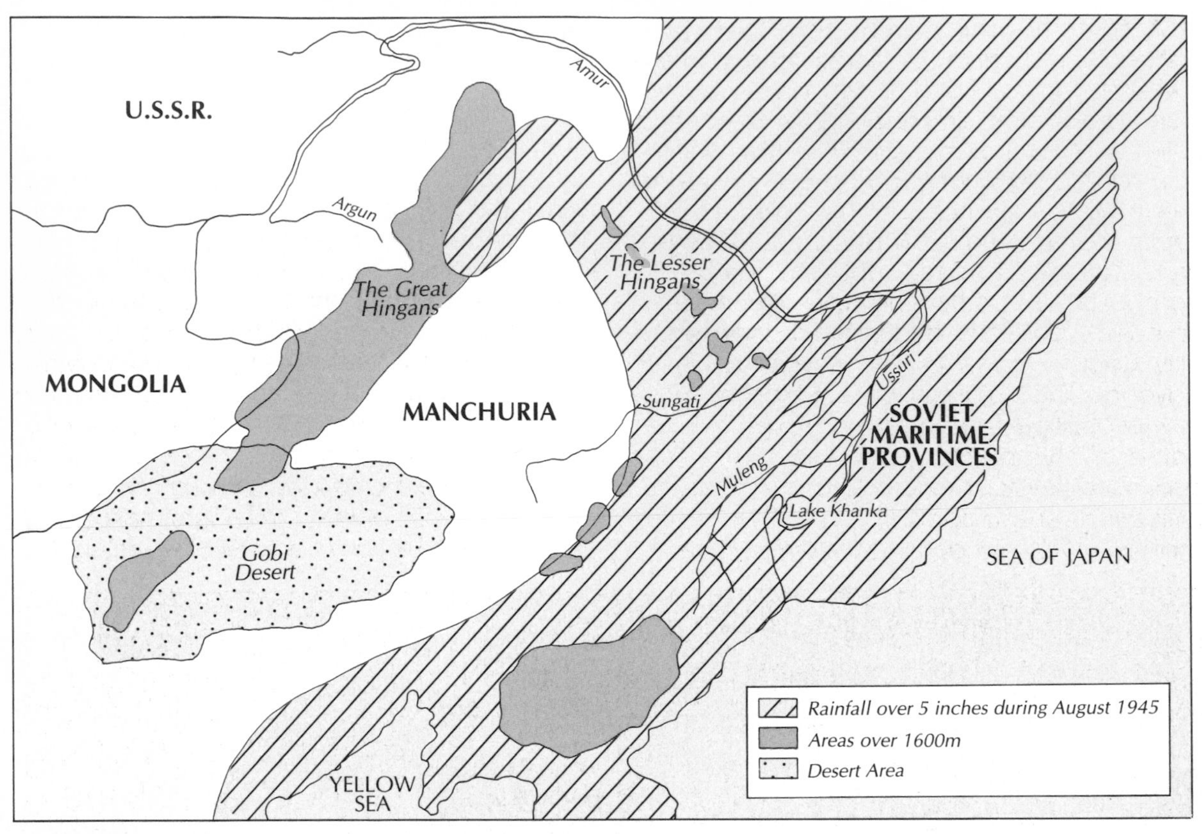

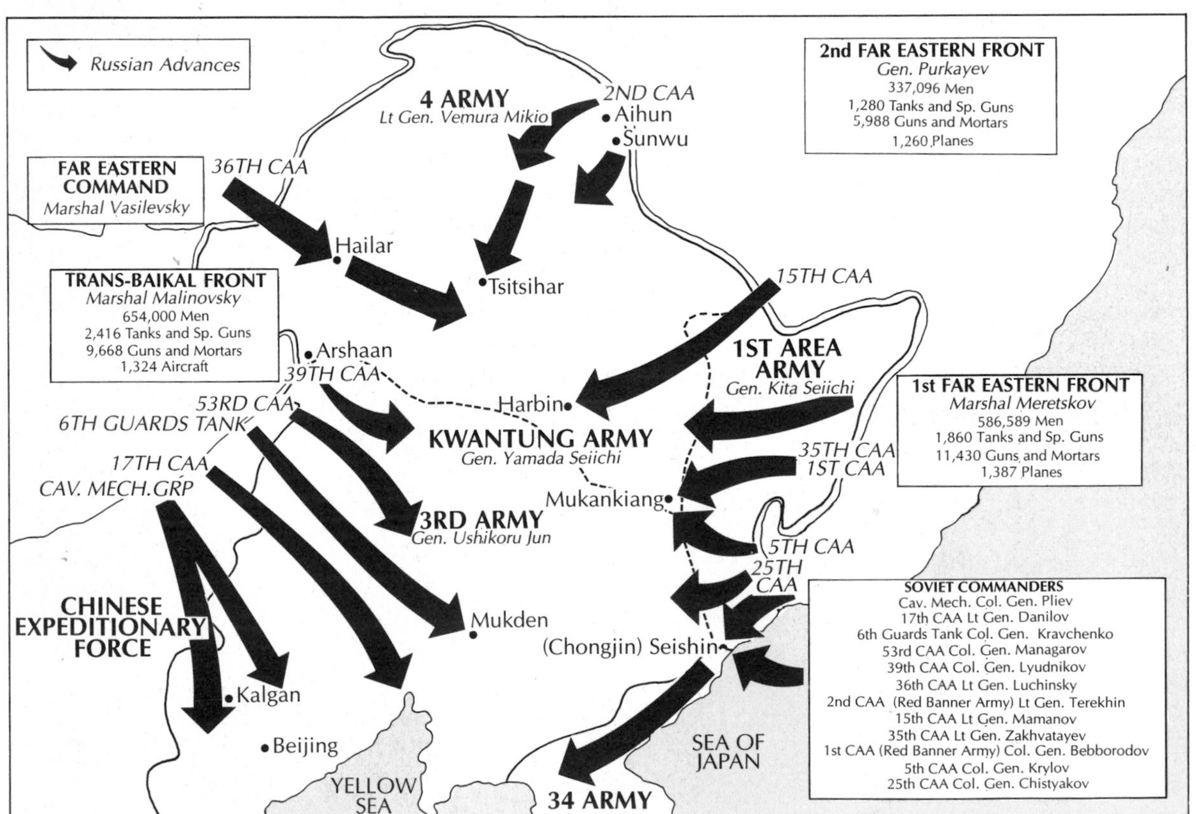

The Soviets sweep into Manchuria on 8th August, 1945, against the Japanese 1st, 3rd, 4th and Kwantung armies. Due to their superior weaponry, the tactical use of surprise and bold command, the Soviets achieve victory before the month is out.

A few months earlier 5th CAA had distinguished itself during fierce fighting in the awkward terrain of East Prussia, and now they were to assault in similar countryside north of Suifeno. Meretskov strengthened the artillery and tank components of the army, making them the key elements in the thrust towards Japanese 1st Area Army HQ at Mutankiang. Krylov decided to forego the advantages of bombardment, partly as he lacked information on enemy positions, and instead attacked in hilly country north of the easiest route of advance. The initial assault was lead by small groups of about a hundred men taken from first echelon rifle battalions. These units were balanced combat teams whose task was to infiltrate deep into Japanese defences. For the main thrust Krylov had 5.4 battalions, 218 guns or mortars and forty tanks or self-propelled guns (SP) per kilometre.

Attacking in heavy rain at 1.00am on 9th August, 5th CAA caught the Japanese by surprise. The assault groups recklessly penetrated deep into the Japanese defences, leaving points of resistance to be taken by the 2nd echelon. For example, the 'Camel' strongpoint was taken by infantry, supported by tanks and 152mm SP guns, later in the morning. By nightfall leading elements of the 5th CAA were fifteen to twenty-two kilometres into the Japanese rear. Having broken the initial Japanese defences, 5th CAA deployed a powerful forward detachment of a tank brigade, two battalions of infantry and a regiment of SP artillery; this force, reinforced when it faced serious opposition, enabled the

Soviet cavalry on the move. The Manchurian campaign was the last major appearance of cavalry in modern warfare. Pliev's Cavalry-Mechanized group emulated the feats of the ancient Mongols in their dramatic advance across the Gobi Desert. Pliev's advance was made possible by the thorough logistical support of Trans-Baikal Front.

Facing page top: men of a Soviet anti-aircraft, who unit had little to do during the Manchurian campaign. The Japanese air force there was heavily outnumbered and consisted of inexperienced pilots in training planes. Wisely the Japanese high command ordered their planes out of the region on the second day of the campaign.

Facing page bottom; the 'Stalin' tank, a powerful armoured fighting vehicle with a 122mm gun and frontal armour roughly four inches thick. Despite its power it was a relatively fast, light vehicle capable of taking on the heaviest German tanks. Its power was wasted against the Japanese, who were equally impotent against the T-34.

Right: a reconnaissance plane of the Soviet air force. Accurate intelligence was only one of the benefits conferred by control of the air. Not only did the Soviet air force provide invaluable close tactical support, thereby facilitating the advance, but they also kept 6th Guards Tank moving by supplying their petrol by air.

bulk of the army to move forward rapidly in march formation. Defeating two Japanese infantry divisions, 5th CAA, supported by the 1st Red Banner Army, entered Mutankiang on 16th August.

At the southern end of the Front, Chistyakov's 25th CAA demonstrated the value of amphibious operations, while the rapid land advance was also supplemented by several airborne assaults. The biggest landing was at Seishin, the second largest city in northern Korea. Three separate landings – on 13th, 14th and 15th August – secured the city for the advancing 393rd Infantry Division. An infantry division, a marine brigade and two maritime battalions held out until 16th August when 393rd Division arrived. Had the campaign lasted longer, it would have been evident that 1st Far Eastern Front had ruined Japanese hopes of a defence based on northern Korea and precluded any chance of the Kwantung Army receiving reinforcements.

The least spectacular role in the campaign was given to 2nd Far Eastern Front commanded by Purkayev. He concentrated his forces for an advance on three axis, ignoring most of the 2130-kilometre frontage. The Front's job was to 'fix' Japanese forces in the north while the two Soviet pincers joined in central Manchuria.

A distinctive feature of Purkayev's campaign is the use made of the powerful Amur River flotilla. The 15th CAA crossed the Amur helped by the flotilla, which then supported a 700-kilometre advance down the Sungari River into Harbin. The 2nd Red Banner Army was the only Soviet army unable to achieve surprise on 9th August. Held up in the Aihun-Sunwu fortified region until 20th August, they still managed to push elements of the army over the Lesser Hingan Mountains to Tsitsihar by the end of the campaign.

Purkayev was also responsible for operations against southern Sakhalin. Here, once again, the Soviets combined an overland advance

A Red Army artillery man loading his weapon. Soviet combat troops deservedly acquired a reputation for dogged defence, but in the Manchurian campaign they demonstrated their capacity for innovative and flexible offensive action. Anyone wishing to see the Red Army as a 'steamroller' would be surprised by the offensive panache displayed in Manchuria.

Facing page top: Red infantry take cover in light woodland prior to resuming the advance. In the First Far Eastern Front small groups of infantry spearheaded the advance, penetrating deeply into Japanese defences. Soviet infantry demonstrated that they had learned to create balanced combat teams with automatic weapons.

Facing page bottom: a Red Army nurse providing first aid on the front line. Soviet women played a much more prominent role in the fighting than their counterparts in the west. Fortunately, the skills of this particular 'angel of mercy' were rarely needed in the Manchurian campaign as Soviet losses were relatively light.

with a thirty-three-ship amphibious expedition. At the eastern extreme of the Front's extensive area, a division landed on Shumsu Island and, by 3rd September, Soviet forces had landed on all the Kuriles islands.

Japan's formal surrender on 14th August did not immediately stop the fighting in Manchuria. For a while it seemed that the Kwantung Army would continue fighting, but wiser councils prevailed and on 19th August Hata signed the surrender document at Vasilevsky's HQ. The Soviet advance continued; as the campaign ended ad-hoc airborne units occupied Manchuria's major cities.

The Kwantung Army had compounded an impossible task by responding ineptly to the Soviet threat. Despite basic weaknesses, such as lacking any air cover, (after two days combat Japanese planes were ordered out of Manchuria), the Red Army should not have won so quickly. The problems faced by 2nd Red Banner Army demonstrate that the Kwantung Army as a whole could have made things harder for the Soviets. Otuzu's plan for a fighting withdrawal was ruined by the disobedience of Ushikoru Jun, commander of 3rd Area Army, who failed to pull back from the frontier zone as ordered.

Nevertheless, the Soviet achievement should not be belittled because of the errors of their opponents; after all, the Red Army had worked hard to bring about these errors. The campaign was a virtuoso performance. It achieved surprise at all levels, created purpose-built forward detachments to maintain the momentum of the advance and displayed the capacity to take the initiative at lower levels of command. Only the precipitous end of the Asian War deprived the Red Army of recognition for an impressive victory. Nevertheless, Stalin's army had delivered the rapid triumph his political objectives required, thereby enabling him to underline the U.S.S.R.'s claim to great-power status in the Far East.

BIBLIOGRAPHY

Blitzkreig in the West

A. HORNE, *To Lose A Battle* (London, 1969)
L. DEIGHTON, *Blitzkrieg* (London, 1979)
T.N. DUPUY, *Options of Command* (New York and London)
P. CALVOCORESSI & G. WINT, *Total War* (London, 1972)
B. BOND, *France and Belgium 1939-1940* (London)

Dunkirk and the Fall of France

W.S. CHURCHILL, *The Second World War* (London, 1948) Book III
M. GILBERT, *Finest Hour – Winston S. Churchill 1939 - 1941* (London, 1983)
F. GROSSMITH, *Dunkirk – A Miracle of Deliverance* (London, 1978)
N. HAMILTON, *Montgomery* (London, 1978)
J. HARRIS, *Dunkirk: the Storms of War* (London, 1980, 1988)
H. GUDERIAN, *Panzer Leader* (London, 1952)

Battle for Crete

C. BUCKLEY, *Greece and Crete 1941* (London, 1952)
A. CLARK, *The Fall of Crete* (London and New York, 1962)
B.H. LIDDELL HART, *The Other Side of the Hill* (London, 1983)
J. LUCAS, *Alpine Elite, German Mountain Troops of World War II* (London, 1980)
T. SIMPSON, *Operation Mercury, The Battle for Crete 1941* (London and Auckland, 1981)

Barbarossa – The Drive to the East

P. CARRELL, *Hitler's War on Russia: the Story of the German Defeat in the East* (London, 1964)
J. ERICKSON, *The Road to Stalingrad: Stalin's War With Germany* (London, 1975) Vol. I
B.I. FUGATE, *Operation Barbarossa: Strategy and Tactics on the Eastern Front, 1941* (California, 1984)
B.A. LEACH, *German Strategy Against Russia 1939-1941* (Oxford, 1973)
A. SEATON, *The Russo-German War, 1941-1945* (London and New York, 1971)
M.L. VAN CREVALD, *Supplying War: Logistics from Wallenstein to Patton* (Cambridge and New York, 1977)

The Siege of Leningrad

J. ERICKSON, *Stalin's War with Germany* (London, 1975-83) Vols I & II
L. GOURE, *The Siege of Leningrad* (Oxford and Stanford, 1962)
H.E. SALISBURY, *The 900 Days: the Siege of Leningrad* (London and New York, 1969)
A. WYKES, *The Siege of Leningrad: Epic of Survival* (London, 1968)

Bataan and Corregidor

J.H. BELOTE & M. WILLIAM, *Corregidor: The Saga of a Fortress* (New York, 1967)
E. MORRIS, *Corregidor, the Nightmare in the Philippines* (London, 1982)
J.D. CLAYTON, *The Years of MacArthur* (New York, 1975)
R. WARD, *Fall of the Philippines* (London, 1971)

Battle of Gazala

C. BARNETT, *The Desert Generals* (London, 1960)
M. CARVER, *Tobruk* (London, 1964)
W. JACKSON, *The North African Campaign* (London, 1974)
R. LEWIN, *Rommel as Military Commander* (London, 1968)
R. PARKINSON, *Auchinleck of Alamein* (London, 1977)
B. PITT (ed.), *The Purnell History of the Second World War* (London, 1967) Vol. III, No. 5

The Battles of El Alamein

C. BARNETT, *The Desert Generals* (London, 1960)
W. JACKSON, *The North African Campaign* (London, 1974)
R. LEWIN, *Rommel as Military Commander* (London, 1968)
M. CARVER, *Alamein* (London, 1962)
B. MONTGOMERY, *El Alamein to the River Sangro* (London, 1952)
B. PITT (ed.) *The Purnell History of the Second World War* (London, 1967) Vol. III, No. 5

Guadalcanal

G. KENT, *Guadalcanal, Island Ordeal* (London, 1971)
T.G. MILLER, JR., *The Cactus Air Force* (New York, 1969)
R. WHEELER, *A Special Valor: The U.S. Marines and the Pacific War* (New York, 1983)
J.L. ZIMMERMAN, *The Guadalcanal Campaign* (New York, 1949)

Stalingrad – The Turning Point

P. CARREL, *Hitler's War on Russia* (Harrap, London)
V.I. CHUIKOV, *The Beginning of the Road* (Macgibbon & Kee, London, 1963)
J. ERIKSON, *Stalin's War on Germany* (Weidenfeld & Nicolson, London, 1983)
G. JUKES, *Stalingrad, the Turning Point* (Macdonald, London, 1968)
G.JUKES, *Hitler's Stalingrad Decisions* (University of California Press, 1985)
E. VON MANSTEIN, *Lost Victories* (Methuen, London, 1958)
L. ROTUNDO, *The Battle for Stalingrad* (Pergamon-Brassey, London, 1989)

Operation Torch

H.C. BUTCHER, *Three Years With Eisenhower* (London, 1946)
J. D'ARCY DAWSON, *Tunisian Battle* (1943)
G.F. HOWE, *North West Africa; Seizing the Initiative in the West* (The U.S. Army in World War II, Mediterranean Theater of Operations {Official History} Department of the Army, Washington D.C., 1957)
K. MACKSEY, *Crucible of Power, the Fight for Tunisia 1942-3* (London, 1969)
I.S.O. PLAYFAIR & C.J.C. MOLONY, *The Mediterranean and Middle East* (British Official History of the Second World War, HMSO; London, 1966) Vol. IV
P. TOMPKINS, *The Murder of Admiral Darlan* (London, 1965)

Kursk – The Clash of Steel

J. ERICKSON, *The Road to Berlin* (London, 1983)
A. SEATON, *The Russo-German War 1941-45* (London, 1971)
F. E. ZIEMKE, *Stalingrad to Berlin* (Washington, 1968)
H.P. WILMOTT, *The Great Crusade* (London, 1989)
I. PAROTKIN (ed.), *The Battle of Kursk* (Moscow, 1974)
G. JUKES, *The Clash of Armour* (London, 1968)

The Battles for Monte Cassino

M. CLARK, *Calculated Risk* (New York, 1950)
J. ELLIS, *Cassino, the Hollow Victory* (London, 1983)
A. KESSELRING, *Memoirs* (London, 1968)
F. MAJDALANY, *Cassino – Portrait of a Battle* (London, 1963)
B. PITT (ed.), *The Purnell History of the Second World War* (London, 1967) Vol. IV
G.A. SHEPPERD, *The Italian Campaign, 1943-1945* (London, 1968)

Burma – From Imphal to Kohima

L. ALLEN, *The Longest War* (London, 1984)
A.J. BARKER, *The March on Dehli* (London, 1963)
G. EVANS & A. BRETT-JAMES, *Imphal – A Flower on Lofty Heights* (London, 1964)

D-Day – The Allied Invasion of Europe

C. RYAN, *The Longest Day - The D-Day Story* (New York and London, 1982)
S. BADSEY, *Normandy 1944 - Allied Landings and Breakout* (London, 1989)
C.D'ESTE , *Decision in Normandy* (New York and London, 1983)
M. HASTINGS, *D-Day and the Battle for Normandy* (London, 1984)
J. KEEGAN, *Six Armies in Normandy* (London and New York, 1982)

Bagration – The Soviet Sledgehammer

G. NIEPOLD, *Battle for White Russia* (London, 1987)
V. LARINOV et al, *World War Two : Decisive Battles of the Soviet Army* (Moscow, 1981)
Main Front : Soviet Leaders Look Back on World War Two (London, 1987)

Arnhem – The Bridge Too Far

C. RYAN, *A Bridge Too Far* (London and New York, 1974)
J. FROST, *A Drop Too Many* (London, 1982)
R. URQUHART, *Arnhem* (London, 1958)
J. SIMS, *Arnhem Spearhead* (London, 1978)

Battle of the Bulge

B.L. LIDDALL HART, *The Other Side of the Hill* (London, 1983)
C.B. MACDONALD, *The Battle of the Bulge* (New York and London, 1984)
J. PIMLOTT, *The Battle of the Bulge* (London, 1983)
T.N. DUPUY, *Options of Command* (New York and London, 1984)

The Battles of Mandalay and Meiktila

B. PERRETT, *Tank Tracks to Rangoon – The Story of British Armour in Burma* (London, 1978)
G. EVANS, *Slim as Military Commander* (London, 1969)
R. LEWIN, *Slim, The Standardbearer* (London, 1976)

Manchuria – The Forgotten Victory

B. PITT (editor), *History of the Second World War* (London, 1968) Vol. VI
D.M. GLANTZ, *August Storm : the Soviet 1945 Strategic Offensive in Manchuria* and *August Storm: Soviet Tactical and Operational Combat in Manchuria* (Leavenworth Papers Nos. 8 and 7, Kansas, 1983)
V. LARINOV (and others), *World War II: Decisive Battles of the Soviet Army* (Progress Publishers, Moscow, 1984)